An American Guide
to British
Social Science Resources

by
Herbert M. Levine
and
Dolores B. Owen

The Scarecrow Press, Inc.
Metuchen, N.J.   1976

Library of Congress Cataloging in Publication Data

Levine, Herbert M
    An American guide to British social science resources.

    Includes index.
    1. Social scientists--United States. 2. Social sci-
ence research--Great Britain. 3. Social sciences--Library
resources--Great Britain--Directories. 4. College teachers
--Leaves of absence--Handbooks, manuals, etc. 5. Social
sciences--Societies, etc. --Great Britain--Directories. I.
Owen, Dolores B. , joint author. II. Title.
H62. L443   300'. 25'41   76-22690
ISBN 0-8108-0950-8

Dedicated to
Andrew Jackson Bullock
and Paul T. Nolan

CONTENTS

v

PREFACE

The primary purpose of the Guide is to provide basic
information about important social science library resources
in Britain and methods by which they can be efficiently util-
ized. The book is intended to be a handy reference source
for American social scientists planning or conducting research
in Great Britain. It is written for the academic needs of historians, political scientists, economists, genealogists, and
sociologists who heretofore have been dependent on scattered
sources for information. Additional subjects are included
which will assist the researcher in adjusting to British customs and accommodations.

The Guide is designed to solve some of the more important problems facing the American researcher. The foreign scholar in Britain encounters two major difficulties:
settling down and gathering information in a limited amount
of time. The scholar will find information in the Guide
which will help him make travel arrangements, obtain passports, secure proper academic credentials, and locate housing. It also provides information on taxes, banking, currency conversion, and establishing a base of operations. If
the scholar's time is limited, this aspect of the Guide will
hopefully assist him in utilizing it efficiently.

The Guide had its origins in the personal experience
of one of the authors on sabbatical leave in Britain. Although he had been to Britain for short visits before, he encountered problems the answers to which became the basis
of this publication. He also met other Americans who had
experienced similar difficulties. Although he had read several guides to Britain, none dealt with the particular problems of the American academic there for research purposes.
Even books written for teachers on sabbatical are not re-
search-oriented. British guide books to libraries do not present a sufficient amount of specific information of interest to
the American researcher, although some do contain extensive
descriptions of library holdings.

Since the book required special information about libraries, we agreed that two different backgrounds were needed: that of the social scientist and that of the librarian. The book is, therefore, a joint effort, and each author shares equally the credit and the blame, where either is due.

Information came from published sources, questionnaires, and interviews. We gathered all the relevant published information about British libraries and archives we could find and selected the sources we believed would be most helpful to the American social scientist. The idea was not to present all the sources--just the most important. Which sources were important, which were marginal, and which were irrelevant became a subject of considerable discussion. We consulted with individuals in the United States and in Britain about the particular institutions to be included. We decided that social science should include primarily sources in history, politics, sociology, economics, and genealogy, with some references also to geography, statistics, and the humanities. One difficulty was that the term social science is not generally regarded in Britain as including history, and we occasionally had to indicate to British scholars what we meant. On the basis of information obtained in the United States, a preliminary entry was prepared for each institution. That entry indicates the name, address, telephone number, underground stop (in London), subject coverage, access, publications, duplication facilities, and services of the institution. Each preliminary entry and a request that corrections be made were sent to the institution concerned. The response was excellent. About 250 letters were sent and 230 answers received.

Letters were also sent to professional associations and societies. The secretaries of these organizations were asked what services were supplied to members and what special assistance could be offered to visiting academics.

The postal inquiries to libraries, record offices, associations, and societies were supplemented with personal visits in the United States and in Britain. We met with officials at the British Information Service and the British Tourist Authority in New York. The reason for these visits was to obtain basic information and to learn which questions are most asked by American academics who plan to conduct research in Britain.

We traveled throughout Britain in the summer of 1975 and ultimately covered more than 3,000 miles to visit those

viii

institutions about which we felt we needed more information. We gave particular attention to the important library and archive resources, such as the British Library, the Public Record Office, major university libraries, the National Library of Scotland, and the National Library of Wales. We also went to small, out-of-the-way libraries and record offices. Specifically, we visited institutions in London, Oxford, Cambridge, Boston Spa, Lichfield, Stafford, Birmingham, Durham, Edinburgh, St. Andrews, Aberdeen, Inverness, Glasgow, Manchester, Liverpool, Aberystwyth, Cardiff, and Brighton. Interviews with librarians and archivists were conducted, and tours of libraries and record offices were arranged. These tours were sometimes extensive, as was the case at the British Library Reference Division and Lending Division, and the Gateshead Public Library. Even photographic and duplicating departments were investigated. At the Public Record Office, for example, the Head of the Photographic Services conducted us on an extensive tour of his modern, well-equipped offices. Although the nature of the trip precluded much advance warning or appointment, the reception was always courteous and warm.

Much academic research is a cooperative and collegial enterprise. We could never have completed this book without the active cooperation of individuals on both sides of the Atlantic. Although it is often difficult to distinguish between the personal and professional assistance given to us, we want to thank Allan and Susie Stewart and David and Ann Carlton for helping us to cope with the many difficulties we encountered in this project.

Other people in Britain to whom we are most grateful are Mr. Geoffrey D. M. Block (Conservative Research Department), Mrs. Patricia Bradford (Churchill College, Cambridge), Mr. T. S. Cardy (Gateshead Public Library), Mr. Richard Cheffins (British Library Lending Division), Mr. James Davie (Daily Telegraph), Mr. Peter A. Hoare (University of Glasgow), Mr. R. Illsley (Norfolk County Library), Mr. David Jervis (British Library), Mr. Peter Knowlson (Liberal Party), Mr. Charles Ritcheson (American Embassy), Mr. K. J. Smith (Public Record Office), Mr. Peter Smith (London and South Eastern Library Region), and Dr. M. I. Williams (National Library of Wales).

We were helped by many people in the United States. We want to thank our colleagues at the University of Southwestern Louisiana, particularly Dr. Vaughan Baker, Mr. Dennis Gibson, Dr. Donn M. Kurtz II, Dr. William McGrath, and Dr. Paul T. Nolan. Dr. Ray P. Authement and Dr. Sammie W. Cosper of the USL Administration approved our sabbatical leaves.

Mrs. D. M. Paul, Information Officer at the British Information Office in New York, discussed with us the questions most asked by American academics planning extended study in Britain. We also wish to thank Miss Gabrielle Hollier, Mr. Larry Robertson, Mr. Travis Owen, and Mr. Mitchell Ward.

Mrs. Sonya Abington typed our original inquiry letters and some of the draft material. Ms. Margaret Blumberg typed the final manuscript copy.

Because of the generosity and concern of our friends, colleagues, and people we met along the way, the quality of the book has improved. For saving us from mistakes, we say thanks. We recognize our responsibility for any errors the reader may find.

INTRODUCTION

An American Guide to British Social Science Resources is organized into three chapters and two appendices. Chapter I deals with the particular problems of scholars who plan to conduct research in Britain for a period of several weeks to a year. Information about touring, car rentals, sightseeing, hotels, resorts, and theaters should be sought in travel guide books.

Chapter I is divided into two sections: "When in the United States" and "When in Britain." The first section provides basic information about passports, travel arrangements, the British Embassy and Consulates, financial matters, and British information sources in the United States. It describes how advanced planning can save time getting settled and conducting research. The second section discusses housing arrangements, telephone facilities, and mail services in Britain. It indicates alien registration and work permit procedures, health care, school arrangements for children, and tax responsibilities. Information about typing and copying is also provided, and sources for writing markets are indicated. A schedule of holidays is included. The services provided by the American Embassy in Britain and a list of Government Bookshops conclude the chapter.

Chapter II is a description of the major British library and record office resources of interest to social scientists. This chapter constitutes the largest part of the book. The chapter is introduced by a preliminary section which should be read before examining a particular entry. That section describes how to use the guide by providing an explanation for each category of the entry. It also offers a quick-guide to important collections and sources of photographs, prints, and press clippings.

Chapter III describes the professional associations, societies, and political parties which social scientists may want either to join or visit. Special attention is given to services which these organizations provide for visiting scholars. There are appendices containing a select list of British universities and an alphabetical list of institutions.

Chapter 1

PLANNING THE TRIP

A. When in the United States

Preparations can be made in the United States which will save money and time and simplify work in Britain. Early attention should be given to travel, passport, academic credentials, housing, climate, packing, banking, and mail.

1. Travel

Most people crossing the Atlantic do so by air carrier. Fares vary enormously, depending on length of stay, affiliation with an organization, and the flexibility of one's travel schedule.

Charter flights are offered by many organizations, and usually this service provides the cheapest way to get to Britain. To be eligible for most charters, a person must have been a member of the organization chartering the plane for a minimum of six months. In the past, the American Association of University Professors, the American Historical Association, and the Modern Languages Association have conducted charter operations.

Another inexpensive way to get to Britain is by the use of Travel Group Charters (TGC's). TGC flights are available to anyone who books his ticket at least sixty-five days in advance. No affinity to an organization is necessary. All TGC flights are offered on a round-trip basis; no one-way trips are permitted.

The selection of this kind of charter during the fall and winter months is not as extensive as in the summer. The Council on International Education Exchange (CIEE) not

1

only offers many TGC flights, but also acts as a clearing-house for information on flights offered by other organizations. CIEE has two offices: 777 United Nations Plaza, New York, New York 10017, telephone: (212) 661-0310; and 235 East Santa Clara Street #710, San Jose, California 95113, telephone: (408) 287-8240. CIEE offers various services for students and faculty, including tours, discounts for travel within Europe, and guide books.

The Civil Aeronautics Board has approved a new type of charter flight, the "one-stop inclusive tour charter." This charter arrangement, which has no affinity requirement, can be as much as fifty per cent cheaper than standard coach flights. This is a combination package of airline tickets, hotel accommodations, and sometimes ground transportation or entertainment. Tickets must be booked thirty days in advance for foreign flights. Passengers must stay a minimum of six nights in a foreign city, but there is no maximum period. Travel agents have detailed information about this kind of charter flight.

A new type of fare, called APEX (Advance Purchase Excursion Fare), is now available. To use the APEX plan, an advance non-refundable deposit of twenty-five per cent must be made. A full payment is required two calendar months prior to departure. APEX tickets are valid for not less than twenty-two nor more than forty-five days, and no stopovers are permitted. No change in dates or cities can be made without a penalty.

In addition to the APEX plan, airlines offer fourteen to twenty-one day and twenty-two to forty-five day excursion fares. With these arrangements no advance booking is required. Passengers should investigate the difference in cost between the excursion and APEX fares to see if there is a significant saving.

Youth fares on scheduled carriers offer savings, but this service is limited to individuals under twenty-two years of age at the time of departure. The youth fare is round-trip and allows no stopovers. Reservations are confirmed five days prior to departure.

Icelandic Airline offers low-cost transportation to Luxembourg on modern jet aircraft. Passengers should compare the cost of going to Luxembourg and then to Britain with the cost of a direct flight to Britain.

The most expensive way to get to Britain by air is on a regular scheduled flight. The advantage of using this service is that it provides freedom to change a schedule at any time.

The airlines offer a variety of plans for travel, but regulations and prices change frequently because of the competitive character of the industry. It is wise to consult with a travel agent or representatives of a student union or travel committee on a university campus early in the planning of a trip.

Although travel by air carrier offers advantages of time and money, some people prefer a sea voyage. Not many ships make a regular trans-Atlantic run. The Queen Elizabeth II is one of the last big ships to make regular summer crossings. Passage on cargo ships is not inexpensive, but full information on schedules and costs can be obtained from a travel agent. One advantage of sea travel is that baggage allowances are more generous than the forty-four-pound maximum for economy fare air travelers.

2. Passports, Visas, and Other Documents

Citizens of the United States must have a valid passport to be admitted into Great Britain. To obtain a passport, a citizen or national of the United States must apply in person to either a passport agency, a clerk of any federal court, a clerk of any state court of record, a judge or clerk of any probate court, or a postal clerk designated by the Postmaster General (postal clerks have been designated only in certain areas). United States Passport Agency offices are located as follows:

Boston, Mass.	John F. Kennedy Building Government Center 02203
Chicago, Ill.	219 South Dearborn Street 60604
Honolulu, Hi.	Room 304 Federal Building 96813
Miami, Fla.	51 S. W. First Avenue 33130
New Orleans, La.	344 Camp Street 70130
New York, N. Y.	630 Fifth Avenue 10020
Los Angeles, Calif.	1004 Federal Office Building 300 North Los Angeles Street 90012
Philadelphia, Pa.	Room 4426 Federal Building 600 Arch Street 19106

San Francisco, Calif.   Room 1405 Federal Building
                               450 Golden Gate Avenue
                               94102
Seattle, Wash.   500 Union Street 98101
Washington, D.C.   1425 K Street, N.W. 20524

Family passports are available. A wife or husband
who is to be included in the passport must appear in person
with the applicant and also sign the application. Unmarried
children under the age of eighteen are not required to appear
in person. Applicants must show proof of United States citi-
zenship, which could be a previous passport, a certified copy
of a birth certificate, or a certificate of naturalization. Applicants should also have with them identification (e.g., driver's license, social security card, or credit card).

Duplicate, signed photographs taken within six months
of the date of application, portraying a good likeness of and
satisfactorily identifying the applicant, must be presented
with the application. Both photographs must be signed on
the front along the left-hand side without marring the fea-
tures. When a husband and wife and/or children are to be
included in the same passport, a group picture is preferred.
Separate photographs, however, may be submitted. The
photographs may be in color or black-and-white. They must
be full face and printed on thin unglazed paper with a light,
plain background. Photographs should not be larger than
three by three inches nor smaller than two and one-half by
two and one-half inches in size.

Although a passport is required for entrance into
Britain, no visas or international certificates of vaccination
are necessary for Americans. If an American visitor is also planning to travel first in countries where smallpox or
other vaccinations are required, he may have to provide
proof of vaccination before being permitted entry into Britain.

The conditions of entry mentioned above pertain to
American citizens. Other nationals should consult the near-
est British Consulate.

3. Brit3sh Information Sources in the United States

Authoritative sources of information about Britain
which Americans may consult in the United States are the
British Information Services, British Tourist Authority, and

the British Embassy and Consulates.

a. British Information Services

Information concerning British government, economics, industry, science, education, and other specific topics related to Britain can be obtained from British Information Services with addresses in the following cities:

845 Third Avenue, New York, New York 10022
3100 Massachusetts Avenue, N.W., Washington, D.C. 20008
33 North Dearborn Street, Chicago, Illinois 60602
Equitable Building, 120 Montgomery Street, San Francisco, California 94104

b. British Tourist Authority

General tourist information can be obtained from the British Tourist Authority located at the following addresses:

680 Fifth Avenue, New York, New York 10019
Suite 2450 John Hancock Center, 875 North Michigan Avenue, Chicago, Illinois 60611
612 South Flower Street, Los Angeles, California 90017

The British Tourist Authority can provide information and is an essential source for visiting academics. The Authority supplies lists of its offices in Britain. It furnishes information about hotels, apartments, travel, sightseeing, major events, discount schemes on British Rail, and car rentals. Some maps and tourist publications are offered without charge; the Authority also sells good British guide books.

c. British Embassy and Consulates

The British Embassy and British Consulates provide assistance to Americans on specific matters, not easily dealt with elsewhere. The locations and telephone numbers of the Embassy and Consulates are as follows:

Washington, D.C. (Embassy) 3100 Massachusetts Avenue, N.W. 20008; telephone: (202) 462-1340
Atlanta, Georgia Suite 912, 225 Peachtree Street, N.E. 30303; telephone: (404) 524-5856/8
Boston, Massachusetts Suite 4740 Prudential Tower, Prudential Center 02199; telephone: (617) 261-3060

Chicago, Illinois 33 North Dearborn Street 60602;
    telephone: (312) 346-1810/7
Houston, Texas Suite 2250, 601 Jefferson 77002;
    telephone: (713) 223-2301
Los Angeles, California 3701 Wilshire Boulevard 90010;
    telephone: (213) 385-7381
New York, New York 845 Third Avenue 10022;
    telephone: (212) 752-8400
St. Thomas, Virgin Islands P.O. Box 687, Charlotte
    Amalie 00801
San Francisco, California 9th Floor, Equitable Life
    Building, 120 Montgomery Street 94104;
    telephone: (415) 981-3030
San Juan, Puerto Rico Room 1014 Banco Popular Center,
    10th Floor Hato Rey, G.P.O. 2157 00926;
    telephone: (809) 767-4435

4. Academic Preparation

To prepare for the research period in Britain, the
foreign scholar should obtain the proper academic documents
and write to those libraries and associations he expects to
consult in Britain. It would be wise for him to communicate
with American professional organizations and government
agencies. He may also want to investigate British writing
markets.

a. Academic Documents

The visiting academic expecting to spend more than a
few weeks in Britain should have two different kinds of letters of introduction from his home institution. The first
letter should be written by a university official directing or
supervising the research. It will be helpful in avoiding red
tape when he arrives in Britain and is interviewed by an immigration official. The official must be satisfied that each
visitor has sufficient means of support, is able to meet the
cost of the return trip to the United States, and does not intend to settle permanently in Britain. This letter should indicate the specific nature of the work planned, e.g., sabbatical research project, study, etc., the anticipated length of
stay, and the source of financial support.

The second letter should be a general letter of introduction designed primarily for librarians and archivists rather than for an immigration official. This second letter should

also be written by a university official directing or supervising the work to be conducted. The letter should mention
the status of the scholar, his need to consult libraries, archives, or other sources, and his integrity to use those resources. It is wise to have several copies of this kind of
letter.

   b. Writing Ahead to British Libraries and Associa-
      tions

   Time can be saved by writing ahead to libraries and
associations. With sufficient notice admission tickets can be
arranged and books can be placed on reserve for immediate
use. The advantages of writing ahead are discussed in
Chapter 2, pp. 26-27.

   c. American Professional and Governmental Organi-
      zations

   American social scientists should consult with their
various professional associations to determine what assistance
those associations provide. Some associations have ties with
their British counterparts. Some are able to put the researcher in touch with people working in their discipline,
either in the United States or in Great Britain, or in both.

   One association involved in this academic area is the
American Political Science Association (APSA). In the Fall
1974 issue of PS, an APSA publication, the Association ex-
pressed interest in developing on a continuing basis a roster
of members traveling abroad. This roster would assist
other national political science associations, universities,
and agencies in meeting such individuals for the purpose of
inviting them to attend or speak at seminars and meetings.

   Political scientists might also be interested in the
British Politics Group, founded at the 1974 APSA convention.
The organization has established as one of its first priorities
the improvement of communications among students of British politics. It publishes a register of ongoing research on
the United Kingdom. A newsletter provides information on
such subjects as conferences, grant opportunities, research
activities in progress, publishing outlets, and personnel
changes. Inquiries about the group should be directed to
Dr. Jorgan Rasmussen, Executive Secretary, British Politics
Group, Department of Political Science, 509 Ross Hall, Iowa
State University, Ames, Iowa 50010.

Another source of preliminary investigation is the
United States Information Agency (USIA) Volunteer Speaker
Program. The Speakers Division of the USIA recruits members who are willing, while traveling abroad on other than
government grants, to lecture under U.S. Embassy or USIA
auspices on a volunteer basis. Visitors may be asked to
talk before professional groups, to participate in seminars
or panel discussions, to lecture at universities, or to attend
social events offering opportunities for the informal exchange
of ideas with colleagues in the same field.

No travel grants are offered. USIA posts, however,
usually offer speakers a modest honorarium, per diem, and
travel expenses for any detours from their planned itinerary.
Inquiries about the program should be sent to USIA, Information Center Service, Speakers Division, 1717 H Street, N.W.,
Washington, D.C. 20547.

d. Writing Markets

American scholars might wish to write for British
journals or newspapers. Some of the British journals welcome contributions in the form of articles and reviews from
Americans on sabbatical in Britain. Those who wish to write
should consult the particular publication for information. An
indispensable guide is The Writers' and Artists' Year Book
(London: Adam and Charles Black). The book contains a
list of markets for books, journal articles, and newspaper
articles in Britain and elsewhere. In addition to consulting
that yearbook, scholars might want to write directly to the
editor of a British journal, indicating their projects and
qualifications.

5. Housing

In this section, attention is given to what can be done
in the United States to arrange for housing in Britain. Another section on housing, which describes different types of
accommodations, is located in the "When in Britain" section
of this chapter.

Locating suitable housing accommodations in Britain
is a difficult task facing the foreign visitor. The advantages
of making pre-trip housing commitments are that time is
saved and rental costs will probably be relatively low. The
disadvantage of booking from the United States is that one

cannot see what he is selecting but must depend upon the description of others.

Among methods for obtaining accommodations in Britain while still in the U.S. are the following: 1) consulting a friend or colleague who has spent time in Britain; 2) advertising in British newspapers or magazines; 3) writing to a university accommodations office; 4) writing to an agency in the United States which arranges for housing overseas; 5) making short-term reservations at a hotel in Britain; and 6) requesting information of Tourist Information Centres.

a. Friends and Colleagues

Faculty members and students might have contacts in Britain and could secure information about the availability of apartments or houses and about the proximity of the suggested area to the place of major research effort. This method of finding housing often produces the best results, since the information and description are generally reliable.

b. Advertising

Some newspapers and magazines carry advertisements from American academics seeking housing in Britain. An advertisement can be placed in the New York Review of Books, New Statesman, Spectator, The Times (London), Evening Standard, London Weekly Advertiser, or provincial newspapers. In addition to the usual information the advertisement should indicate the length of stay. It is sometimes possible to exchange housing with a Briton visiting in the United States.

c. University Accommodations

A foreign academic can receive assistance from the university accommodations office of any British university. Universities frequently make their housing available during vacation periods to individuals who may or may not be associated with that university. Many university accommodations offices also retain a list of accommodations available in the surrounding area. The names of major universities and their addresses can be found in Appendix A.

d. American Agencies

Two companies in the United States can be helpful in

locating housing. University Holidays Limited/AAD Associates, P.O. Box 2093, Eads Station, Arlington, Virginia 22202, telephone: (703) 521-2240, offers individuals, families, and groups a wide selection of holiday accommodations at many universities throughout Great Britain. These accommodations range from a single bedroom with a full English breakfast to a self-catering flat with several bedrooms. Rooms are available for a single night, a long weekend, or a holiday season.

Vacation Exchange Club, 350 Broadway, New York, New York 10013, offers people from all over the world the opportunity to exchange houses. The club publishes a directory, issued in December and February. Subscribers advertise their homes and indicate the desired location of an exchange house. There is a charge for advertising in the directories.

e. Short-Term Reservations

For those individuals who want to inspect housing before making commitments, an option is to make reservations at a British hotel for the first few days after arrival. This procedure is particularly useful if the researcher's family accompanies him. A list of hotels can be obtained from a travel agency or from the British Tourist Authority. It should be remembered that hotel rooms, particularly in London, are expensive. Requests can be made to the Tourist Authority for budget-price accommodations.

f. Tourist Information Centres

The British Tourist Authority will provide a booklet listing the towns and cities in the United Kingdom which have Tourist Information Centres. The booklet indicates the address, telephone number, and basic services offered, including whether the particular agency will arrange accommodations. Some of these, particularly outside London, will help locate long-term accommodations for visitors.

6. Climate

Although Britain is located as far north as Newfoundland, the Gulf Stream waters flowing near the coast affect and warm the climate. Extreme conditions are rare. In winter, polar continental air will sometimes pass over the

country, bringing excessive cold. In summer, southerly air-
streams have been known to drive the temperature in southern
England as high as ninety degrees Fahrenheit.

The Highlands generally receive more rain than other
areas, although the entire country enjoys much rainfall which
is fairly well distributed throughout the year. In general,
April, May, and June are the driest months; August, October, and December are the wettest. The number of days of
snowfall each year ranges from as many as thirty in northeast Scotland to as few as five in southwest England.

Climate averages for Britain, by month, are as follows:

	J	F	M	A	My	Jn	Jl	Ag	S	O	N	D
Average daily temp. (°F)	39	40	43	48	54	60	63	62	57	50	44	41
Average daily low (°F)	35	35	36	40	45	51	54	54	49	44	39	36
Average daily high (°F)	43	45	49	55	62	68	71	70	65	56	49	45
Average humidity (%)	85	82	79	75	73	73	73	76	80	85	86	86
No. of days of rain	15	15	14	13	12	12	13	13	12	16	16	16

When one is in Britain, he may obtain weather information and forecasts by telephone. The number in London is
01-246 8091. For most other areas, one must dial the proper exchange and 8091. A list of the exchange numbers may
be found in Whitaker's Almanack.

7. What to Take

The traveler to Britain will need to know the household effects to take, the customs regulations on these articles, the effect of voltage on electrical appliances, and the
availability of typewriters and stationery supplies.

a. Household Effects

Many apartments and homes come furnished with linen, blankets, crockery, silverware, and cooking utensils. Towels are generally not provided except at hotels.

b. Customs Regulations

Visitors to Britain who plan to spend less than a year can enter the country with personal, household, and professional effects without any customs duty charge or value-added tax if these effects are solely for their own or their dependents' private or professional use and are to be re-exported on their departure. It is possible that they will be asked to leave a recoverable deposit as security for the tax on new or valuable articles. As an alternative procedure, they can arrange to have the articles sealed and forwarded under a carrier's bond to the port of exportation at their own expense.

Those visitors planning to spend more than a year in Britain may take into the country at no duty charge personal and household effects solely for their own or dependents' use. The Customs Officer must be satisfied that these items are solely for continued personal use and have been in the visitor's possession and use outside the United Kingdom for some time (usually twelve months, but three months in the case of most clothing or textile goods or articles of very small value).

American visitors who leave from the United States for Britain are allowed to take into the country without duty payment the following items: 400 cigarettes, or 200 cigarillos, or 100 cigars, or 500 grams of tobacco; one liter of alcoholic beverages over 38.8 proof or fortified or sparkling wine plus two liters of still table wine; two ounces of perfume; one-fourth liter of toilet water; and £10 worth of other goods.

Certain goods are prohibited or restricted. These include counterfeit money, addictive drugs, firearms and ammunition, flick knives, plants, bulbs and certain vegetables and fruits, radio transmitters (including walkie-talkies), meat and poultry (not fully cooked), most mammals including domestic animals, and birds. The landing of animals in Britain must be authorized by a license issued by an appropriate government department. Information about taking animals into the country can be obtained from any British Consulate or the British Information Services in New York.

Americans may take into Britain notes in any currency, travelers' checks, and letters of credit without limit.
When leaving Britain, visitors may take with them sterling
of Scheduled Territory notes up to an aggregate value of £25,
as well as foreign currency notes up to a total value of £300.
They may also take out any foreign currency notes which
were brought in with them.

c. Electrical Appliances

Electric appliances should be checked for voltage
specifications before being transported to Britain. In Britain,
the voltage generally in use varies from 220 to 250 volts al-
ternating current. American equipment might require trans-
formers since it usually operates on lower voltages. Items
with motors, e.g., electric shavers, food-mixers, refrigera-
tors, vacuum cleaners, and floor polishers, are relatively
easy to convert.

Items with timing devices, e.g., clocks, automatic
washing machines and cookers, most types of record players
and hi-fi components, are difficult to convert. Items with
heating elements might need an expensive transformer.
American television sets are convertible only at great expense. There are many television rental companies in Britain, so visitors wishing to have a television set should consider this option. Users of television sets must possess an
annual license, which can be purchased at any post office.

d. Typewriters and Stationery Supplies

Light-weight portable typewriters can be taken with
the researcher on his trip, but there are many stores which
rent and sell new or used typewriters. Stationery stores are
available in abundance. Although a variety of typing paper
is manufactured, the standard size differs from the 8-1/2 by
11-inch American standard, which is difficult to obtain and
when available is usually of low quality. The standard size
British typewriter paper measures 8-1/4 by 11-3/4 inches.
Graduate students who are required to type their dissertations or theses on a particular size paper should consider
taking a sufficient quantity with them. Other stationery
items, such as typewriter ribbons, pens, etc., are easy to
locate.

8. Banking and Money

Visitors have a variety of methods available to them
for handling their money. It should be remembered that the
relative value of British and American currency fluctuates.
Americans who plan to spend several months in Britain
might, therefore, find it desirable not to change all their
American dollars into British sterling at one time.

For long stays in Britain, a bank account would be
helpful and a letter of introduction from the visitor's home
bank will expedite the process of opening an account. Although an American check can be deposited in a British bank
account, it normally takes several weeks for the check to
clear and be converted into British currency. A faster
method is to request the British bank to wire the American
bank (higher fees are charged for this service) or to purchase a sterling draft before leaving the United States. The
draft is immediately negotiable and can be put directly into
an account.

Travelers' checks are probably more useful for short
visits. These can be purchased in the United States either
in American or British currency denominations. It is good
to remember here, too, that the value of currency fluctuates, and thought should be given to what kind of travelers'
checks to obtain. Either kind is readily accepted in Britain.

It is sensible to have some British currency in hand
upon arrival in Britain so that first-day expenses can easily
be met. British money can be purchased in most American
banks and some travel agencies.

Credit cards are useful in Britain as they sometimes
allow for the immediate cashing of American personal checks
up to five hundred dollars. The services provided for each
card should be ascertained before departure. Bills for
American credit cards used in Britain are eventually converted into dollars. Often the rate of exchange for the bill
is not the same as on the day of the purchase, but rather
the rate as of the day that the credit card company makes
its conversion from pounds to dollars. It can take as long
as three months from the day of purchase for a bill to be
received from the credit card company. Some firms add a
small charge (about one or one and a half per cent) for this
kind of transaction.

Overseas visitors can exchange money in banks and bureaux de change. Hotels, shops and restaurants will also exchange money, but generally at an unfavorable rate. A passport or visa is required for identification to change money.

Normal banking hours in England and Wales are Monday to Friday, 9:30 A.M. to 3:30 P.M. In Scotland, the hours are Monday to Wednesday, 9:30 A.M. to 12:30 P.M., 1:30 P.M. to 4:30 P.M.; Thursday, 9:30 A.M. to 12:30 P.M., 1:30 P.M. to 3:30 P.M., 4:30 P.M. to 6:00 P.M.; Friday, 9:30 A.M. to 3:30 P.M. In Northern Ireland, banks are open Monday to Friday, 10:00 A.M. to 12:30 P.M., 1:30 P.M. to 3:30 P.M. Air and rail terminals at major cities often contain banks which are open more hours on more days of the week.

9. Mail

If a mailing address is essential, visitors should consider using the General Delivery of the Post Office in any British city. Letters and parcels to be called for can be addressed to any major post office in Britain. The words "To Be Called For" or "Poste Restante" should appear in the address. Poste Restante is provided solely for the convenience of travelers and may not be used in the same town for more than three months.

It is not even essential to know in advance the location of the main post office. The words "Main Post Office" appearing in the address will direct the letter to the proper location. In London, a letter addressed to Poste Restante, Main Post Office, will be directed to King Edward Building, King Edward Street, London EC1A 1LP. Because of London's large population, it is possible to have mail sent to Poste Restante, Trafalgar Square B.O., 24-28 William IV Street, London WC2N 4DL, but that name and address, rather than Main Post Office, should appear on the envelope or package. Letters are generally not held for periods longer than two weeks before being returned to the sender. General delivery is a good short-term method to obtain mail if a location has not been determined in advance of departure.

B. When in Britain

        Even with prior planning, it is not always possible to
arrange for housing or to complete alien registration forms
in advance. Visitors should become familiar with legal responsibilities and should know about services and facilities
in Britain.

1. Housing

        In the previous section suggestions were made for ad-
vance planning to locate housing. It is not always possible
to make these advance commitments. This section describes
how to locate housing after the visitor has arrived in Britain.

        Some aspects of housing in Britain should be kept in
mind. Prices tend to be higher in the summer months than
at other times of the year; hotel rooms, apartments, and
houses are more expensive in central London than in other
parts of Britain. Accommodations are available which provide a variety of facilities.

        It is more difficult to obtain a telephone in Britain
than in the United States. Success depends on the location
of the city and whether a telephone has already been installed for a previous tenant. If a telephone is installed for
the first time in an apartment or house, the cost of installation might be as much as one-hundred dollars. If a phone,
although disconnected, is already in place, the installation
cost is much less. The Post Office, which handles telephones in Britain, does not give estimates. Some apartment
buildings, however, have pay telephones.

        To locate accommodations in Britain, the following
sources can be examined: newspapers and magazines, Tourist Information Centres, accommodation agencies and estate
agents, and notices on posting boards.

        a. Newspapers and Magazines

        Newspapers and magazines publish want-ads for apart-
ments and house rental. Of particular interest in London is
the London Weekly Advertiser. The "good buys" are taken
up quickly, so it is advisable to get a copy of the paper as
soon as it appears. Other sources are indicated in the ear-

lier section on housing.

b. Tourist Information Centres

Tourist Information Centres, which have been described above, are located throughout Britain. In most large cities, they can provide hotel and guest house accommodations. Many tourist offices have names and addresses of lessors of accommodations for long-term users.

In London there is a London Tourist Board office at Victoria Station (near platform 15) which is open daily, offering hotel accommodations. For budget and student accommodations, visitors must go to 8-10 Buckingham Palace Road, London SW1W ODU (located near Victoria Station), which is open only from June to October. At other times of the year, budget and student accommodations are arranged at Platform 15 of Victoria Station. No telephone reservations are made; it is necessary to go personally to the office.

c. Accommodation Agencies and Estate Agents

Accommodation agencies and estate agents offer apartments and houses for rental and sale. A list of companies can be found in the classified telephone directory. Generally, a fee equal to one week's rent is charged for locating a place, but this cost might be worth the time saved. It should be noted that most of these offices are closed on weekends.

d. Notices

One source for locating accommodations is notices which are posted on boards outside stores, such as newsagent's dealers and stationery stores, where individuals place messages advertising apartments or rooms for rent. If the visitor knows the particular area of a city in which he prefers to live, he might want to peruse these notices. This method of finding accommodations is time-consuming, but it does provide another option.

2. Legal Requirements

Americans planning to spend several months in Britain should be familiar with regulations governing alien registration, work permits, and driver's licenses.

a. Alien Registration

Immigration officials might request long-term visitors
to register with the police. Usually registration is required
within ten days of arrival. In London the place to register
is the Metropolitan Police Office, 10 Lamb's Conduit Street,
London WC1N 3X. Addresses of registration locations outside London will be furnished by immigration officials.

Immigration officials will require the information described in the section on letters of introduction. A few pass-
port-size photos are required. If necessary, these can be
obtained from a coin-operated camera at the registration
building. Academic scholars on a summer trip are generally
not required to register.

b. Work Permits

Most people who go to Britain for employment are required to hold work permits issued by the Department of Employment. The permit must be obtained by the prospective
employer for a named worker. It is issued for a specific
job for a stated period which may not exceed twelve months.
Teachers and language assistants coming to schools in Britain for periods up to twelve months under approved exchange
schemes do not need work permits. Specific questions about
work permits should be directed to the British Embassy or
Consulates.

c. Driver's License

A valid American driver's license or international
driving permit will be accepted in Britain for a period of
one year. After that year a visitor is regarded as a resident and must obtain a provisional driving license and take
the driving test.

3. Taxes

Americans who plan to spend several months in Britain should consult their accountants in the United States to
determine their tax status. Income tax inquiries for Britain
should be addressed to the Secretary, Board of Inland Revenue, Somerset House, London WC2R 1LB. Customs and
Value Added Tax (VAT) inquiries should be directed to the
Secretary HM Customs and Excise, King's Beam House,

Mark Lane, London EC3R 7HE.

Britain has double taxation agreements with the United States. These agreements provide that the income of certain classes arising in one country is, subject to certain conditions, exempt from tax or taxed at a reduced rate in that country if it flows to a resident of the other.

Under present rules governing sabbaticals, half of income received from the American university is liable to United Kingdom income tax, unless the work done in Britain is entirely unconnected with normal duties of employment in the United States. Generally, if the purpose of sabbatical leave is to increase the person's professional standing and value to his institution, and if the sabbatical stay in Britain is more than 183 days in any fiscal year commencing April 6, he is subject to United Kingdom income tax. (Article XIX of the Double Taxation Convention Between the United States and the United Kingdom has no standing for academics because the article refers to students.) Article XI (2) applies to academics. This article provides that if the academic is in the United Kingdom for less than 183 days in any fiscal year commencing April 6, no United Kingdom tax will be charged. Each fiscal year is considered separately. This provision applies to academics who receive any part of their salary. They will be entitled to full U.K. personal allowances in computing their liability to U.K. tax. They can claim, under the Double Taxation Convention, credit for U.K. tax against U.S. tax through the U.S. Internal Revenue Service. Whether income from research grants and fellowships is taxable in the U.K. depends upon the precise terms and conditions of the grants and fellowships, and no general rule can be given.

Americans may take advantage of VAT rebates for goods purchased in Britain and exported either personally or by mail. VAT is a general turnover tax on consumption and applies to a wide range of goods and services supplied in the course of a business and to imported goods but not to imported services. VAT is calculated as a percentage of the value of the supply, generally the actual amount paid excluding VAT itself. The single standard rate of VAT is eight per cent, and for certain luxury items, twenty-five per cent.

Certain purchases by overseas visitors to Britain can be exported free of VAT under the personal export and over-

the-counter schemes. One scheme provides relief from VAT
on motor vehicles purchased by overseas visitors for temporary use in Britain and subsequent exportation. Department stores which export goods will generally provide the
proper VAT forms. If the store ships merchandise directly,
the procedure is simple. If the visitor takes purchases with
him, he must show the merchandise and the form to the
Customs Official at the point of embarkation. If baggage is
checked through at a British airport before the Customs Official inspects the goods and rebate forms, no rebate is
forthcoming.

4. Health Care

        Americans who travel to Britain wholly or mainly to
seek medical treatment are expected to pay for it privately
and might be asked by immigration authorities to produce
evidence that they have made arrangements to do so. Medical care to non-residents is limited to treatment of emer-
gencies which arise during the period of the stay in Britain.
This emergency treatment is provided under the National
Health Service. Non-residents must pay for most dental
costs, however.

5. Schools

        American visitors can enroll their children in British
schools, which are organized into two categories: 1) the
system of public education, which is comprised of schools
owned and maintained by public education authorities and
schools owned by private (usually religious) organizations but
maintained out of public funds; and 2) independent private
schools (including what are called Public Schools), which receive no grant from public funds. There are also a few
schools which are not maintained by local education authorities but receive direct grants from the government. Tuition
is charged in these schools.

        Within the public system of education, free services
are provided to all children from the age of five to eighteen,
who are normally or temporarily residents in the United
Kingdom without respect to nationality. Some educational
authorities provide free nursery schools for children between
the ages of two and five. Local authority nursery school
policy varies widely, however. Parents from the United

States wishing to send their children to schools in the public educational system should write to the Chief Education Officer of the education authority in the area in which they intend to live.

The Department of Education and Science publishes List 70, a list of independent schools in England and Wales. List 70 is available from Pendragon House Inc., 220 University Avenue, Palo Alto, California 94301, or it can be consulted in the British Information Services Library.

For Scotland, there is no equivalent List 70. A list of independent schools can be obtained from The Secretary, Scottish Education Department, St. Andrew's House, Edinburgh EH1 3DQ.

6. Holiday Schedule

On bank holidays most libraries are closed. University schedules vary, but generally they are from October 1 to the end of June, with about one month holiday at Easter and one month at Christmas. The schedule for bank holidays is as follows:

England and Wales

New Year's Day
Good Friday
Easter Monday
The last Monday in May
The last Monday in August
Christmas Day
December 26
December 27 (if December 25 or 26 is a Sunday)

Scotland

New Year's Day
January 2
January 3 (if January 1 or 2 is a Sunday)
Good Friday
The first Monday in May
The first Monday in August
Christmas Day
December 26 (if December 25 is a Sunday)

Northern Ireland

New Year's Day
March 17
March 18 (if March 17 is a Sunday)
Easter Monday
July 12
The last Monday in August
Christmas Day
December 26
December 27 (if December 25 or 26 is a Sunday)

7. American Embassy and Consulates

The American Embassy and Consulates will advise or help if an American citizen is in serious difficulty or distress. They do not, however, perform the work of travel agencies, information bureaus, banks, the police, and accommodation bureaus. They do not hold mail for American citizens, since that function is performed by the Post Office.

The Embassy and Consulates can provide a list of attorneys if requested to do so. They can locate appropriate medical services and inform next of kin if an American is injured or becomes seriously ill.

The American Embassy (24/31 Grosvenor Square, London W1A 2LH; telephone: 01-499 9000) operates a Speakers' Bureau. At various times, the Cultural Attaché receives requests for speakers in a variety of fields. Faculty and students can register with the Speakers' Bureau if they wish to be considered for such engagements.

8. Government Bookshops

Government bookshops are located in London and other major cities. These stores contain publications of Her Majesty's Stationery Office (HMSO). HMSO is also the United Kingdom agent for European Community publications, and for those of the principal international organizations. HMSO publishes a monthly catalog listing the publications that can be purchased in the stores. The American agent for British Government publications is Pendragon House, Inc., 220 University Avenue, Palo Alto, California 94301.

Her Majesty's Stationery Office is located at Atlantic House, Holborn Viaduct, London EC1P 1BN. The mailing address for orders is The Government Bookshop, P.O. Box 569, London SE1 9NH. Telephone orders may be placed by calling 01-928 1321.

Government bookshops are found in the following locations:

England

258 Broad Street
Birmingham B1 2HE

50 Fairfax Street
Bristol BS1 3DE

49 High Holborn
London WC1V 6HB

Brazennose Street
Manchester M60 8AS

Scotland

13a Castle Street
Edinburgh EH2 3AR

Wales

109 St. Mary Street
Cardiff CF1 1JW

Northern Ireland

80 Chichester Street
Belfast BT1 4JY

Chapter 2

LIBRARIES AND ARCHIVES

A. How to Use This Section

This section contains entries for the institutions holding the most important social science collections in Great
Britain. The criterion for selecting an institution is the
value it has to social scientists. Not all library and archival
collections in the United Kingdom, therefore, are indicated
here.

The length and detail of each entry vary because of:
1) the overall importance of the collection to social scientists, and 2) the kind of information available about the institution. Lengthy citations are given some institutions, such
as the British Library and the Public Record Office, because
of the great importance of their holdings. Other institutions
with much smaller collections sometimes have substantial entries because of the unique quality of their collections.

The data for each entry were obtained from questionnaires, published sources, and personal interviews. This
procedure presented some difficulties. In some cases no
quantification or classification of holdings has ever been
made, and the librarians themselves do not know how many
books or periodicals are contained in their collections. In
all cases, however, the authors have sought to present an ac-
curate compilation.

The best way to understand the meaning of each library entry in the guide is to spend some time reading the
description of each category in this section. The categories
include the institution, address, telephone, underground stop
(for London), holdings, subject coverage, access, publications, duplication, and services.

Institutions: Institutions include universities, public and private libraries, record offices, newspapers, societies and political parties. The institutions are listed alphabetically according to location.

To make the Guide more usable cross-references are given. Sometimes a library is part of a university, and the entry is filed under the particular university rather than the library name. The School of Oriental and African Studies Library, consequently, is described under London, University of London, School of Oriental and African Studies. Cross-referencing is also used when the formal name of a library is not the same as the institution which houses it. The library at the London School of Economics, for example, is officially named British Library of Political and Economic Science.

Among the institutions, record offices present the greatest difficulty because of recent boundary changes. On April 1, 1974, a law was enacted which reorganized the counties of the United Kingdom. Some of these counties were combined with others, some changed their jurisdiction, and some disappeared as legal entities. Record office material has been moved or retained without any uniform pattern. The dust has not yet settled from the reorganization, but the entries for record offices are based on the most recent information available to the authors.

In part, because the restructuring has not been completed, there is some confusion as to where some county record offices will be located. The entry for the record office sometimes includes the new county jurisdiction. Where the old county has become a division of a larger unit and the record office has been retained in the old location, a separate entry has often been made. To the maximum extent possible, cross-references are provided.

The reader will find that some societies are included in this chapter and others in the next. Many societies have libraries, and dual entries appear in a few instances. The criterion for including a society here is whether its collection is an important social science resource.

Address: Library collections for a single institution are often housed in different locations. These are indicated sometimes in the address category, but often later in the entry. If the location of a library is to change, the new address is also indicated.

Telephone: Telephone entries include the STD number (area code), which should be used only for long distance
calls. In this Guide the STD number appears before the
hyphen in the telephone listing.

Underground: The underground stops have been listed
for London. The London Underground, however, does not
extend to all locations in London.

Holdings: Holdings include books, pamphlets, periodicals, microforms, records (printed and manuscript),
manuscripts, documents, press clippings, maps, plans,
prints, photographs, paintings, and recordings. There is
little consistency among institutions in reporting this category. In some entries, therefore, books are listed alone
and in others are included with reports or pamphlets.
Where exact figures have been furnished, they are cited.
Where no figures were provided, we only record the fact
that a particular form of material is held. Some record offices have supplied their holdings variously in terms of numbers of documents, volumes of documents, linear feet, cubic
feet, rooms, or even tons. The purpose of including a figure is to give the reader a rough idea of the extent of the
collection. A figure presented in whatever form is better
than none. The figures for the holdings include the total
collection (not merely the social science holdings) unless
otherwise specified.

Subject Coverage: The major collections in social
science for each institution are included in this section.
Some of the library collections are so enormous that only a
few of the significant holdings are mentioned. Here again,
the amount of information provided depends in large part on
the response of the institution. More thorough data can be
sought in the publications category.

Access: This section indicates whether a collection
is open to the public, is available to scholars conducting advanced research, necessitates payment of a fee, and requires
a letter of introduction. The hours of operation are also included both for regular sessions and for holiday periods.
Unusual periods during which a library is closed are recorded in this section.

Since research time is limited for the American schol-

ar in Britain, the general rule is that he should write or
telephone ahead to the institution holding the materials he
needs. Time can be saved by postal or telephone inquiries,
and in some cases such inquiries are essential. In this way
readers' tickets can be secured in advance; books can be
placed on reserve for a specified date; and other information can be obtained. In some cases staff and space limitations are such that an appointment is required. If the scholar appears on the premises unannounced, he might find that
he must return at another time. The researcher should
consider taking with him a letter of introduction, as described on pages 6-7.

Publications: The term publication is given broad interpretation. This entry category lists formally published
bibliographies, monographs, typewritten catalogues, handlists, etc. Both current and out-of-print publications are
included. If the entry makes no specific mention of the publisher, it can generally be assumed that the institution is
the publisher. If a work describing some aspect of the collection is published elsewhere, that fact is recorded in this
category.

Duplication: Extensive coverage of duplication services is included because American researchers often plan
to microfilm or photocopy materials for study at their home
institutions. Usually duplication devices are not used as ex-
tensively as in the United States; consequently, rapid service
cannot be assured. For example, the Public Record Office
has a large staff and many modern copying machines in its
Photographic Division, but a period of three to six months
is often required for microfilm work to be processed. Other
institutions vary in their speed in executing copying orders,
so individuals planning to copy material should give attention to this category.

This section also contains price information for copying services. Because Britain is experiencing serious in-
flation, the entries do not contain specific figures. The ad-
jectives used to describe prices are low, moderate, moderately high, and expensive. For full-size copying at the time
of writing (summer 1975), low meant two to three pence per
sheet; moderate, five pence; moderately high, six pence; expensive, seven pence and over.

Services: This category records whether material
circulates. The term "to circulate" is used in its American

library context, meaning to be loaned. The category also indicates the kinds of inquiries which are answered, the nature of research assistance provided, and the interlibrary loan opportunities offered. Other specialized information is explained.

Most British libraries are associated with the British Library Lending Division (BLLD). Visiting academics should note that the BLLD offers one of the best national interlibrary loan services in the world. The lending system in the United States is decentralized, and researchers often must wait for weeks to get a book from another library. Such is not the case with BLLD. The BLLD has modern telex and postal facilities and prides itself on processing the bulk of its orders within twenty-four hours of receipt. It has a remarkable ninety-four per cent satisfaction rate and operates an international service.

B.   Quick Reference Guide

Major Collections: The following institutions attract most American researchers in the social sciences:

Bodleian Library (Reference No. 191)
British Library (No. 95)
British Library of Political and Economic Science
    (No. 138)
Cambridge University Library (No. 24)
Institute of Historical Research (No. 164)
Public Record Office (No. 147)
Royal Commission on Historical Manuscripts (No. 150).

Photographic and Print Collections: Many libraries contain photographs and prints. Those with large holdings are the following:

Bath Reference Library (No. 8)
Birmingham Public Libraries (No. 15)
Bishopsgate Institute Library (No. 91)
Brighton Area Libraries (No. 17)
British Broadcasting Corporation Reference Library
    (No. 93)
Cambridge County Record Office (No. 23)

Canning House Library (No. 97)
Central (London) Office of Information (No. 98)
City of Cardiff (County of South Glamorgan) Public Libraries (No. 27)
Department of the Environment, Property Services Agency Library (No. 106)
Durham University Library (No. 47)
East Sussex County Library (No. 73)
Gateshead Public Libraries (No. 60)
Greater London Council Maps, Prints, and Photographs (No. 111)
Guildhall Library (No. 115)
Hampshire County Library (No. 220)
Hereford Cathedral Library (negatives) (No. 70)
Hertfordshire Record Office (No. 71)
House of Lords Record Office (No. 122)
Imperial War Museum Libraries and Archives (No. 123)
India Office Library (No. 124)
Institute of Contemporary History and Wiener Library (No. 127)
Labour Party Library (No. 129)
London Borough of Bexley (No. 133)
London Borough of Tower Hamlets Libraries Department (No. 136)
Manchester Public Libraries (No. 178)
Ministry of Overseas Development, Directorate of Overseas Surveys (No. 109)
National Library of Wales (No. 2)
National Monuments Record (No. 144)
Norfolk County Library (No. 187)
The Polish Library (No. 146)
Royal Air Force Museum (No. 148)
Sheffield City Libraries (No. 203)
Society of Antiquaries of London Library (No. 153)
Southampton City Record Office (No. 209)
Treasury and Cabinet Office Library (No. 159)
University of Newcastle Upon Tyne Library (No. 183)
University of Reading, Institute of Agricultural History and Museum of English Rural Life (No. 198)
West Sussex Record Office (No. 36)
Westminster Abbey Muniment Room and Library (No. 173)
William Salt Library (No. 212)

Press Clippings: British newspaper libraries contain extensive sources of newspaper clippings, but these are generally for internal use, and are not listed in the Guide.

Other library collections which contain large holdings of press clippings are the following:

> Commonwealth Institute Library and Resources Centre (Reference No. 100)
> Conservative Research Department Library (Conservative Party) (No. 102)
> House of Commons Library (No. 120)
> House of Lords Record Office (No. 122)
> Imperial War Museum Library and Archives (No. 123)
> Institute of Contemporary History and Wiener Library (No. 127)
> International Institute for Strategic Studies (No. 128)
> Labour Party Library (No. 129)
> London Borough of Tower Hamlets Libraries Department (No. 136)
> Norfolk County Library (No. 187)
> Plaid Cymru (Welsh National Party) (No. 29)
> Royal Institute of International Affairs Library (No. 151)
> Scottish Conservative Central Office (No. 51)

Resident Library: For those scholars in search of solitude and quiet for writing or conducting research, attention should be directed to St. Deiniol's Library in Hawarden (Reference No. 39). Low-cost accommodations are provided for both short-term and long-term users. The library is located a few miles from Chester.

C. Record Offices and Other Genealogical Resources

The public record offices are the richest sources of genealogical information in Britain. The Reorganization Act of April 1, 1974, caused many of the county boundary lines in Great Britain to be changed. As a result, record offices which were once independent units have, in some cases, come under the administration of a central office. In these instances the entries in this book are included under the name of the central office. Dual entries will occasionally be found. The dates of records held in the various record offices are not given in every entry, but wherever possible an indication of the earliest material available has been noted.

Among the genealogical resources available in British record offices are ecclesiastical records, bishops' transcripts, wills, records of Quarter Sessions and Petty Sessions courts, custumal records, muniments, visitations, and manorial records. The meanings of these terms are not always clear to the American.

Ecclesiastical records generally refer to the records of the Church of England, the Church in Wales, the Episcopal Church in Scotland, and the Church of Ireland. The searcher can expect parish registers of the Church of England to contain entries of baptism, marriage, and burial. Non-conformist church registers vary with the sect, but usually contain records of birth or baptism or both, marriage, and burial. Registers for the Roman Catholic Church are written mostly in Latin and record births, baptisms, marriages, and some deaths or burials. The entries for baptisms occasionally give the names of the sponsors at christening and make reference to the parents' marriage.

Bishops' transcripts are copies of parish registers. These are like the originals, except that there are frequent omissions. Occasionally, when the originals have been destroyed, the transcripts are the only remaining records.

Wills give the name of the deceased and usually his/her residence and occupation. The date on which the will was made and the date of its proving are given, as well as the names of the heirs and the executors or administrators.

Quarter Sessions court records provide a record of crimes, of the administration of the courts, and of land tax assessments. The records of crimes give the name, residence and occupation of the defendant, the name of the plaintiff, and the name of each witness. Jury lists for each court session give names, residences, and sometimes occupations of the jurors. Petty Sessions courts are the courts of summary jurisdiction of justices of the peace. Occasionally these records are available.

Custumal records refer to the collection of the customs of a manor.

Muniments are documentary records or archives, but in law, the term refers specifically to title deeds to property.

Visitation refers to the ceremonial visit of an official

for purposes of inspection. It can mean the document which
records the results of the visit of a herald to individuals
within his province. The herald may investigate the right to
bear arms or hear claims for grants of arms.

In the older sense, manorial records refer to a ter-
ritorial or jurisdictional unit. Modern usage refers to a
specific estate. The control held over tenants by the lord of
a manor was exercised through the manor court. Manorial
records are those pertaining to the business of the manor and
criminal and civil cases heard in the manor court. Manorial
rolls contain legal evidence of servitude.

Most record offices will answer short postal queries,
but extensive searching must be done by the individual.
Only rarely are charges made for the use of the records,
but in some cases the record office staff will conduct a
search for which a fee is charged.

Genealogical material will also be found in libraries,
church archives, and private collections. A list of genealogical resources and record offices included in this Guide
follows:

England

Aylesbury:	Buckinghamshire Record Office
Beverley:	Humberside County Record Office
Bristol:	Bristol Record Office
Cambridge:	Cambridge County Record Office
	Gonville and Caius College Library, Cambridge
Canterbury:	Cathedral Archives and Library, Canterbury
Carlisle:	Cumbria County Council Archives Department
Chelmsford:	Essex Record Office
Chester:	Cheshire Record Office
	Chester City Record Office
Chichester:	West Sussex Record Office
Dorchester:	Dorset Record Office
Durham:	Durham County Record Office
Exeter:	Devon Record Office
Gateshead:	Gateshead Public Libraries
Gloucester:	Gloucestershire County Record Office
Grimsby:	Grimsby Borough Record Office
Guildford:	Surrey Record Office

Hereford:	County Council of Hereford and Worcester Record Office
Hertford:	Hertfordshire Record Office
Huntingdon:	County Record Office, Huntingdon
Kingston Upon Hull:	Kingston Upon Hull Record Office
Leeds:	Leeds City Libraries
Leicester:	Leicestershire Record Office
Lewes:	East Sussex Record Office
Lichfield:	Lichfield Joint Record Office
London:	Corporation of London Records Office
	Greater London Record Office (London Section)
	Greater London Record Office (Middlesex Section)
	Guildhall Library
	Office of Population Censuses and Surveys
	Public Record Office
	Society of Antiquaries of London Library
	Society of Genealogists
	Surrey Record Office and Kingston Borough Muniment Room
	Westminster City Libraries
Maidstone:	Kent Archives Office
Matlock:	Derbyshire Record Office
Newcastle Upon Tyne:	Northumberland Record Office
Northallerton:	North Yorkshire County Record Office
Northampton:	Northamptonshire Record Office
Norwich:	Norfolk County Record Office
Nottingham:	Nottinghamshire Record Office
Oxford:	Oxfordshire County Record Office
Plymouth:	West Devon Record Office
Portsmouth:	Portsmouth City Record Office
Preston:	Lancashire Record Office
Reading:	Berkshire Record Office
Ripon:	Ripon Cathedral Library
Salisbury:	The Diocesan Record Office
Sheffield:	Sheffield City Libraries
Shrewsbury:	Salop Record Office
Southampton:	Southampton City Record Office
Stafford:	Staffordshire County Record Office
Taunton:	Somerset Record Office
Trowbridge:	Wiltshire County Record Office
Truro:	Cornwall County Record Office

Wigan:	Wigan Record Office
Winchester:	Hampshire County Record Office
Worcester:	The County Council of Hereford and Worcester Record Office
York:	York City Archives

Scotland

Dumfries:	Dumfries Museum
Edinburgh:	General Register Office for Scotland Scottish Record Office
Glasgow:	Glasgow District Libraries, The Mitchell Library

Wales

Aberystwyth:	Cardiganshire Record Office
Caernarvon:	Gwynedd Archives Service
Cardiff:	City of Cardiff (County of South Glamorgan) Public Libraries Glamorgan Archive Service
Carmarthen:	Carmarthenshire Record Office
Cwnbran:	Gwent Record Office
Deeside:	Clwyd Record Office
Haverfordwest:	Pembrokeshire Record Office
Llangefni:	Llangefni Area Record Office

Northern Ireland

| Belfast: | General Register Office |

Isle of Man

| Douglas: | Isle of Man General Registry The Manx Museum Library |

Channel Islands

| Guernsey: | The Greffe |

D. Libraries and Archives

ABERDEEN

1 **Institution** University of Aberdeen Library
  Address King's College, Aberdeen AB9 2UB
  Telephone 0244-40241
  Holdings 650,000 books; 30,000 pamphlets; 7,000 periodicals

Subject Coverage: The collection is rich in material relating to the Scottish Highlands (including family papers) and particularly in antiquities of the northeast of Scotland. The subjects of the faculties of the university are covered with strong holdings in history and topography. The library holds the McBean Jacobite Collection; the Gregory Collection of the history of science and medicine; the O'Dell Collection of railway material.

Access: The library is primarily for the use of the members of the university; others may use the reference materials. American scholars should have a letter of introduction. The library is open Monday to Friday, 9:00 A.M. to 1:00 P.M.; Saturday, 9:00 A.M. to 5:00 P.M. during the fall and spring academic term. For the summer term, the hours are Monday to Friday, 9:00 A.M. to 11:00 P.M.; Saturday, 9:00 A.M. to 5:00 P.M. At other times, the library is open Monday to Friday, 9:00 A.M. to 5:00 P.M.; Saturday, 9:00 A.M. to 1:00 P.M. Manuscripts and special collections may be consulted only Monday to Friday, 9:00 A.M. to 4:30 P.M. Inquiries should be directed to the Librarian.

Publications: Aberdeen University Studies and Aberdeen University Review are among the most important publications issued. There are also an Annual Report, a Library Handbook, and monthly accessions lists.

Duplication: Facilities are available for both full-size and micro-copying.

Services: All telephone and mail inquiries are answered. Staff members are available to assist researchers who wish to consult manuscript material. Non-members of the university must make special arrangements to borrow from the library.

ABERYSTWYTH

2 **Institution** National Library of Wales
  Address Aberystwyth, Cardiganshire SY23 3BU

Telephone   0970-3816
Holdings   2,000,000 books; pamphlets; 6,000 periodicals;
               2,000 microfilms; 30,000 manuscripts; 180,000 maps,
               prints, photographs, and drawings; 3,500,000 ar-
               chives; 1,000 slides

Subject Coverage: The library is a copyright library and has
the world's largest collection of books in the Welsh language or
books relating to Wales.   It also contains special material relating to other Celtic countries.   Among the special collections
are the Sir Idris Bell Collection on papyrology, the Sir Charles
Thomas-Stanford Collection (incunabula, Euclid, and Civil War
tracts), the Herbert Millingchamp Vaughan Collection (Jacobitism,
genealogy, Italian history and literature), and a complete set of
the works of the Gregynog Press.   The Department of Manuscripts includes a version of Chaucer's Canterbury Tales, manuscripts of Bede's Ecclesiastical History, and the Hengwrt-Peni-
arth Manuscripts (the finest collection of Welsh manuscripts in
a single location).   The library is a repository for manorial
records, records of the Court of Great Sessions of Wales (1542-
1830); the archives of the Presbyterian Church of Wales, the archives of the Anglican Church in Wales, many collections of
family and estate papers, and the diaries and correspondence of
David Lloyd George.

Access: Admission is by a reader's ticket.   An application
form can be obtained from the Librarian.   Visiting American
academics should have a letter of introduction specifying the
kinds of material needed.   The library is open Monday to Friday, 9:30 A.M. to 6:00 P.M.; Saturday, 9:30 A.M. to 5:00 P.M.

The library is divided into three parts: the Department of Printed Books, Department of Manuscripts and Records, and the Department of Prints, Drawings and Maps.

Publications: Bibliotheca Celtica, A Register of Celtic Publications (annual); National Library of Wales Journal (semi-annual);
Handlist of Manuscripts (annual); and Annual Reports (containing
preliminary descriptions of accessions).

Duplication: Duplication facilities are excellent and include a
photostat camera, a Xeroxing service, and micro-copying devices.   Duplicating costs are relatively inexpensive, and orders
are processed rapidly.

Services: Books do not circulate.   Information is given by telephone or mail.   Ultra-violet lamps for reading manuscripts are
available.

ABERYSTWYTH

3   Institution   The University College of Wales Library

Address   Aberystwyth, Dyfed SY23 2AX
Telephone   0970-2711
Holdings   325,000 volumes; 2,900 periodicals; 846 microforms

Subject Coverage: The library has a collection of U.S. literature, history (centered around 1850-1880), and foreign relations.
French Revolution material is well represented, as is West
African literature (e.g., microfilm of Sierra Leone newspapers,
1880-1935) and consular dispatches, 1858-1906. English medieval history is included, especially of the 13th and 14th centuries. There is a full collection of League of Nations and UN
publications and good holdings in diplomatic history since 1890
in the Department of International Politics. A considerable collection of Command Papers and House of Commons Papers is
also held by the library.

Access: The library is housed in various buildings. The Law
Library, the Social Sciences Library, and most science libraries
are on the Penglais campus. The humanities, except for European languages, literature, and art, are retained in the Old College by the sea, awaiting their eventual transfer to the new library on the Penglais campus.

American scholars may use the collection with the permission
of the Librarian. References are required. Visitors may not
borrow from the library. During the academic year, the libraries are open Monday to Friday, 9:00 A.M. to 10:00 P.M.;
Saturday, 9:00 A.M. to 1:00 P.M. During vacation, the hours
are Monday to Friday, 9:00 A.M. to 1:00 P.M., 2:00 P.M. to
5:30 P.M.; Saturday (except in July and August), 9:00 A.M. to
1:00 P.M. All the libraries close for a week at Christmas
and Easter. Visitors should always ascertain the opening hours
of the libraries, since there may be some variation.

Publications: Publications include a list of the library's pre-
1701 books, a Union List of Periodicals in Aberystwyth Libraries,
A Guide to the College Libraries, regular accessions lists,
broadsheets, and handlists.

Duplication: Full-size copying services are available at moderate cost. Photographic prints, slides, and microfilms can be
supplied, provided the terms of the Copyright Act are observed.

Services: Interlibrary loan service is provided. A readers'
advisory service is available for the humanities, social sciences,
and law.

ALDERSHOT

4   Institution   Prince Consort's Army Library
     Address   Knollys Road, Aldershot, Hampshire GU11 1PS
     Telephone   0252-24431, ext. Montgomery 381/382

Holdings   40,000 books; 24 periodicals; maps

Subject Coverage: The collection includes military history, regimental history, military science and organization, and biographies of political figures and service personnel. The library houses the military books presented by HRH The Prince Consort. These have been added to by the Aldershot Military Society and the Army Library Service. The library also contains maps and material relating to the history of the army in Aldershot.

Access: British service personnel may use the library, but other researchers must apply in writing for an appointment ahead of time. Inquiries should be directed to the Librarian. A letter of introduction from the home institution would be useful. The library is open Monday to Thursday, 9:00 A.M. to 1:00 P.M., 2:00 P.M. to 5:30 P.M.; Friday, 9:00 A.M. to 1:00 P.M., 2:00 P.M. to 5:00 P.M.

Publications: A booklet entitled Prince Consort's Library 1860-1960 was issued to mark the library's centenary.

Duplication: No copying facilities are available at present.

Services: Military history books printed before 1945 are lent only if the library possesses duplicates. The general collection circulates to service borrowers through personal and postal loans.

AYLESBURY

5   Institution   Buckinghamshire Record Office
     Address   County Hall, Aylesbury, Buckinghamshire HP20 1UA
     Telephone   0296-5000
     Holdings   books; records

Subject Coverage: The record office contains official records of the county and private papers. It is also the Diocesan Record Office for the county of Buckingham. Among official records are Quarter Sessions (from 1678), County Council (from 1889), and Lieutenancy. Among the transferred records of official bodies functioning within the county are Archdeaconry of Buckingham, Parish, Coroners, Poor Law Guardians, District Councils, Petty Sessions, School Board, Constabulary, and non-conformist. The non-conformist church records include Baptists, Independents or Congregational, Wesleyan, Primitive Methodists (thirty-three congregations in all) registers of birth or baptisms and burials, 1765 to about 1837. Quaker records include registers of births, marriages, and burials, 1656 to 1837. The collection contains private deposits of personal, family, estate, and business records. There is a small collection of standard reference and local history works in the Search Room.

Access: The record office is open to the public. Inquiries should be directed to the Archivist. The hours are Monday to Thursday, 9:15 A.M. to 5:30 P.M.; Friday, 9:15 A.M. to 5:00 P.M. A prior appointment is not necessary, but persons visiting the office for the first time are advised to seek an interview with a member of the staff if they are contemplating extensive research.

Publications: Education Records (1961); Records of the Archdeaconry of Buckingham (1961); Catalogue of Maps (1961); Handlist of Buckinghamshire Inclosure Acts and Awards, by W. E. Tate (1947); Calendar of Quarter Session Records, 1678-1724, 6 vols.; Notes for Genealogists.

Duplication: Full-size copying facilities at high cost are available. Orders for photostatic copies of large documents cannot be executed at the office. Arrangements can, however, be made for work to be done professionally, but a delay of up to six weeks is entailed. Arrangements for photographing can be made in consultation with the record office, but the office has no photographic service of its own.

Services: Catalogues and lists of official classes of private deposits will be found in the Search Room. Material does not circulate.

BANGOR

6	Institution	Bangor Public Library
	Address	Ffordd, Gwynedd, Bangor, Gwynedd LL57 1DT
	Telephone	0248-53479
	Holdings	34,290 books; 70 periodicals

Subject Coverage: The library includes works on local history, archaeology, and many aspects of Welsh life.

Access: The library is open to the public. Tickets, obtainable from the library, are necessary to borrow material. Inquiries should be made to the City Librarian. The library is open Monday, Tuesday, Thursday, Friday, 10:30 A.M. to 7:00 P.M.; Saturday, 9:30 A.M. to 4:00 P.M.

Publications: None.

Duplication: Copying facilities are not available.

Services: Inquiries made by telephone or mail will be answered.

BANGOR

7	Institution	University College of North Wales

Address   Bangor, Gwynedd LL57 2DG
Telephone   0248-51151
Holdings   400, 000 books; 3, 500 periodicals; microforms;
             300, 000 manuscripts

Subject Coverage: The library holds publications on economics,
history, philology, social theory, and institutions. It is strong
in Welsh history, language, and literature. There are several
important collections, including the Bangor Cathedral Library
(1, 100 volumes printed before 1700 and four incunabula) and
archives consisting of over 300, 000 manuscripts relating to
North Wales.

Access: The library is open to visiting academics for reference
only, on approval of the Librarian. A letter of introduction is
recommended. During the academic year, the library is open
Monday to Friday, 9:00 A.M. to 10:00 P.M.; Saturday, 9:00
A.M. to 12:30 P.M.; Sunday, 2:00 P.M. to 5:00 P.M. During
vacation, the hours are Monday to Friday, 9:30 A.M. to 5:00
P.M.; Saturday, 9:00 A.M. to 12 noon.

Publications: The library issues an Annual Report and has published a Catalogue of the Bangor Cathedral Library, comp. by
E. Gwynne Jones and J. R. V. Johnston (1961).

Duplication: Full-size and micro-copying facilities are available
at low cost and without long delays.

Services: Telephone and postal inquiries will be answered.
The collection circulates only to members of the university.
The library cooperates with the British Library Lending Division
and the regional library bureau.

BATH

8   Institution Bath Reference Library
    Address   18 Queen Square, Bath, Avon BA1 2HP
    Telephone   0225-28144
    Holdings   79, 000 books; 350 periodicals; 793 microforms;
                 537 manuscripts; newspapers; maps; prints; photo-
                 graphs

Subject Coverage: The library has a good general collection and
special collections on Bath and Somerset, and works on Gloucestershire and Wiltshire. French Revolution newspapers and material on Napoleon are also held. There are early printed books
including several incunabula and private press books. Resources
covering public health, military history, English history, and
the Oppenheim and Miles Collection of 19th century travels can
be found here. In addition there are prints, maps, photographs,
and manuscripts.

Access: The library is open to the public. The hours are Monday to Friday, 10:00 A.M. to 8:00 P.M.; Saturday, 9:30 A.M. to 5:00 P.M. Inquiries should be made of the Director.

Publications: Among the publications of the library are Printed Books, 1476-1640 (1968); Catalogue of Incunabula (1966); Select List of Books on Bath (1975); Bath Guides, Directories and Newspapers (1973); Philately: A Catalogue of the Library of the Bath Philatelic Society and Books in Bath Reference Library (1973); Bath: Architecture and Planning (1975).

Duplication: Full-size copying equipment is available, but there are no facilities for micro-copying. Copies are made at moderate cost.

Services: Inquiries by telephone or by mail will be answered.

BELFAST

9   Institution   Belfast Public Libraries
    Address   Central Library, Royal Avenue, Belfast BT1 1EA
    Telephone   0232-43233
    Holdings   635,628 books; 1,970 periodicals; microforms;
                    manuscripts; newspapers; maps

Subject Coverage: There is a large collection of local history material (over 40,000 items). Among the most important are the F. J. Bigger Collection of Irish history; archaeology and antiquarian material; J. S. Crone Collection of Irish books, pamphlets, and periodicals; and the collections of Grainger, Horner, Riddell, Doyle, and Moore. There is a large collection of Irish and Belfast newspapers from 1761; maps, plans, letters, manuscripts, and cuttings; and topographical, trade, and telephone directories. There is also material on law and heraldry. Early Belfast printed books can be found, and the library houses the Northern Ireland Branch of the Library Association Library. The library is a depository for publications of HMSO, UN, UNESCO and for both the unclassified and declassified reports of the American, British, and European atomic energy authorities. Also included are British and Irish patent specifications and abridgments from other countries and standard specifications from Britain, Canada, Rhodesia, Nyasaland, Australia, and New Zealand and those of the Ministry of Defense, Directorate of Technical Development, and the ASTM (American Society for Testing & Materials).

Access: Visiting scholars are welcome to use the collection, and arrangements can be made for borrowing material. Inquiries should be directed to Chief Librarian. The library is open Monday, Thursday, 9:30 A.M. to 8:00 P.M.; Tuesday, Wednesday, Friday, 9:30 A.M. to 5:00 P.M.; Saturday, 9:30 A.M. to 1:00 P.M.

Publications: The library has issued Catalogue of the Joseph Bigger Collection.

Duplication: Full-size copying facilities are available.

Services: Current information files are maintained for commodities and for countries. The material is gathered from newspapers and periodicals and from the publications of foreign banks and embassies.

BELFAST

10 Institution   General Register Office
    Address   Oxford House, 49-55 Chichester Street, Belfast
                    BT1 4HL
    Telephone   0232-35211
    Holdings   books; records; reports

Subject Coverage: The collection contains records of births, deaths, marriages, and adopted children's certificates. It holds the Registrar General's Annual Reports for Northern Ireland since 1924, for England and Wales since 1891, for Scotland since 1953, and for the Irish Republic since 1938; abstracts of statistics for the United Kingdom and Irish Republic since 1935 and 1931 respectively; census reports for Northern Ireland; reports from the various Northern Ireland departments; vital statistics of Northern Ireland since 1922; census of population as follows: 1841, 1851, 1861, 1871, 1881, 1891, 1901, 1911, 1926, 1937, 1951, 1961, 1966, and 1971; Ulster Year Books; annual reports from the United States and European and Commonwealth countries; U.S. statistical publications; Demographic Year Books (1948-1973); and World Health Statistics. The Medical Sections contain material relating to diseases and methods of coding deaths.

Access: The collection is open to the public. Inquiries should be directed to the Registrar General. Office hours are Monday to Friday, 9:00 A.M. to 4:45 P.M.

Publications: Quarterly Returns; Registrar General's Annual Report.

Duplication: Full-size copying facilities are available. The cost is moderate, and usually processing can be completed within one day.

Services: The office supplies copies of birth, death, marriage, and adopted children's certificates.

BELFAST

11 Institution   Public Record Office of Northern Ireland
    Address   66 Balmoral Avenue, Belfast BT9 6NY
    Telephone   0232-661621
    Holdings   10, 000 books; 1, 000 pamphlets; 50 periodicals;
                   2, 000 microforms; 500, 000, 000 documents; news-
                   papers

Subject Coverage: The record office contains works on the historical, political, social, and economic development of Northern
Ireland. The period covered is from about 1650. Many pre-
1900 Irish papers were destroyed in 1922, and the surviving
papers are the basic source. The post-1920 records of the
Northern Ireland administration reflect every function of the
government. Ecclesiastical collections include administrative
records for the Church of Ireland dioceses of 1) Down and Con-
nor and Dromore, 2) Clogher, and 3) Derry. In addition there
is material from the Roman Catholic Diocese of Clogher which
includes correspondence dealing with political events in the
nineteenth century. This archive may be examined only with
the written consent of His Lordship the Bishop. The archive
of the Society of Friends contains a number of registers of
births, deaths, marriages, wills and inventories dating from
the 17th century. There are no Roman Catholic registers, but
these are available on microfilm in the National Library of
Ireland, Dublin. Records of business and industry form one of
the most substantial classes of records in the office. These
range from hundreds of account books and ledgers of large
firms to a few documents of one-man concerns. Some collections reflect the growth of the mercantile business in Ireland
as well as other forms of industry and trade from the late 17th
century. The Foster/Massereene Papers (concerning the politics of the 1798 Rebellion and the passing of the Act of Union);
the diaries of William Johnston of Ballykilbeg (1847 to 1870 and
1873 to 1902); the political papers of Frederick, 1st Marquis of
Dufferin and Ava (about 53, 000 documents and 750 volumes including correspondence) will also be found in the collection.

Access: Researchers are welcome to use the resources on the
premises. Inquiries should be directed to the Deputy Keeper
of the Records (letter preferred). At present a fifty-year rule
is in operation, but the office expects to come into line with
English practice very soon, so that documents more than thirty
years old may be seen by the public. The hours are Monday
to Friday, 9:30 A.M. to 4:45 P.M.

Publications: The publications include Annual Reports (with abstracts of manuscript material acquired during the year); Educational Facsimiles and Local History Studies; The Ashbourne
Papers, 1869-1913; Irish Unionism, 1885-1923. A complete
list is contained in HMSO Sectional List no. 24.

Duplication: Full-size and micro-copies can be obtained.

Services: The collection does not circulate. Much of the library was developed as a study aid to those using public records.

BELFAST

12 Institution   The Queen's University Library
   Address   Belfast BT7 1NN
   Telephone   0232-45133
   Holdings   688,000 books and pamphlets; 7,000 periodicals

Subject Coverage: The library includes material on law, social science, and education. There are a number of special collections, including the MacDouall Sanskrit Collection; the John Ross (Rosenzweig) Hebrew Collection; Hibernica Collection of history and literature (notably the Henry, O'Rahilly, and Simms Collections); Savory (Huguenot) Collection; Samuel Simms Collection on the history of medicine (housed in the Queen's University of Belfast Medical Library, Institute of Clinical Science, Grosvenor Road, Belfast BT12 6BJ; telephone: 0232-22043); Bishop Thomas Percy Library; part of Adam Smith's library.

Access: Researchers are admitted at the discretion of the Librarian. A letter of introduction is recommended. The hours are Monday to Friday, 9:00 A.M. to 11:00 P.M.; Saturday, 9:00 A.M. to 12:30 P.M. during the academic year. Library hours during vacation are Monday to Friday, 9:00 A.M. to 5:30 P.M.; Saturday, 9:00 A.M. to 12:30 P.M. The library is closed the last full week in June.

Publications: Northern Ireland Legal Quarterly; Statistical and Social Enquiry Society of Ireland Journal (annual), although not library publications, are available for exchange.

Duplication: Full-size copying is available at moderate cost.

Services: The collection circulates to members of the university only.

BEVERLEY

   Institution   East Riding Record Office
                  See: BEVERLEY, Humberside County Record
                  Office (Reference No. 13)

BEVERLEY

13 Institution   Humberside County Record Office

Address   County Hall, Beverley, North Humberside HU17 9BA
Telephone   0482-887131
Holdings   several hundred books; several hundred pamphlets;
               records

Subject Coverage: The collection includes official and semi-
official records of the new county of Humberside and of its
predecessor authority, the East Riding County Council. Family
and estate papers from the same area are included, notably
those of the Beaumont family dating from the 15th century, the
Eastoft family dating from the 16th century, and Beaumont of
Carlton Towers which contains a confirmation of an exchange
of lands from the 11th century. Title deeds, maps, plans, and
surveys are also included. Parish records from the Archdeaconry of East Riding include baptism, marriage, and burial
registers from the 16th century of nearly one hundred parishes.
A list of these parishes with the dates of the earliest and latest
entries is available. It should not be assumed that consecutive
registers between these dates are held. There is a small reference library for the use of staff and researchers.

Access: The collection is open to the public. Inquiries should
be directed to the Archivist. The hours are Monday to Thursday, 9:00 A.M. to 1:00 P.M., 2:00 P.M. to 5:00 P.M.; Friday, 9:00 A.M. to 1:00 P.M., 2:00 P.M. to 4:15 P.M.

Publications: Brief Guide to the Contents of the Humberside
County Record Office (1974); summary lists (in preparation).

Duplication: Full-size copying and photographic facilities are
available. The cost varies according to the size of the document.

Services: None of the material is available on loan. Copies of
lists of holdings are available without charge on request. Telephone and postal inquiries are answered.

BEXLEY

Institution   London Borough of Bexley Library Service
               See: LONDON, London Borough of Bexley Library
               Service (Reference No. 133)

BIRMINGHAM

14 Institution   Birmingham Law Library
    Address   8 Temple Street, Birmingham B2 5BT
    Telephone   021-643 9116
    Holdings   43,000 books; 70 periodicals; manuscripts; news-
                  papers; 20 sets of law reports

Subject Coverage: The library, which is the private collection
of the Birmingham Law Society, contains extensive holdings of
law publications, including the history of law and early law
books. Some of the manuscript material dates from the 12th
century, and many of the resources are unobtainable elsewhere.

Access: Visiting scholars are permitted to use the collection
on the premises. Inquiries should be addressed to the Librarian. A letter of introduction is recommended. The hours are
Monday to Friday, 9:30 A.M. to 5:00 P.M.

Publications: The Birmingham Law Society has published The
Birmingham Law Library: Historical Notes on the Contents of
the Law Library.

Duplication: Full-size copying facilities are immediately available, but the cost is high.

Services: The collection circulates only to members of the
Birmingham Law Society.

BIRMINGHAM

15 Institution   Birmingham Public Libraries
    Address   Central Libraries, Paradise, Birmingham B3 3HQ
    Telephone   021-235 4511
    Holdings   963, 000 books; 10, 000 periodicals; 94, 500 micro-
                   forms; 170, 000 manuscripts; 18, 500 maps, photo-
                   graphs; 134 incunabula

Subject Coverage: The library resources include works in history, topography, philosophy, and religion; a Local Studies Library (printed and manuscript items relating to Birmingham, including the Boulton and Watt Collections); Social Sciences Library (British and U.S. Patents); Sir Benjamin Stone Collection
(photographs). The library is a depository for UN publications
and the Birmingham Diocesan Record Office.

Access: The Reference Library is open to the public, but
readers requiring books from the stacks may be asked to provide identification. Inquiries should be directed to the City Librarian. The hours are Monday to Friday, 9:00 A.M. to 8:30
P.M.; Saturday, 9:00 A.M. to 5:00 P.M.

Publications: Catalogue of the Birmingham Collection, 1918-
1931 (2 vols.); Periodicals in the Commercial Library (1966);
Birmingham Before 1800: Six Maps (1968); a series of technical bibliographies and guides to various departments and services.

Duplication: Complete photographic service is available.

Services: The library provides interlibrary loan service. Inquiries by telephone or mail will be answered.   There are
specialists in each subject department.

BIRMINGHAM

16 Institution   University of Birmingham Library
    Address   P.O. Box 363, Edgbaston, Birmingham B15 2TT
    Telephone   021-472 1301
    Holdings   950,000 volumes; 7,000 periodicals; 2,500 micro-
                   forms; 20 manuscript collections

Subject Coverage: The library has strong collections in commerce, social science, and law.   The resources support the
teaching and research of the university's academic departments
and special centers, which include the Centre of West African
Studies, Centre for Russian and East European Studies, Institute
of Local Government Studies, Centre for Urban and Regional
Studies, and others.   The special collections of interest to social scientists include the manuscripts of Joseph, Austen, and
Neville Chamberlain; John Galsworthy; Francis Brett Young;
Harriet Martineau; Cadbury Papers; Shishkin Papers.

Access: Visiting scholars may use the library for reference.
Inquiries should be addressed to the Librarian.   A letter of introduction is recommended.   Special collections may be consulted only Monday to Friday, 9:00 A.M. to 5:00 P.M.   During
the academic year, the library is open Monday to Friday, 9:00
A.M. to 9:00 P.M.; Saturday, 9:00 A.M. to 12:30 P.M.   During vacation, the hours are Monday to Friday, 9:00 A.M. to
5:00 P.M.; Saturday, 9:00 A.M. to 12:30 P.M.   The library is
closed on Saturday during August.

Publications: Guide to the Library; Regulations; Special Guides;
Quick Lists; Catalogue of the Cadbury Papers (1973); John Galsworthy: Catalogue of the Collection (1967) are among the publications issued by the library.   A complete list, which includes
publications about the library, is available.

Duplication: Photocopying and microfilming facilities are available.

Services: Circulation of the collection is restricted to members of the university.

BOSTON SPA

    Institution   British Library Lending Division
                   See: LONDON, British Library (Reference Divi-
                   sion) (Reference No. 95)

BRIGHTON

17	Institution	Brighton Area Libraries
	Address	Church Street
		Brighton BN1 1VE
	Telephone	0273-691195
	Holdings	270,000 books; 25,000 pamphlets; 600 periodicals; microforms; manuscripts; newspapers; 1,100 maps; 18,000 photographs

Subject Coverage: The library has an excellent general collection and several important special collections. Among these are the Bloomfield Collection (manuscripts and incunabula); Lewis Collection (foreign books and periodicals); Matthews Collection (Oriental books); Cobden Pamphlets (rare items relating to politics and economics); Ackerman Collection (illustrations, 1780-1830); Sussex Collection (includes a photographic survey). The collection of photographs contains local scenes, pictures of buildings, and old postcards (arranged by content of the picture). The library is a depository for the tapes of Radio Brighton, which are kept on file permanently. The library itself produces tapes of interviews with individuals who can make a contribution to the local history of the area.

Access: The library is open to the public. Visiting scholars are permitted to use the collection for reference. Inquiries should be addressed to the Area Librarian. A letter of introduction would be helpful. The hours are Monday to Friday, 10:00 A.M. to 7:00 P.M.; Saturday, 10:00 A.M. to 4:00 P.M.

Publications: Catalogue of Manuscripts and Printed Books Before 1500 (1962); Brighton in Retrospect (1974).

Duplication: Full-size copying facilities are immediately available at moderately high cost.

Services: The lending collections circulate to those who hold library tickets. Tickets are accepted from other library authorities in Great Britain. An individual may obtain a ticket if he can produce a recommendation or a local address. The library cooperates with the British Library Lending Division. Copies of photographs can be purchased.

BRIGHTON

Institution	Institute for Development Studies
	See: BRIGHTON, University of Sussex Library (Reference No. 18)

BRIGHTON

18 Institution   University of Sussex Library
    Address   Brighton BN1 9QL
    Telephone   0273-66755
    Holdings   450, 000 books and pamphlets; 2, 000 periodicals;
                   microforms

Subject Coverage: The library supports the faculties of the
university. The collection includes Sessional Papers (1801-
1900); Parliamentary Papers from 1964; Command Papers from
1901 (incomplete); British Standards; European Communities
publications; official publications of Kenya, Tanzania, and
Uganda; League of Nations Documents and British political party
pamphlets. The Institute of Development Studies (at the university) and the University of Sussex Science Policy Research
Unit have libraries that are separate from the university library. The Institute of Development Studies is a depository
for UN, UNESCO, FAO, and GATT publications, and the Science Policy Research Unit holds resources in history, sociology,
economics, and statistics of science.

Access: Visiting scholars are permitted to use the library resources if they have proper recommendations. Inquiries should
be addressed to the Librarian. The hours are Monday to Friday, 9:00 A.M. to 9:45 P.M.; Saturday, 10:00 A.M. to 6:00
P.M.; Sunday, 1:30 P.M. to 7:30 P.M. during the academic
year. During vacation, the hours are Monday to Friday, 9:00
A.M. to 5:30 P.M.

Publications: The university library issues pamphlets covering
the resources of particular subject collections.

Duplication: Full-size copying facilities are available.

Services: The collection circulates only to members of the
university. Literature searches will be conducted for all readers.

BRISTOL

19 Institution   Bristol Record Office
    Address   Council House, College Green, Bristol BS1 5TR
    Telephone   0272-26031, ext. 440/441/442
    Holdings   books; pamphlets; periodicals; microforms; records

Subject Coverage: The office is the official repository for the
records of the city (and former county) of Bristol. These include archives of the Corporation of Bristol and of the Diocese
of Bristol, as well as public records of a local nature, manorial and tithe documents, and private archives. Among the Official Archives are Charters and Custumals, records relating to

Lieutenancy and Shrievalty, administrative records, financial
records, judicial records, and the records of various statutory
authorities, such as the Local Board of Health, School Boards,
and Urban and Rural District Councils, which have been transferred to the Bristol Archives Office.

Access: The record office is open to the public. Application
should be made to the City Archivist, preferably in writing.
The Search Room hours are Monday to Thursday, 8:45 A.M. to
4:45 P.M.; Friday, 8:45 A.M. to 4:15 P.M.; Saturday, 9:00
A.M. to 12 noon (by appointment).

Publications: The office has published Guide to the Parish Records of the City of Bristol and County of Gloucester, ed. by
Irvine Gray and Elizabeth Ralph (1963); Guide to the Bristol
Archives Office, ed. by Elizabeth Ralph. Details of accessions
since the publication of, or not included in, the latter Guide are
published annually in the Transactions of the Bristol and Gloucestershire Archaeological Society.

Duplication: Full-size and micro-copying facilities are available.

Services: Postal and telephone inquiries are answered. Where
appropriate inquirers are encouraged to carry out their own research or to employ a record agent, since staff time is limited.
Talks are given on sources, and quarterly exhibitions of archives are mounted at the City Museum. Researchers may use
the collection only on the premises.

BRISTOL

20	Institution	University of Bristol, Wills Memorial Library
	Address	Queen's Road, Bristol BS8 1RJ (Note: after Janu-ary, 1976, Tyndalls Avenue, Bristol)
	Telephone	0272-24161
	Holdings	530,000 books; 120,000 pamphlets; 4,500 peri-odicals; microforms; manuscripts

Subject Coverage: In addition to serving the faculties of the
university (which include law and social science), the library
contains material on business history, historical chemistry (including alchemy), Anglo-Norman relations, English cartography,
and many important historical works on geology and engineering. It contains the John Addington Symonds Collection, the
Pinney Papers and other West Indian records (especially 17th
and 18th centuries), notebooks and sketchbooks of I. K. Brunel.
There are works on the Wars of the Roses, English economic
history in the 16th and 17th centuries, and U.S. and Latin
American history. It also houses a collection of autographed
Penguin books given by Sir Allen Lane from his private library.

Access: The library is open to members of the university, but other researchers can make application to the Librarian and are admitted at his discretion. A letter of introduction is advisable. The library is open Monday to Friday, 8:45 A.M. to 9:00 P.M.; Saturday, 8:45 A.M. to 1:00 P.M. during the academic year. During short vacations, the hours are Monday to Friday, 8:45 A.M. to 7:00 P.M.; Saturday, 8:45 A.M. to 1:00 P.M. During long vacations, the library is open Monday to Friday, 8:45 A.M. to 5:00 P.M.

Publications: The library publishes Annual Reports, Accessions Lists, and a Guide to the Library.

Duplication: The library can provide full-size copies but has no facilities for micro-copies.

Services: The collection circulates to members of the university only, or through interlibrary loan. Inquiries will be handled either by telephone or through the mail.

BROMLEY

| Institution | London Borough of Bromley Public Libraries |
| | See: LONDON, London Borough of Bromley Public Libraries (Reference No. 134) |

CAERNARVON

21	Institution	Gwynedd Archives Service, Caernarvon Area Record Office
	Address	County Offices, Shirehall Street, Caernarvon, Gwynedd LL55 1SH
	Telephone	0286-4121, ext. 235
	Holdings	books; pamphlets; periodicals; microforms; records; newspapers

Subject Coverage: The collection contains a comprehensive range of material on Welsh history (particularly North Wales local history and local newspapers). The holdings include official county records (Quarter Sessions from 1541); private deposited records from 1176 (family, estate, and business papers); local authority papers (including Guardians of the Poor, police, and large accumulations of quarrying records). The record office also holds microforms of records found elsewhere.

Access: The service is open to the public. Inquiries should be directed to the Archivist. Appointments should be made to assure admission as search rooms are frequently full. The hours are Monday, Tuesday, Thursday, Friday, 9:30 A.M. to 12:30 P.M., 1:30 P.M. to 5:00 P.M.; Wednesday, 9:30 A.M. to 12:30 P.M., 1:30 P.M. to 7:00 P.M.

Publications: Bulletin (annual); miscellaneous calendars; guides; reproductions of documents; postcards; general books on local history.

Duplication: Full-size copying is available at moderate cost. Photographs can also be provided.

Services: An education service for liaison with schools and colleges can be arranged. Material does not circulate.

CAMBERLEY

22 Institution   Royal Military Academy Sandhurst, Central Library
    Address   Camberley, Surrey GU15 4PQ
    Telephone   0276-63344, ext. 367/368
    Holdings   100,000 books; 250 periodicals; microforms

Subject Coverage: The library contains works on war studies, military technology (held in a special branch library), international affairs, and contemporary Britain. There is a special Soviet Studies Collection.

Access: Visiting academics would be permitted to use the collection. Inquiries should be directed to Headquarters. A letter of introduction is recommended. The library is open Monday, Tuesday, Thursday, 8:30 A.M. to 12:30 P.M., 1:30 P.M. to 7:30 P.M., 8:00 P.M. to 10:00 P.M.; Wednesday, Friday, 8:30 A.M. to 12:30 P.M., 1:30 P.M. to 7:00 P.M.; Saturday, 8:30 A.M. to 12:30 P.M.; Sunday, 2:00 P.M. to 5:00 P.M.

Publications: The library issues a Library Handbook; Guide to the Classification System; selected articles of military interest; recent military additions lists.

Duplication: Photo-copying facilities are available.

Services: The collection does not circulate but is available for interlibrary loan.

CAMBRIDGE

23 Institution   Cambridge County Record Office
    Address   Shire Hall, Castle Hill, Cambridge CB3 0AP
    Telephone   0223-58811, ext. 281
    Holdings   2,250 books; several hundred pamphlets; 12 periodicals; 200 microforms; 6,200 feet of records; several hundred Ordnance Survey maps and plans; several hundred aerial photographs

Subject Coverage: The collection contains records of all kinds relating to Cambridgeshire and the Isle of Ely, including parish

records and land drainage records, but excluding diocesan and
probate records which are held at University Library, Cambridge. There is a reference library on local and archival subjects. The branch office, containing records for the former
county of Huntingdonshire, is the County Record Office (Grammar
School Walk, Huntingdon PE18 6LF; telephone: 0480-52181, ext.
42). See: Reference No. 74.

Access: The record office is open to the public. Inquiries
should be directed to the County Archivist. The hours are
Monday to Thursday, 9:00 A.M. to 5:15 P.M.; Friday, 9:00
A.M. to 4:15 P.M.; Thursday (by appointment), 5:15 P.M. to
9:00 P.M.

Publications: Annual Reports (including lists of accessions);
Guide to Educational Records in the County Record Office, Cambridge (1972).

Duplication: Full-size and micro-copying facilities are available
on demand. The cost is moderate. Other types of photocopying are also provided.

Services: Telephone and postal inquiries are answered.

CAMBRIDGE

24 Institution   Cambridge University Library
    Address   West Road, Cambridge CB3 9DR
    Telephone   0223-61441
    Holdings   3,000,000 books and pamphlets; 17,000 periodicals;
                   50,000 microforms; 15,000 manuscripts; 700,000
                   maps

Subject Coverage: The library contains resources in all subjects and all languages. It is a National Copyright Deposit Library. It has an extensive collection of early printed books and
contains both Western and Eastern manuscripts. Among the
many important special collections are Far Eastern books (books
in Chinese, Japanese, and Korean including the Chinese books
of Sir Thomas Wade and the Japanese books of W. G. Aston);
Acton Library (the collection of the first Lord Acton, Regius
Professor of Modern History, 1885-1902); Armorial bindings;
Madden Collection (ballads, consisting of 16,354 broadsides).

There are many separate college and departmental libraries at
Cambridge, each with a distinctive collection. For a description of these, see A. N. L. Munby, Cambridge College Libraries. Cambridge: W. Heffer and Sons, Ltd., 2d ed., 1962.
Among these libraries are the following:

Christ's College Library (50,000 volumes): incunabula, Charles
Lesingham Smith Collection (early scientific works); Sir Stephen

Gazelee Collection (Coptic studies); William Robertson Smith
Oriental Library.

Churchill College Library (21,000 volumes): political, military,
and scientific archives of the late 19th and 20th centuries. The
Churchill College Archives include a major collection of the papers of Churchill and some papers of Attlee and of Bevin, and
a large collection of papers of other 20th century British political figures.

Clare College Fellows Library (8,000 volumes): Cecil Sharp
manuscripts and a collection of folk music.

Clare College Forbes Library (8,000 volumes): principally for
undergraduates.

Corpus Christi College Library (20,000 volumes): Anglo-Saxon,
later medieval, and Reformation material; incunabula.

Downing College Library (10,000 volumes): manuscripts relating to the city and University of Cambridge; naval history;
law; Civil War and Commonwealth newspapers.

Emmanuel College Library (53,000 volumes): library of Archbishop Sancroft; incunabula; manuscripts; Bishop Liturgical Collection.

Fitzwilliam Museum Library (25,000 volumes): manuscript and
early printed music; autograph compositions.

Girton College Library (60,000 volumes): Newall Collection
(Scandinavian material); Frere Collection (Hebrew manuscripts);
Cam Collection (medieval history); Crews Collection (Judaeo-
Spanish material); Fegan Collection (bibliography).

Gonville and Caius Library (40,000 volumes): manuscripts related to medieval law; 17th century heraldic and genealogical
records; East Anglican local history and topography.

Jesus College Library (10,300 volumes): incunabula; medieval
manuscripts on north-country monasteries; Civil War tracts;
military science. Older works are found in Old Library, modern material in College Library.

Kings' College Library (140,000 volumes): Pote Collection
(Oriental manuscripts); Keynes Library (philosophy and history
of thought); Rowe Music Library; incunabula.

Magdalene College Old Library: manuscripts of works by
Thomas Hardy, Rudyard Kipling, T. S. Eliot; manuscripts of
14th century Apocalypse; incunabula, including Caxton's second
edition of Chaucer's Canterbury Tales; early theological works.

Magdalene College Pepys Library (3, 000 volumes): Pepys' own collection with his catalogue; medieval manuscripts; naval manuscripts; historical manuscripts (mainly 16th and 17th centuries); incunabula; calligraphic collection; prints of London and Westminster.

Newnham College Library (50, 000 volumes): incunabula; early editions of 16th and 17th century chroniclers, dramatists, and poets.

Pembroke College Library (40, 200 volumes): medieval manuscripts; papers of Gray, C. Stuart, William Mason, R. Storrs.

Peterhouse Library (25, 000 volumes): medieval manuscripts (on deposit in University Library); incunabula; Ward Collection (English history and literature); Temperley Collection (European history).

Queens' College Library (33, 000 volumes): incunabula; Milner Collection (works on Reformation history); divinity.

St. Catharine's College Library (24, 000 volumes): manuscripts; incunabula; 17th century political and religious tracts; Spanish books and manuscripts of 16th and 17th centuries.

St. John's College Library (100, 000 volumes): Otway Collection (17th century pamphlets); Sir Soulden Lawrence Collection (law); mathematical works of historical interest; Thomas Gisborne Collection (18th century books).

Selwyn College Library (30, 000 volumes): pamphlets relating to 19th century English church history; theology; papers and correspondence of Brooke Foss Westcott.

Sidney Sussex College Library (7, 300 volumes): manuscripts; incunabula; early works on mathematics.

Trinity College Library (150, 000 volumes): manuscripts (Greek, 10th century Gospels, Canterbury Psalter, Oriental works); incunabula; Aldis Wright Collection (Hebrew manuscripts); canon law and Bibles; Julius Hare Collection (German theology); law; papers of William Whewell; 19th century manuscripts including those of Sir James Frazer; Houghton Papers (Richard Monckton Milnes); Macaulay Collection (mostly printed books with some manuscripts).

Trinity Hall Library (11, 000 volumes): college archives; canon law; Larman Bequest (books and manuscripts concerning Reformation and Tudor periods); heraldry.

Among the department and institute libraries are the following:

African Studies Centre

Centre of South Asian Studies
Department of Applied Economics
Faculty of Modern and Medieval Languages, Department of
    Slavonic Studies
Institute of Criminology
The University Archives (housed in the University Library)

Access: In general, a visiting scholar must have permission
and a prior appointment to use the resources of the college libraries and of the University Library in Cambridge. Inquiries
should be made, by letter, to the librarian connected with the
specific collection the researcher desires to consult. A letter
of introduction is recommended. The hours differ among the
various libraries. The University Library is open Monday to
Friday, 9:00 A.M. to 10:00 P.M. during the academic year.
During vacation, the hours are Monday to Friday, 9:00 A.M.
to 7:00 P.M.; Saturday, 9:00 A.M. to 1:00 P.M.

Publications: Current Serials Available in the University Library and in Other Libraries Connected with the University;
Library Classification Schemes; Readers' Handbook; Catalogues
of Manuscripts: ...; Catalogues of Books: ...; Catalogues of
Exhibitions.

Duplication: Full-size and micro-copying facilities are available
at the University Library, and full-size copying is provided in
some college libraries. If a researcher expects to acquire
copies of material, he should inquire ahead of time.

Services: Only members of the university are allowed to borrow from the collections.

CANTERBURY

25 Institution   Cathedral Archives and Library, Canterbury
    Address   Precincts, Canterbury, Kent CT1 2EG
    Telephone   0227-63510
    Holdings   40,000 books; 6 periodicals; microforms; 500,000
                  manuscripts

Subject Coverage: The library contains resources in early theology, history, and paleography. It is also a repository for the
archives of the Dean and Chapter (from the 8th century); the
Diocese (14th to 19th century); the City Corporation of Canterbury (14th to 19th century). The collection includes manuscripts,
incunabula, and early printed books.

Access: Inquiries should be directed to the Archivist by letter
or telephone. A letter of introduction is necessary. Admission is available only by appointment. The hours are Monday
to Friday, 9:30 A.M. to 12:45 P.M., 2:00 P.M. to 4:30 P.M.
The library is occasionally closed for exhibitions.

Publications: None.

Duplication: Full-size and micro-copying facilities are available.

Services: The collection does not circulate.

CANTERBURY

26 Institution   University of Kent at Canterbury Library
    Address   The University, Canterbury, Kent CT2 7NU
    Telephone   0227-66822
    Holdings   85,000 books and pamphlets, 950 periodicals,
                   microforms

Subject Coverage: The library contains resources in economics, history, law, sociology, and statistics. The special collections include the Lloyd George Collection, a European Documentation Centre, and a Centre for the Study of Cartoons and Caricature.

Access: Visiting scholars may use the collection for reference upon application. Inquiries should be directed to the Librarian. A letter of introduction is recommended. The hours are Monday to Friday, 9:00 A.M. to 10:00 P.M.; Saturday, 9:00 A.M. to 9:00 P.M.; Sunday, 2:00 P.M. to 9:00 P.M. during the academic year. During vacation, the hours are Monday to Friday, 9:00 A.M. to 9:00 P.M.; Saturday, 9:00 A.M. to 5:00 P.M. It is closed one week at Christmas; Friday to Monday, Easter; and Monday, late summer Bank Holiday.

Publications: Library Handbook (available to users only).

Duplication: Full-size copying facilities (self-service) are available at low cost. Micro-copying services are provided at low cost, but require up to one month for processing.

Services: The collection circulates only to members of the university. Other services, except interlibrary loan, are available to all users.

CARDIFF

27 Institution   City of Cardiff (County of South Glamorgan) Public
                   Libraries
    Address   Central Library, The Hayes, Cardiff CF1 2QU
    Telephone   0222-22116
    Holdings   800,000 books; 56,000 pamphlets; 2,000 periodicals;
                   1,000 microfilms; 6,000 manuscripts; 2,000 maps
                   and prints; 100,000 illustrations; 40,000 deeds and
                   documents

Subject Coverage: The library is a repository for manorial records and has extensive collections relating to Wales and border counties. Government publications, British Standards, and British patent abridgements are also collected. The library holds the Book of Aneurin, one of the earliest literary manuscripts in the Welsh language, incunabula, press books, and fine bindings.

Access: The library is open to the public. A ticket is necessary to borrow material. Tickets from other authorities are accepted on a reciprocal basis. Inquiries should be directed to the City Librarian. The library is open for reference Monday to Friday, 9:30 A.M. to 8:00 P.M.; Saturday, 9:30 A.M. to 5:30 P.M. The Central Lending Library is open Monday to Saturday, 9:30 A.M. to 5:30 P.M.

Publications: Union Locating Index of Periodicals, Glamorgan and Monmouthshire; subject lists; quarterly select list of additions.

Duplication: Full-size and micro-copying facilities are available.

Services: Telephone and postal inquiries will be answered. The library is a member of the Wales Regional Library Scheme and cooperates with the British Library Lending Division.

CARDIFF

28 Institution   Glamorgan Archive Service
    Address   Glamorgan Record Office, County Hall, Cathays
                   Park, Cardiff CF1 3NE
    Telephone   0222-28033
    Holdings   books; periodicals; records

Subject Coverage: The records include those of the County Council, Quarter Sessions, Petty Sessions, Turnpikes, and Boards of Guardians. There are also estate papers and industrial records. Among the special collections are Swansea Gaol Journals of Governor, Surgeon, and Chaplain, 1729-1878 (33 vols.) and the Minutes of the South Wales and Monmouthshire Branch of the British Medical Association, 1871-1943 (6 vols.). The service is a repository for Society of Friends records for Wales and border counties.

Access: The collection is open to the public. Inquiries should be directed to the Archivist. The hours are Monday to Thursday, 9:00 A.M. to 5:00 P.M.; Friday, 9:00 A.M. to 4:30 P.M. Advance notice of a visit is appreciated.

Publications: Iron in the Making; Dowlais Iron Company Letters, 1782-1860, ed. by M. Elsas (1960); Annual Report; accessions lists; Glamorgan, 1536-1974: Aspects of a Changing

County (1974).

Duplication: Full-size copying facilities are available.

Services: Postal and telephone inquiries are answered. Material does not circulate.

CARDIFF

29 Institution   Plaid Cymru (Welsh Nationalist Party)
    Address   8 Queen Street, Cardiff CF1 4BU
    Telephone   0222-31944
                   See also: Plaid Cymru, p. 238
    Holdings   books; pamphlets; press clippings

Subject Coverage: The party holds a comprehensive collection of literature on contemporary aspects of Welsh society, with particular emphasis on economics, industry, and the Common Market. Literature is available in English and Welsh. There is no library, but the Research Department has a newspaper clipping file on matters of interest to the party. The bulk of the collection is on contemporary affairs. Material of historical interest (from about 1920) is held at the National Library of Wales in Aberystwyth.

Access: The collection is not open to the public, but may be used with special permission for advanced research. Application should be directed to the Research Officer to examine the material at Cardiff. To use the Welsh Nationalist Collection at Aberystwyth, application must be made to the General Secretary of the party. The party office is open Monday to Friday, 9:00 A.M. to 5:00 P.M.

Duplication: Duplication can be made only by arrangement.

Services: The material does not circulate. The Research Department may arrange meetings with specialists in the subject that a visiting scholar is studying. These specialists may be either political figures or scholars.

CARDIFF

30 Institution   University College, Cardiff
    Address   P.O. Box 98, Cardiff CF1 1XQ
    Telephone   0222-44211
    Holdings   400,000 volumes; 2,600 periodicals

Subject Coverage: The library, in addition to supporting the faculties of the university, contains works on the history and literature of Wales, the Welsh language, and related Celtic subjects. Among the special collections is the Salisbury Library.

Access: Visiting scholars are permitted to use the collection
with permission of the Librarian. A letter of introduction is
recommended. The hours are Monday to Friday, 9:00 A.M.
to 10:00 P.M.; Saturday, 9:00 A.M. to 1:00 P.M. during the
academic year. During the Christmas and summer vacations,
the hours are Monday to Friday, 9:00 A.M. to 5:00 P.M.
During the first half of the Easter vacation, the library is open
Monday to Friday, 9:00 A.M. to 5:00 P.M.; Saturday, 9:00 A.M.
to 1:00 P.M. During the second half of the Easter vacation,
the schedule for the academic year is followed.

Publications: The library issues an Annual Report; accessions
lists; a list of periodicals; readers' guides.

Duplication: Full-size and micro-copying facilities are available.

Services: Inquiries made by mail are answered. The library
cooperates in interlibrary loan service.

CARLISLE

31 Institution   Cumbria County Council Archives Department
   Addresses   The Record Office, The Castle, Carlisle, Cumbria
                 CA3 8UR; and The Record Office, County Offices,
                 Kendal, Cumbria LA9 4RQ
   Telephones   0228-23456, ext. 316 (Carlisle); 0539-21000 (Kendal)
   Holdings   books; microfilms; records

Subject Coverage: The record offices contain resources in history, law, and the social sciences; records of the county and
city; Quarter Sessions; Poor Law Union records; many church,
business, and private deposits, including some personal political
papers.

The Carlisle office contains Quarter Sessions records (1668-
1962); minutes of the County Council and its committees (from
1889); Carlisle city records (local Board of Health and Burial
Board from 1850, gas and waterworks companies, 1818-1869,
Town Clerk's letter books, 1836 to about 1950, minutes of the
Corporation and its committees, 1835-1950). Lieutenancy rec-
ords, although incomplete, contain militia books and returns for
Cumberland and Eskdale Wards (1796-1830).

The Kendal office contains Westmorland Quarter Sessions records
(from 1729); County Council records (beginning in 1889, but at
present no modern records are held); County Council deeds; records of the Lake District Planning Board.

In the record office library at Carlisle are volumes from the
Carlisle Law Library, Lords and Commons Journals, Parliamentary History of England, 1066-1802 and Parliamentary Debates, 1803-1832, Rolls series Record Commission, and Public

Record Office publications to 1909. The Curwen Library at
the Kendal Record Office contains valuable printed material for
the local history of Lancashire, Yorkshire, Cumberland, and
Westmorland, as well as works useful for the study of legal
history, heraldry, and genealogy.

Access: Records deposited at Carlisle and Kendall are immediately available at the respective offices. No appointment
is necessary, although a preliminary letter is helpful.

Manuscripts from the Dean and Chapter library may be made
available at the Carlisle office on receipt of prior notice.

The records of Lord Egremont from Cockermouth Castle can
also be made available at Carlisle, but a week's notice is required for them to be brought from Cockermouth. The offices
are open Monday to Friday, 9:00 A.M. to 5:00 P.M.

Publications: Bibliography of the History and Topography of
Cumberland and Westmorland, by H. W. Hodgson (1969);
Fleming-Senhouse Papers, by E. Hughes (1961).

Duplication: Full-size and micro-copying facilities are available
at moderate cost. Small full-size copying orders can be done
immediately. Microfilms take approximately one month depending on the size of the order.

Services: Original records may not be borrowed, but microfilmed material may be transferred temporarily to libraries or
similar institutions.

CARMARTHEN

32	Institution	Dyfed Archive Service
	Addresses	Carmarthenshire Record Office, County Hall, Carmarthen SA31 1JP

Pembrokeshire Record Office, The Castle, Haver-
fordwest SA61 1QZ
See also: HAVERFORDWEST, Pembrokeshire
Record Office (Reference No. 68)

Cardiganshire Record Office, Swyfa'r Sir, Marine
Terrace, Aberystwyth SY23 2DE

Telephones   0267-4261, ext. 160 (Carmarthen); 0437-3707
(Haverfordwest); 0970-7581, ext. 257 (Aberystwyth)

Holdings   books; records

Subject Coverage: The collections in Carmarthen and Haverfordwest consist of deposited manuscript material relating to the
former county area in addition to official authorities. In Cardiganshire, the holdings are based largely on the administrative

records of the former County Council.

Access: The collections are open to the public. Inquiries should be addressed to the County Archivist. The hours are Monday to Thursday, 9:00 A.M. to 5:00 P.M.; Friday, 9:00 A.M. to 4:15 P.M.

Publications: Carmarthenshire Studies: Essays Presented to Major Francis Jones, ed. by Tudor Barnes and Nigel Yates; Pembrokeshire Letters; Elizabethan Pembrokeshire.

Duplication: Full-size copying facilities at moderate cost are available. Micro-copying services can also be provided.

Services: The collection does not circulate. The Dyfed Archives Service offers lectures and exhibitions.

CHANNEL ISLANDS See: GUERNSEY

CHELMSFORD

33 Institution   Essex Record Office
    Address   County Hall, Chelmsford, Essex CM1 1LX
    Telephone   0245-67222, ext. 2104
    Holdings   5, 000 books; 6, 000 pamphlets; newspapers;
                   2, 000, 000 archives and papers

Subject Coverage: In addition to holding original records of the county, the office contains resources relating to genealogy, topography, and the history of Essex. There are also printed reports of other county record offices and archive repositories, important historical journals and local historical publications, and county newspapers.

Access: Researchers are permitted to use the collection, but preferably by appointment. Inquiries should be made of the County Archivist. A letter of introduction is recommended. The office is open Monday, 9:15 A.M. to 8:45 P.M.; Tuesday to Thursday, 9:15 A.M. to 5:15 P.M.; Friday, 9:15 A.M. to 4:15 P.M.

Publications: Among the publications of the Essex Record Office are Catalogue of Maps in E.R.O., 1566-1855 (reprint, 1969); Second Supplement to Catalogue of Maps in E.R.O. (1964); Third Supplement to Catalogue of Maps in E.R.O. (1968); Essex Parish Records, 1240-1894; Guide to Essex Record Office (1969). A general catalogue of publications is available from the office.

Duplication: Full-size copies are available at high cost. Micro-copies are provided at moderate cost. The record office provides many forms of photocopying.

<u>Services:</u> The collection does not circulate.

CHESTER

34 Institution   Cheshire Record Office
    Address   The Castle, Chester CH1 2DN
    Telephone   0244-602559/60 (County Archivist)
    Holdings   2,800 books, pamphlets, and periodicals; 400 reels
                   of microforms; 8,500 feet of records; documents;
                   newspapers; maps

<u>Subject Coverage:</u> The record office holds a variety of archival
groups, among which are County Council records (19th and 20th
centuries); private collections (13th to 20th centuries); Diocesan
records (16th to 20th centuries); Ecclesiastical Commissioners'
records (15th to 20th centuries); Society of Friends: Cheshire
Monthly Meeting records (17th to 19th centuries); Methodist records (18th to 20th centuries); Statutory Authorities (Poor Law
Guardians; Borough, Urban, and Rural District Councils; Weaver
Navigation, 18th to 20th centuries); ecclesiastical parish records
(16th to 20th centuries); township and civil parish records (17th
to 20th centuries); Quarter Sessions (16th to 20th centuries);
militia records (18th to 19th centuries); public records (Coroners'
Districts; Hospital Management Committees; Insurance Committees; Land Tax Commissioners; crew lists and log books of
merchant ships registered at Runcorn, 19th to 20th centuries);
probate records (from 15th century); school records (from 16th
century).

The collection also includes records on microfilm, among which
are Census Returns, 1841, 1851, 1861, 1871; Ecclesiastical
Census, 1851; Non-conformist Registers, 1648-1837; Chester
Eyre and Quo Warranto Rolls, 1299-1499; Hearth Tax Returns,
1663, 1664, 1668, 1674; Diocese of Chester Visitation Records,
1578, 1694; Diocese of Lichfield Bishop's Registers, 1298-1553;
Thomas Bulkeley of Bulkeley's Civil War Memoranda Book, 17th
century; Randle Holme's genealogical and historical manuscripts
collection; Thomas Middleton of Hyde's scrapbooks on Hyde and
district, 19th to 20th centuries; <u>Altrincham Division Chronicle</u>
(weekly newspaper), 1889-1890; <u>Altrincham and Bowdon Guardian</u>
(twice weekly newspaper), 1895-1900; <u>Macclesfield Stockport and</u>
<u>Congleton Chronicle</u> (weekly newspaper), 1836-1848.

The collection includes printed maps, among which are <u>Cheshire:</u>
Saxton, 1577; Blaeu, 1645; Speed, 1662; Bowen, 1763; Burdett,
1777; Greenwood, 1819; Swire and Hutchings, 1830; Bryant,
1831; <u>Chester:</u> Lavaux, 1745; Weston, 1789; Wood, 1833; also
Ordnance Survey maps, one-inch, two-inch, six-inch, and twen-
ty-five-inch from 1833. There is also a small collection of
source material.

Access: Researchers are permitted to use the collection on the premises. Inquiries should be directed to the County Archivist. A letter of introduction is recommended. Opening hours are Monday, 9:15 A.M. to 9:00 P.M.; Tuesday to Friday, 9:15 A.M. to 5:15 P.M.; Saturday, 9:15 A.M. to 12:30 P.M.

Publications: Guide to the County Record Office and Chester Diocesan Record Office; summary lists of various record groups (available free on request).

Duplication: Full-size copies at moderate cost can be supplied in two to three days. Dyeline, microfilm, and other photographic reproductions can be supplied by arrangement. Costs and time necessary for processing vary.

Services: The staff is prepared to answer specific reference questions, but in-depth searches must be conducted by the inquirer. The collection does not circulate. Extended searches not exceeding one hour may be undertaken for a fee.

CHESTER

35	Institution	Chester City Record Office
	Address	Town Hall, Chester CH1 2HJ
	Telephone	0244-40144, ext. 2108
	Holdings	books; pamphlets; periodicals; records

Subject Coverage: The office contains the official records of Chester Corporation (from c. 1175) which include material relating to most aspects of the city's history; Chester Rural District Council and Tarvin Rural District Council. Records of private families, businesses, and institutions, relating mainly to the city of Chester, are also held. Notable special collections are the records of the Chester Blue Coat Hospital (1700-1951); Chester Council of Social Welfare (1872-1960); Chester Royal Infirmary (1755-1947); Chester College of Education (1839-1967). There is a reference library containing works about Chester, Cheshire, and neighboring counties; general historical publications; and general reference material. The Chester Archaeological Society Library is also housed in the record office.

Access: The collection may be consulted only in the Students Room. Inquiries should be addressed to the City Archivist. The office is open Monday to Friday, 9:00 A.M. to 1:00 P.M., 2:00 P.M. to 5:00 P.M.

Publications: Guide to the Charters, Plate and Insignia of the City of Chester, by M. Groombridge; The Chester Mystery Plays, by H. Boulton; Chester, 1066-1971: Contemporary Descriptions by Residents and Visitors, by D. M. Palliser; Chester Schools: A Guide to the School Archives with a Brief History of Education in the City from 1539 to 1972, by A. M. Kennett.

Duplication: Full-size copying facilities are available at moderate cost. Small copying orders can be completed on short notice.

Services: The material is not available for loan. Telephone and postal inquiries will be answered.

CHICHESTER

36 Institution   West Sussex Record Office
Address   County Hall, Chichester, Sussex PO19 1RN
Telephone   0243-85100, ext. 351
Holdings   4,000 books; 2,000 pamphlets; 25 periodicals; 100 microforms; records; manuscripts; maps; prints and drawings; photographs

Subject Coverage: Records held include those of families, estates, local authorities, courts of justice, probate authorities, parishes, and Poor Law Guardians. The office contains a small collection of photographs, prints, and drawings. There is also a small reference library.

Access: The office is open to the public. Inquiries should be directed to the County Archivist. It is advisable to write or telephone before making a first visit. The hours are Monday to Friday, 9:15 A.M. to 12:30 P.M., 1:30 P.M. to 5:00 P.M.

Publications: The office publishes catalogues of its major collections including The Crookshank Collection, ed. by Francis W. Steer (1960); The Greatham Archives, ed. by A. A. Dibben (1962); The Hawkins Papers, ed. by Francis W. Steer (1962). A list of publications is available from the office.

Duplication: Full-size copying facilities at moderately high cost are available.

Services: None of the material is available on loan, but telephone and mail inquiries are answered.

CWMBRAN

37 Institution   Gwent Record Office
Address   County Hall, Cwmbran, Gwent NP4 2XH
Telephone   06333-67711, ext. 243
Holdings   books; pamphlets; records

Subject Coverage: The record office contains the official records of the former county of Monmouth, including courts of law and

local administration. Other records comprise those of local
families, estates, and institutions.

Access: The record office is open to the public. Inquiries
should be directed to the County Archivist. The Search Room
is open Monday to Thursday, 9:30 A.M. to 5:00 P.M.; Friday,
9:30 A.M. to 4:00 P.M. Prior notice of intention to visit is
not necessary, but is appreciated.

Publications: Annual Reports; Guide to the Records.

Duplication: Full-size and micro-copying facilities are available.

Services: Inquiries by mail and telephone will be answered,
provided no prolonged research is required.

DEESIDE

38 Institution   Clwyd Record Office
    Address   The Old Rectory, Hawarden, Deeside, Clwyd CH5
                   3NR
    Telephone   0244-532364
    Holdings   2,000 books; 500 pamphlets; records

Subject Coverage: The new county of Clwyd was formed on
April 1, 1974 from Flintshire, most of Denbighshire, and the
Edeyrnion district of Merioneth. The Clwyd Record Office
(comprising the former Flintshire Record Office and the Denbighshire Archives Department) is in charge of the public and
official records of Flintshire and Denbighshire from the 16th
century. The collection contains Quarter Sessions (from 1720),
County Council (from 1889), Poor Law (1834-1948), highway,
education (from 1862), Borough and District Council records.
Records for Flintshire are held in the headquarters of the record office in Hawarden, those for Denbighshire in Ruthin (46
Clwyd Street, Ruthin, Clwyd LL15 1HP; telephone: 08242-3077).

The Hawarden office also holds the archives of local families
and estates, some dating from medieval times, and collections
of business and industrial records--mostly for Flintshire, but
including much Denbighshire material. Similar collections are
beginning to accumulate at Ruthin.

The County Archivist acts as Hon. Archivist to St. Deiniol's Library, Hawarden, and deals with the listing and production of
the Glynne-Gladstone Manuscripts and other collections deposited
there.

Access: Most documents can be produced without prior notice,
but those scholars with long-term projects or with limited research time are advised to make an appointment. At least two

days' notice must be given for access to papers at St. Deiniol's
Library. Access to certain classes of official records is restricted. The hours are Monday to Thursday, 8:45 A.M. to
12:45 P.M., 1:30 P.M. to 5:00 P.M.; Friday, 8:45 A.M. to
12:45 P.M., 1:30 P.M. to 4:30 P.M. The Ruthin office is
open Monday to Thursday, 8:30 A.M. to 12:30 P.M., 1:30
P.M. to 5:00 P.M.; Friday, 8:30 A.M. to 12:30 P.M., 1:30
P.M. to 4:30 P.M. Inquiries should be directed to the County
Archivist.

Publications: Guide to the Flintshire Record Office (1974);
Clwyd in Old Photographs (1975); H. M. Stanley and Wales
(1972); Hand List of the County Records (1955); Farmhouses
and Cottages (1964).

Duplication: Full-size copies can be provided on demand at
moderate cost. Photographic services are also furnished.

Services: The collection does not circulate.

DEESIDE

> Institution   Flintshire Record Office
>   See: DEESIDE, Clwyd Record Office (Reference
>   No. 38)

DEESIDE

39 Institution   Saint Deiniol's Library
   Address   Hawarden, Deeside, Clwyd CH5 3DF
   Telephone   0244-532350
   Holdings   100,000 books; 50 periodicals

Subject Coverage: The library, based originally on W. E. Gladstone's Collection, holds works in theology, history, philosophy,
and literature. The special collections include the letters of
Gladstone and his family, the personal papers of Archbishop
Green of Wales, and 19th century studies. A large pamphlet
collection is on permanent loan from the National Liberal Club,
Gladstone Library. The library, containing a strong collection
in medieval, Tudor, and Stuart studies, holds Royal Historical
and Camden Societies material, Rolls and Manuscripts Commission series, and HMSO publications. The entire Loeb Classical
Library, Greek and Latin, is also held.

Access: This is a residential library and has accommodations
for thirty guests. It is for the use of scholars who reside
there while conducting research. Inquiries should be addressed
to the Warden. The library is open all year. Research need
not be limited to the holdings of the library, since scholars in
any field are welcome to use the facilities.

Publications: None.

Duplication: Full-size copying facilities are available at moderate cost, and orders will be processed upon request.

Services: The collection does not circulate. The library cooperates with the British Library Lending Division.

DORCHESTER

40 Institution   Dorset Record Office
    Address   County Hall, Dorchester, Dorset DT1 1XJ
    Telephone   0305-3131
    Holdings   300 books; pamphlets; 5 periodicals; records

Subject Coverage: The record office holds Quarter Sessions, Petty Sessions, manorial, estate, family, parish, business, and probate records of Dorset. A small reference library for staff and researchers is available.

Access: The office is open to the public. Advance notice of a visit is appreciated. The hours are Monday to Friday, 9:00 A.M. to 5:00 P.M. Inquiries should be directed to the County Archivist.

Publications: None.

Duplication: Full-size copying facilities are available.

Services: The material can only be used on the premises. A limited search will be made in response to a postal inquiry.

DOUGLAS

41 Institution   Isle of Man General Registry
    Address   Finch Road, Douglas, Isle of Man
    Telephone   0624-3358
    Holdings   records

Subject Coverage: The general registry contains the High Court Records, original Acts and Resolutions of Tynwald, Grants of Representation to the estates' decedents, original plans and valuation of Manx estates and many other documents relating to the history and development of the Isle of Man. The registry also contains statutory records of births registered in the Isle of Man (from 1878); records of Church of England baptisms (1611-1878); statutory records of marriages registered in the Isle of Man (from 1884); Church of England marriage records (1629-1849); Church of England and Dissenters marriage records (1849-1883); statutory records of deaths (from 1878); records of Church of England burials (1610-1878); adopted children

registers (from 1928); wills (from 1847); deeds to property in
the Isle of Man (from 1847).

Access: The registry is open to the public. Inquiries should
be directed to the Chief Registrar. The hours are Monday to
Friday, 9:00 A.M. to 1:00 P.M., 2:15 P.M. to 4:30 P.M.

Publications: Census Reports; Chief Registrar's Annual Report ... of Births, Marriages and Deaths.

Duplication: Full-size copying facilities are available.

Services: No material is available on loan. Telephone and
mail inquiries are answered.

DOUGLAS

42	Institution	The Manx Museum Library
	Address	Kingswood Grove, Douglas, Isle of Man
	Telephone	0624-5522
	Holdings	15,000 books and pamphlets; 50 periodicals; 6,000 deposits of manuscripts; newspapers

Subject Coverage: The library contains works relating to the
Isle of Man, including political and economic history, geography,
folklore, archaeology, and the Manx language. There are also
manuscript maps, the public records of the Isle of Man, and
Manx newspapers from 1793. Census records are held from
1821-1871 (at ten-year intervals), but those for 1841 are incomplete. Other records include wills (1828-1846) and deeds to
property in the Isle of Man (1600-c.1846).

Access: Scholars are welcome to use the collection. Inquiries
should be made of the Librarian or Director. The library is
open Monday to Saturday, 10:00 A.M. to 5:00 P.M.

Publications: Journal of the Manx Museum (annual); Bibliography of Literature Relating to the Isle of Man; Manx Archaeological Survey (6 parts); Ancient Monuments Handbook; Early
Maps of the Isle of Man; guides to the museum and Branch Folk
Museums.

Duplication: Full-size copying facilities are available only
through the Government Office. No immediate service is provided.

Services: The collection does not circulate.

DUMFRIES

43	Institution	Dumfries Museum

Address   Corbelly Hill, Dumfries DG1 2AD
Telephone   0387-3374
Holdings   50 books; pamphlets; microforms; records; manu-
             scripts; newspapers

Subject Coverage: The collection includes files of local newspapers and magazines from 1773; local manuscript diaries from
the mid-18th century; several tons of burgh archives, mainly
from 1506, but some from 1300; almost complete run of burgh
court books, Town Council Minutes, and related material from
1506; almost complete sets of accounts, jail books, anchorage
books from 1631; some 20,000 loose documents, boxed and
calendared according to subjects (petitions, accounts, jail documents, military documents, etc.), up to 1720. (Documents between 1720 and 1900 are arranged by bundles and subject in
record boxes.) Microfilm of most of the earlier material is
in stock (and may also be obtained from the University of Edinburgh Library). The collection also contains microfilm of Kirk
Session Minutes from 1615 and of local customs records from
1660 to 1832.

Access: Application to use the collection must be made by the
researcher. Admission is with permission of the Curator of
Museums.

Publications: Papers in Transactions of Dumfries and Galloway
Natural History and Antiquarian Society (since 1862); leaflets.

Duplication: Full-size copying facilities are available.

Services: Information can be provided, documents copied, and
desks and documents made available to researchers. Material
is not normally loaned.

DUNDEE

44 Institution   University of Dundee Library
    Address   Dundee DD1 4HN
    Telephone   0382-23181
    Holdings   300,000 books and pamphlets; 4,564 periodicals;
                  microforms; manuscripts

Subject Coverage: The library resources are strong in the
social sciences and include a special collection on the history
of medicine. It has the Brechin Diocesan Library which contains incunabula, illuminated manuscripts, and the Leng Collection of Scottish philosophy. The faculties of the university are
fully covered.

Access: Visiting scholars may use the library upon application
to the Librarian. A letter of introduction from the home institution is recommended. The hours are Monday to Friday,

9:00 A.M. to 10:00 P.M.; Saturday, 9:00 A.M. to 12:00 noon
during the academic year. During vacations, the hours are
Monday to Friday, 9:00 A.M. to 5:00 P.M.; Saturday, 9:00
A.M. to 12:00 noon.

Publications: Only an Annual Report and Accessions Lists are
issued by the library.

Duplication: Both full-size and micro-copies are available, and
the cost is moderate. Full-size copying is provided on demand;
other forms of copying may take time to process.

Services: Both telephone and postal inquiries are answered.
The collection circulates only to members of the university,
but others may consult reference material.

DURHAM

45	Institution	Durham County Library
	Address	County Hall, Durham DH1 5TY
	Telephone	0385-64411, ext. 599
	Holdings	1,595,341 books and pamphlets; 330 periodicals; microforms; newspapers

Subject Coverage: The library holds two local history collections. The Durham Branch Library holds material on the county and Durham City. The Darlington Branch Library contains
works on the town and surrounding area. There is also a Railway Collection at Darlington.

Access: The library is open to the public. Inquiries should be
directed to the Librarian. The hours of the County Library and
the branches are Monday to Friday, 10:00 A.M. to 7:00 P.M.;
Saturday, 10:00 A.M. to 5:00 P.M.

Publications: The library publishes several catalogues, e.g.,
Local History (1973), a series on various aspects of local history (1971-   ), and occasional book lists.

Duplication: Full-size copying facilities are available at Darlington and Durham.

Services: The library lends books to ticket holders and accepts
those issued by other library authorities.

DURHAM

46	Institution	Durham County Record Office
	Address	County Hall, Durham DH1 5UL
	Telephone	0385-64411, ext. 253
	Holdings	books; periodicals; microforms; records

Subject Coverage: The record office contains many official and
public records. It has also been designated by the Bishop of
Durham as the diocesan repository for parish records. The official records include County Council, Quarter Sessions, Clerk
of the Peace (including enclosure awards and plans), Petty Sessions, Coroners, manorial, Municipal Corporation, Urban District Council and Local Board of Health, Rural District Council
and Rural Sanitary Authority, Civil Parish, Highway Administration (including Turnpike Trust), Ecclesiastical Parish (including
records of parish officers), Board of Guardians, Hospital Management Committee, National Coal Board (including records of
old colliery companies), School Board, School Log Books,
School Building Plans. The private record collection contains
records of families, estates, non-conformist churches and industries. The Search Room contains a small library of local
history books and other works of reference, and is intended to
assist people using the documents.

Access: The record office is open to the public. Inquiries
should be directed to the County Archivist. No appointment is
necessary except to use the microfilm reader. The hours are
Monday to Thursday, 8:45 A.M. to 4:45 P.M.; Friday, 8:45
A.M. to 4:15 P.M.; second Tuesday of each month, 6:00 P.M.
to 8:45 P.M. Anyone using the record office for the first time
is advised to make preliminary written inquiry about the availability of sources.

Publications: Durham County Record Office.

Duplication: Full-size copying facilities are provided at moderate cost. Micro-copies and photographs are also available.

Services: Material is to be used only on the premises. Postal
and telephone inquiries will be answered.

DURHAM

47   Institution   Durham University Library
     Address   Palace Green, Durham DH1 3RN
     Telephone   0385-61262/3
     Holdings   450,000 books; 3,000 periodicals; 4,000 manu-
                    scripts; 100,000 microforms; 2,000 prints, maps,
                    plans, printed ephemera

Subject Coverage: The library collection is found in three
physical locations, but most of the material is in the main
building. The resources support the faculties of the university
and include many special collections, such as those of Prof.
Gunn (Egyptology); Mr. H. J. Cant and Prof. Yetts (Far Eastern); Bishop Cosin, Dr. Routh and Dr. Winterbottom (all of
which contain older printed books and manuscripts relating
chiefly to theology with some politics, history, atlases, re-

ligious controversy, archeology, and topography). An important special collection housed in the Oriental Section of the library is the Sudan Archive (manuscripts and printed material on the former Anglo-Egyptian Condominium). The library is a depository for European Economic Communities publications and for selective subjects from HMSO.

The Mid-East Centre (Documentation Section) collects the official publications of both public and private organizations located in the Middle East. This collection, giving comprehensive coverage of the Mid-East, is acquired mostly through gift or exchange and includes bank reports, ephemera, and material from government and industry. Many of these resources are not available elsewhere. Inquiries should be made to the Documentations Officer.

Access: Visiting scholars are permitted to use the collection on written application to the Librarian. A letter of introduction is recommended. For unusual material, a letter ahead of time would insure that staff is available to aid the scholar and that the needed works can be retrieved beforehand to avoid delay. The hours are Monday to Friday, 9:00 A.M. to 10:00 P.M.; Saturday, 9:00 A.M. to 12:30 P.M. during the academic year. During vacation, the hours are Monday to Friday, 9:00 A.M. to 5:00 P.M.; Saturday, 9:00 A.M. to 12:30 P.M. The library is closed Christmas to New Year's Day and Good Friday to Easter Monday. The Oriental Section, which contains the Sudan Archive, is open Monday to Friday, 9:00 A.M. to 5:30 P.M. during the academic year.

Publications: Among the publications issued are Durham University Journal; Inaugural Lectures; A Union List of Periodicals in the Learned Libraries of Durham, by G. S. Darlow (1962); Summary List of the Additional Manuscripts, by D. Ramage (1963); Maps of Durham, 1576-1872, in the University Library, Durham, by R. M. Turner (1954); Supplement, by A. I. Doyle (1960); Durham Topographical Prints up to 1800: An Annotated Bibliography, by P. M. Bevedekz (1968). There are descriptions of special collections found in The Durham Philobiblon and The Durham University Journal. A list is available at the library.

Duplication: Full-size copying facilities are available, and processing usually takes a day. The cost is moderately low. Micro-copies can be provided at a slightly higher cost, and the delay can be up to three months.

Services: The library has a liberal interlending policy and cooperates with the British Library Lending Division. For loans abroad, the library would prefer to send microfilm rather than the work itself. The collection circulates only to members of the university.

EALING

>   Institution   London Borough of Ealing Library Services
>   See: LONDON, London Borough of Ealing Library
>   Services (Reference No. 135)

EDINBURGH

48   Institution   General Register Office for Scotland
      Address   New Register House, Edinburgh EH1 3YT
      Telephone   031-556 3952
      Holdings   2,000 books and pamphlets; 20 periodicals; records

Subject Coverage: The office contains original records of population and vital statistics relating to Scotland, supplemented by printed reports for the United Kingdom, and some British Commonwealth and foreign countries. The records include civil registers of births, deaths, and marriages in Scotland (from 1855); old parish registers (16th century to 1854); decennial census enumeration books (from 1841). Census records are available only up to 1891.

Access: Researchers may use the material on the premises on payment of a fee. Inquiries should be directed to the Registrar General for Scotland. The hours are Monday to Thursday, 9:30 A.M. to 4:30 P.M.; Friday, 9:30 A.M. to 4:00 P.M.

Publications: Reports of the Registrar General for Scotland (weekly, quarterly, and annual); Estimates of the Population of Scotland (annual); Reports on Censuses of the Population of Scotland (after each census); Life Tables (decennial); Occupational Mortality (decennial).

Duplication: Copying facilities are not available.

Services: The material may only be used on the premises. Inquiries relating to Scottish vital statistics or census records are answered. Analyses of vital statistics will be prepared. Information from the registers and the open census records is issued in the form of official extracts of individual entries.

EDINBURGH

49   Institution   National Library of Scotland
      Address   George IV Bridge, Edinburgh EH1 1EW
      Telephone   031-226 4531
      Holdings   3,000,000 books and pamphlets; 8,000 periodicals;
                     30,000 volumes of manuscripts; 210 newspapers;
                     1,000,000 maps (located in the Map Room, National
                     Library of Scotland Annex, 137 Causewayside,
                     Edinburgh EH9 1PH)

Subject Coverage: The library has been a copyright library
since 1710. It receives all British and Irish publications, including Parliamentary Papers and publications of the UN and
some other international agencies. In consequence, it can provide all material on the social sciences within the range of
British publishing, supplemented by selected foreign purchases.
The library contains a rich collection of manuscripts dealing
with Scottish history and civilization and an almost complete run
of ordnance survey maps of Scotland and England. Among the
notable collections are the following of interest to social scientists: Alva (16th and 17th century law); Blaikie (Jacobite
pamphlets, broadsides, proclamations, and books on Jacobitism); Blair (Celtic or Scottish interest); Campbell (Celtic folklore, tales, and poetry); Ferguson (books from the 16th to 18th
centuries); Lauriston (Scottish books, pamphlets, and chap-
books); Payne (books relating to Francis Bacon); Roseberry
(early Scottish books and pamphlets); Keiller (books on witchcraft and demonology from the 15th century); Lyle (books on
ships and shipping); Macdonald (books on heraldry); Wordie
(polar exploration). In addition, Blair College Library (theological books and books from Scots College Library in Paris)
has been placed on deposit in the library.

The Manuscript Collection contains the Lauriston Castle Library
(records of the incorporation of Candlemakers of Edinburgh and
the papers of the Mackenzies of Delvine); letters of Thomas
Carlyle; the Morton Cartulary (including the writs of the Doug-
lases of Lochleven from the 12th century); letters of Sir Walter
Scott; letters of Robert Louis Stevenson (which may only be consulted with special permission).

Access: Visiting scholars must apply for permission to use the
collection. Inquiries should be directed to the Superintendent
of Reference Services. The Reading Room is open Monday to
Friday, 9:30 A.M. to 8:30 P.M.; Saturday, 9:30 A.M. to 1:00
P.M. The Map Room is open Monday to Friday, 9:30 A.M. to
5:00 P.M.; Saturday, 9:30 A.M. to 1:00 P.M.

Publications: Catalogue of Manuscripts Acquired Since 1925,
vol. 1 (1938); vol. 2 (1966); vol. 3, Blackwood Papers, 1805-
1900 (1968); Summary Catalogue of the Advocates' Manuscripts;
Short-title Catalogue of Books Published Abroad to 1600; List
of Books Printed in Scotland Before 1700, by H. G. Aldis, rev.
ed.; and catalogues of exhibitions and facsimiles (list available).

Duplication: Full-size and micro-copying facilities are available. A price list is provided on request.

Services: The collection does not circulate.

EDINBURGH

50 Institution   Royal Society of Edinburgh
    Address   22/24 George Street, Edinburgh EH2 2PQ
    Telephone   031-225 6057
    Holdings   200,000 books (this includes the bound periodicals
                   which account for about 90% of the holdings)

Subject Coverage: The collection leans heavily toward scientific
material, although there are some social science publications
included. The library has photographs of the past presidents of
the society, a collection of David Hume Manuscripts (13 vols.),
and the James Hutton Manuscripts (2 vols.) on agriculture.

Access: A researcher must have a letter of introduction from
his home institution to use the library. The hours are Monday
to Friday, 9:30 A.M. to 5:00 P.M. Inquiries should be addressed to the Executive Secretary and Librarian.

Publications: Transactions of the Royal Society of Edinburgh;
Proceedings of the Royal Society of Edinburgh; Yearbook of the
Royal Society of Edinburgh (which includes library accession
lists); Communications to the Royal Society of Edinburgh.

Duplication: Full-size copying facilities are available at moderate cost. Copies can be obtained on demand.

Services: Borrowing is permitted only to those sponsored by a
reputable institution or a Fellow of the Society. The collection
is not classified as it consists chiefly of periodical titles. Inquiries made by telephone or mail will be answered.

EDINBURGH

51 Institution   Scottish Conservative Central Office
    Address   11 Atholl Crescent, Edinburgh EH3 8HG
    Telephone   031-229 1342
    Holdings   books; pamphlets; press clippings

Subject Coverage: The collection consists mainly of publications
relating to the government of Scotland. It is divided as follows:
politics and government, social, economics, and overseas. The
library holds a set of Hansard (Commons and Lords) since 1970
(earlier volumes have been transferred to the Advocate's Library) and a set of Public Acts and Measures from 1880.
There are extensive press cuttings which cover Scottish affairs
since 1967.

Access: The library is generally not open to the public, but
American scholars would be allowed to use the collection if a
need could be shown. A prior appointment is necessary. Inquiries should be directed to the Chairman. The hours are

Monday to Friday, 9:30 A.M. to 5:30 P.M.

Publications: The office issues party publications and mani-
festoes.

Duplication: Full-size copying facilities are available, and processing is immediate.

Services: The collection may only be used on the premises.

EDINBURGH

52	Institution	Scottish National Party, Research Library
	Address	6 North Charlotte Street, Edinburgh EH2 4HR
	Telephone	031-226 5722
		See also: Scottish National Party, p. 244
	Holdings	150 books and reports; 40 periodicals; 80,000 press clippings

Subject Coverage: The library contains information mostly pertaining to the history, politics, and economics of Scotland.
Most of the material deals with contemporary matters. The
collection includes electoral addresses, political studies, and
information on oil.

Access: Admission is by appointment only. Application should
be directed to the Senior Research Consultant. Admission is
granted generally to those pursuing advanced research who may
not be able to locate information elsewhere. The hours are
Monday to Friday, 9:30 A.M. to 5:00 P.M.

Publications: Research Bulletin; Scots Independent; Catalogue
of Holdings (in preparation).

Duplication: Full-size copying facilities are available at moderate cost.

Services: The collection does not circulate.

EDINBURGH

53	Institution	Scottish Office Library
	Address	New St. Andrew's House, St. James Centre, Edinburgh EH1 3TG
	Telephone	031-566 8400, ext. 5290/4102
	Holdings	40,000 books; 80,000 pamphlets and reports; 1,000 periodicals

Subject Coverage: The library collection includes politics,
economics, Scottish government and administration, town and
country planning, transport, law, industrial development, and

local government. Resources in social work and public health
and research materials in higher education may be found at St.
Andrew's House (Edinburgh EH1 3DH; telephone: 031-556 8501,
ext. 2781).

Access: The library is primarily for the use of the five de-
partments of the Secretary of State for Scotland (Department of
Agriculture and Fisheries for Scotland, Scottish Development
Department, Scottish Education Department, Scottish Home and
Health Department, and Scottish Economic Planning Department).
Visiting scholars may use the library by appointment. A letter
of introduction is recommended. The hours are Monday to
Thursday, 8:30 A.M. to 5:00 P.M.; Friday, 8:30 A.M. to 4:30
P.M.

Publications: The Scottish Office issues government reports on
various aspects of Scottish administration.

Duplication: Facilities for full-size and micro-copying are
available. Full-size copies can be provided the same day, but
micro-copies may take some time.

Services: Inquiries may be made by mail or telephone. The
library first serves individuals in the Scottish Office, then other
government departments, then other libraries. The library cooperates with the British Library Lending Division and the National Library of Scotland Lending Services Division.

EDINBURGH

54 Institution   Scottish Record Office
    Addresses   HM General Register House, Edinburgh EH1 3YY
                    and (Annex) West Register House, Charlotte Square,
                    Edinburgh EH2 4DF
    Telephones   031-556 6585; 031-226 5101 (annex)
    Holdings   books; pamphlets; periodicals; microforms; records;
                    maps; plans

Subject Coverage: The office holds the public records of Scotland, government and legal, from the 13th century; records of
nationalized industries in Scotland; records of courts; local authority and church records; private muniments; and special collections. There is also a reference library of books, periodicals, and pamphlets relating to Scottish records and the work of
the Scottish Record Office. The main legal and older historical
records are preserved in HM General Register House. Modern
records and special collections are housed in the branch repository at the West Register House.

Access: Visiting scholars are permitted to consult any records
which are open to public access in the Historical Search Room
in HM General Register House or in the West Register House

Search Room. All readers are interviewed and issued with a
reader's ticket. Postal inquiries should be directed to the
Keeper of the Records of Scotland. The hours are Monday to
Friday, 9:00 A.M. to 4:45 P.M.; Saturday, 9:00 A.M. to 12:30
P.M. (Historical Search Room only).

Publications: For a list of publications, see HMSO Sectional
List no. 24, British National Archives.

Duplication: Full-size and micro-copying facilities are available.
Details of current fees are provided on request from the Keeper of the Records of Scotland.

Services: The holdings may only be consulted in the Search
Rooms. For persons unable to make a personal search in records, the Scottish Record Office may conduct searches over
such periods and subject to such conditions as the Keeper of the
Records of Scotland may prescribe for particular classes of
records.

EDINBURGH

55 Institution   University of Edinburgh Library
   Address   George Square, Edinburgh EH8 9LJ
   Telephone   031-667 1011, ext. 6611
   Holdings   1,110,000 books; 175,000 pamphlets; 9,000 peri-
                  odicals; 50,000 manuscripts

Subject Coverage: The library covers all subjects, but is particularly strong in the history of economics, medicine, and science; early 17th century literature and Shakespeare. The large
manuscript section includes the David Laing Collection, records
of Scottish firms, and early African material.

Access: Non-members of the university must apply in writing
to the Librarian for permission to use the library. The main
library, serving principally the faculties of arts and social sciences, contains the manuscript and historical materials in all
disciplines. It is open Monday to Thursday, 9:00 A.M. to 10:00
P.M.; Friday, 9:00 A.M. to 7:00 P.M. during the academic
year. At other times, it is open Monday to Friday, 9:00 A.M.
to 5:00 P.M. It is closed on public holidays, during the second
week in August, and for approximately ten days over Christmas
and the New Year.

The sectional libraries for European governmental studies, law,
medicine, music, theology, and veterinary medicine are located
away from the main library and their hours vary slightly.

Publications: Catalogue of the Printed Books in the Library of
the University of Edinburgh, 3 vols. (1918-1923); Edinburgh
University Library, Index to Manuscripts, 2 vols. (Boston,
Mass., 1964).

Duplication: Full-size copies and photography are available.
Details and cost are provided on request.

Services: The University Library engages in interlibrary cooperation through the British Library Lending Division.

EGHAM

56 Institution   University of London, Royal Holloway College Li-
                  brary
    Address   Egham Hill, Egham TW20 0EY
    Telephone   389-4455
    Holdings   120,000 books and pamphlets; 820 periodicals;
                  microforms

Subject Coverage: The library contains works on history, fine
art, politics, economics, and statistics. It has some resources
in British history in the 12th, 17th, and 18th centuries.

Access: The collection is open to the public upon application
to the Librarian. The hours are Monday to Friday, 9:00 A.M.
to 9:00 P.M.; Saturday, 9:00 A.M. to 1:00 P.M.; Sunday, 2:00
P.M. to 6:00 P.M. during the academic year. At other times,
the library is open Monday to Friday, 9:00 A.M. to 5:00 P.M.

Publications: The library issues a guide to the collection.

Duplication: Photocopying facilities are available at moderate
cost.

Services: The library cooperates with the British Library Lending Division.

EXETER

57 Institution   Devon Record Office
    Address   Concord House, South Street, Exeter EX1 1DX
    Telephone   0392-79146
    Holdings   books; records; maps

Subject Coverage: The collection contains official records of the
county of Devon and Diocese of Exeter. Among these records
are Quarter Sessions (from c.1592); County Council (from c.
1893); Lieutenancy (including muster rolls from 1808); Poor Law
Unions; Turnpike Trustees (from c.1753); Highway Boards (from
c.1856). Ecclesiastical records include diocesan (Episcopal
registers from the 13th century); parish (inclosure awards, tithe
awards, bishops' transcripts and school records); Society of
Friends (registers from the 18th century); Unitarian Congrega-
tion (from the 19th century); Methodist (from the 19th century).
Many family, estate, and business records are also found.

There is a small reference library.

Access: The office is open to the public. Inquiries should be directed to the County Archivist. The hours are Monday to Friday, 9:30 A.M. to 5:00 P.M.; first and third Saturdays in each month (except preceding a Bank Holiday), 9:00 A.M. to 12 noon.

Publications: Guide to Official Records; Oakum; Friends Across the Channel.

Duplication: Full-size copying facilities are available at moderate cost.

Services: Inquiries, within reasonable bounds, will be answered by telephone or mail. The collection does not circulate.

EXETER

58	Institution	East Devon Record Office
	Address	Castle Street, Exeter, Devon EX4 3PQ
	Telephone	0392-73047
	Holdings	several hundred books, pamphlets, and periodicals; 300,000 records

Subject Coverage: The collection includes official records of Exeter City (medieval to modern); records of former district councils; East Devon family and estate papers; Exeter City parish records; and some county records.

Access: The record office is open to the public. Hours are Monday to Friday, 9:30 A.M. to 5:15 P.M.; alternate Saturdays, 9:00 A.M. to 12:30 P.M.

Publications: Annual Report (published with Devon Record Office Report).

Duplication: Full-size copying facilities at moderate cost are available. Some microfilming and photography can be arranged.

Services: Documents may be consulted in the Search Room. They are indexed by person, place, and subject. Telephone and postal inquiries are answered.

EXETER

59	Institution	University of Exeter Library
	Address	Prince of Wales Road, Exeter, Devon EX4 4PT
	Telephone	0392-77911
	Holdings	300,000 books; 2,800 periodicals; microforms; manuscripts

Subject Coverage: The main library holds material on sociology, politics, economics, economic history, geography, and history. There are separate libraries for law and education. Included are the Dodderidge Theological Library and the Totnes Parochial Library.

In the Exeter Cathedral Library (Bishop's Palace, Exeter; telephone: 0392-72894) can be found historical material and the Archives of the Dean and Chapter, which include documents dating from the 10th century. This library also contains works on early medicine and science from the 16th century; English history, medieval ecclesiastical history; 15th, 16th, and 18th century political history; and important collections on local history.

The library of the Devon and Exeter Institution (7, Cathedral Close, Exeter EX1 1EZ; telephone: 0392-74727) contains an interesting local history collection and files of local newspapers.

Access: The main library is open to visiting researchers on application to the Librarian. Inquiries may also be directed to the Sub-Librarian, Readers' Services. A letter of introduction is recommended. The library hours are Monday to Friday, 9:00 A.M. to 10:00 P.M.; Saturday, 9:00 A.M. to 1:00 P.M. during the academic year. During vacation, opening times vary. The library of the Devon and Exeter Institution is open Monday to Friday, 9:00 A.M. to 5:00 P.M. The Cathedral Library is open Monday to Friday, 2:00 P.M. to 5:00 P.M.

Publications: The library issues New Accessions Lists every month. In addition, it has published an Index to Theses Submitted to Exeter University Since 1955. The Cathedral Library has issued the Library of Exeter Cathedral, by L. J. Lloyd, with descriptions of the archives by A. M. Erskine.

Duplication: Full-size copies at moderate cost can be provided, but there are no facilities for micro-copies.

Services: Material is loaned only to members of the university. Inquiries will be answered by telephone or mail.

GATESHEAD

60 Institution   Gateshead Public Libraries
    Address   Prince Consort Road, Gateshead NE8 4LN
    Telephone   0632-773478
    Holdings   45,000 books and pamphlets; 500 periodicals; 400
                  microforms; 50,000 manuscripts; newspapers; 500
                  maps; 4,000 photographs and prints

Subject Coverage: The central library is strong in law resources and local history. It is a repository for manorial and legal documents and contains a collection of local photographs, prints and maps, and many works on the history of the area. The Archives Section holds the records of local government authorities, churches, and industry. Among the many important special collections are the Cotesworth Manuscripts and the Ellison Manuscripts. These are 18th century family papers relating to the early history of the coal trade. There are local newspapers from 1744, early pamphlets, and literary works which relate to the area. Parish records include registers of baptisms, marriages, and burials from the 16th century for St. Mary's, Gateshead (some on microfilm) and registers of baptisms (1825-1918), registers of marriages (1825-1929), registers of burials (1825-1924), index to burials (1884-1901) for St. John's, Gateshead Fell. Transcripts of other parish registers and of wills are also found.

The Reference Division contains a Railways Collection which includes almost all of the books published in Britain on the subject and some foreign material. Most of the collection dates from 1960, but there are some retrospective works.

Access: The library is open to the public. Inquiries should be directed to the Librarian. A letter of introduction would be useful. The hours are Monday, Tuesday, Thursday, Friday, 10:00 A.M. to 8:00 P.M.; Wednesday, 10:00 A.M. to 5:00 P.M.; Saturday, 10:00 A.M. to 12:30 P.M., 1:30 P.M. to 5:00 P.M.

Publications: Historic Gateshead: A Select Bibliography (1967); Gateshead Archives (1968); Religion and Religions: A Select Booklist (1969); Local Government Literature (fortnightly abstracting journal); Cotesworth Manuscripts (1971); The Brandling Junction Railway (1973); A History of Gateshead (1973).

Duplication: Full-size copying facilities are available at moderate cost, and processing is immediate. Arrangements can be made for micro-copying, but the delay is approximately five weeks.

Services: The material circulates only to ticket holders, but tickets from other library authorities will be accepted. The library cooperates with the British Library Lending Division.

GLASGOW

61	Institution	Glasgow District Libraries, The Mitchell Library
	Address	North Street, Glasgow G3 7DN
	Telephone	041-248 7121
	Holdings	1,000,000 books; 1,300 periodicals; 20,000 microforms; 11,500 maps

Subject Coverage: The Mitchell Library is strong in Scottish history, poetry, and genealogy. The Glasgow Collection con-

tains the city directories from 1783, parochial records (on
microfilm) from the 17th century, 18th century maps, voters
registration lists from 1858, and valuation rolls from 1913. Of
particular interest in the Music Room is the Kidson Collection.
This holding includes English and Scottish popular music of the
18th and 19th centuries and a large number of broadsides.

The library is a depository for the publications of the UN,
UNESCO, and FAO and has a standing order for all HMSO pub-
lications. The collection of patent specifications for Great Brit-
ain, Australia, Canada, New Zealand, Ireland, and the United
States is separately housed in the Commercial Library (Royal
Exchange Square, Glasgow, telephone: 041-221 1872).

Access: There are no restrictions on the use of the library.
Inquiries should be made of the Director. Opening hours are
Monday to Friday, 9:30 A.M. to 9:00 P.M.; Saturday, 9:30
A.M. to 5:00 P.M. The library is also open Sunday, 2:00 P.M.
to 8:00 P.M. (October to May).

Publications: The Mitchell Library Catalogue of Additions,
1915-1949, 2 vols. (1959); Catalogue of Robert Burns Collection
in The Mitchell Library (1959); The Mitchell Library Catalogue
of Periodicals (1962); Catalogue of Incunabula and STC Books in
the Mitchell Library (1964); Glasgow Public Libraries, 1874-
1966 (1966); Annual Reports and Annual Programme of Lectures.

Duplication: Full-size copying facilities are available at moderate cost, twenty-four hours a day. Charges for photostat
copying are provided on application. Coin-operated copiers are
available for public use.

Services: All telephone and postal inquiries are answered. The
Mitchell Library is associated with forty-two district libraries
with a lending stock of approximately 1,000,000 volumes.

GLASGOW

62   Institution   University of Glasgow Library
     Address   Hillhead Street, Glasgow G12 8QE
     Telephone   041-334 2122
     Holdings   1,100,000 books; 50,000 pamphlets and reports;
                     7,500 periodicals; 12,000 microforms; 10,000
                     manuscripts; photographs

Subject Coverage: The library is very strong in Scottish history. The holdings include several valuable collections, e.g.,
Hunterian Collection (containing incunabula and manuscripts on
the history of medicine); Dougan Collection of early photographic
work; Wylie Collection (history and antiquities of Glasgow); Ferguson Collection (history of chemistry and alchemy); Stirling-
Maxwell Collection (emblem books); David Murray Collection

(bibliography and local history); Euing Collection (early printing, Bibles, and music, including manuscripts and early printed music); Birnie Philip Collection (letters, manuscripts, books, and papers of James McNeill Whistler). The library is a depository for European Economic Communities publications. There is a branch library for Soviet Studies which has a major collection of East European material.

Access: Special readership (which gives visiting academics equal borrowing privileges with members of the university) is available on low-cost subscription by permission of the Library Committee. Inquiry should be directed to the Librarian by letter. During the academic year, the library is open Monday to Friday, 9:00 A.M. to 9:30 P.M.; Saturday, 9:00 A.M. to 12:30 P.M. During Easter and summer vacation, the library is open Monday to Friday, 9:00 A.M. to 5:00 P.M.; Saturday, 9:00 A.M. to 12:30 P.M. During Christmas vacation, the hours are Monday to Friday, 9:00 A.M. to 5:00 P.M.

Publications: Catalogue of the Manuscripts in the Library of the Hunterian Museum, by John Young and P. Henderson Aitken (1908); Printed Books in the Library of the Hunterian Museum: A Catalogue, by Mungo Ferguson (1930); Catalogue of the Wylie Collection of Books (Mainly Relating to Glasgow) (1929); Catalogue of a Collection of Books and Manuscripts Relating to the Darien Scheme (1932); Catalogue of the Ferguson Collection of Books, Mainly Relating to Alchemy, Chemistry, Witchcraft and Gypsies, 2 vols. (1943); Reader's Guide (annual); Directory of Departmental Libraries and duplicated catalogues of special exhibitions.

Duplication: Facilities for full-size and micro-copying are available at moderate cost. Time necessary for duplication depends on the work in hand. Micro-copying may take several weeks.

Services: Books circulate only to members of the library. Reference inquiries by mail or telephone will be answered. The library cooperates with the British Library Lending Division.

GLASGOW

63	Institution	University of Strathclyde, The Andersonian Library (University Library)
	Address	McCance Building, 16 Richmond Street, Glasgow G1 1XQ
	Telephone	041-552 4156
	Holdings	247,000 books; 4,000 periodicals; 90,000 microforms

Subject Coverage: The collection covers all schools of the university, including the School of Arts and Social Studies. The Anderson Collection (the private library of John Anderson) contains history of science works, particularly of the 17th and 18th centuries.

Access: Visiting scholars are permitted to use the collection
if need can be shown. A letter of introduction is advisable.
Inquiries should be directed to the Librarian. Advance notice
is recommended for access to special collections. During the
academic year, the library is open Monday to Friday, 9:30
A.M. to 9:00 P.M.; Saturday, 9:30 A.M. to 12 noon. The
hours are the same during vacation except that closing time
Monday to Friday is 5:00 P.M.

Publications: Report on Research; Library Regulations

Duplication: Both full-size and micro-copying facilities are
available.

Services: Books may be borrowed only by members of the University Library. Consultation facilities for American scholars
will be provided if need can be shown.

GLOUCESTER

64 Institution   Gloucestershire County Record Office
    Address   Shire Hall, Westgate Street, Gloucester GL1 2TG
    Telephone   0452-21444
    Holdings   3,000 books; 20 periodicals; 3,000,000 manuscripts;
                   maps

Subject Coverage: The record office contains official county
records from 1660 relating to both administrative matters and
crime and punishment, and similar archives of Gloucester City
and other boroughs from the 12th century. Among these are
Quarter Sessions, Petty Sessions, Turnpike and Bridge Trusts,
Highway Boards, School Boards, Poor Law Guardians, County
Councils, and district authorities' records. Ecclesiastical records include Dean and Chapter of Gloucester (from the 16th century), Anglican parish records, and non-conformist records
(Baptists, Congregationalists, and Society of Friends, all from
the 17th century). About 3,100 collections of family, estate,
and business archives from the 12th century; maps from 1600;
and the Hyett Collection of Civil War pamphlets are included
among the resources.

Access: Scholars are welcome to use the material for research
purposes. Inquiries should be directed to the County Archivist.
The Shire Hall Search Room is open Monday to Friday, 9:00
A.M. to 5:00 P.M. The Central Library, Brunswick Road
Search Room (diocesan and Gloucester City archives only) is
open Monday, Tuesday, Thursday, 9:00 A.M. to 8:00 P.M.;
Wednesday, Friday, Saturday, 9:00 A.M. to 5:00 P.M.

Publications: Catalogue of Gloucestershire Books (Hyett Collection) (1946); Guide to Gloucestershire Quarter Sessions Archives,
1660-1889: A Descriptive Catalogue (1958); Guide to the Parish

Records of Bristol and Gloucester (1963); Diocese of Gloucester:
A Catalogue of the Dean and Chapter (1967); Diocese of Gloucester: A Catalogue of the Records of the Bishop and Archdeacon
(1968); A Short Handlist of the Gloucestershire Record Office
(1968), updated by Annual Reports of the Gloucestershire Record Office (from 1969); Gloucester Local History Handbook
(1975).

Duplication: Full-size copying, micro-copying, and photostat
facilities are available. Micro-copying and photostat work take
one to three months to complete. Full-size copying can be accomplished in one week.

Services: Material may only be used at the record office.
Mail and telephone inquiries will be answered. There are
ultraviolet lamps for reading manuscripts.

GREAT YARMOUTH

Institution   Norfolk Eastern Divisional Library
               See: NORWICH, Norfolk County Library (Reference
               No. 187)

GREENWICH

Institution   National Maritime Museum
               See: LONDON, National Maritime Museum (Ref-
               erence No. 143)

GRIMSBY

65 Institution   Grimsby Borough Record Office
    Address   Central Library, Town Hall Square, Grimsby,
                   South Humberside DN31 1HG
    Telephone   0472-59161, ext. 253
                   (Note: it is expected that the office will become
                   a section of the Humberside County Record Office
                   serving all South Humberside.)
    Holdings   records

Subject Coverage: The collection includes principally the official records of the Corporation from the 13th century, but
also fishing industry crew lists and apprenticeship registers;
Quarter Sessions and Coroners' records; Grant Thorold Estate
Papers; Capt. S. M. Burton Papers; Peter Dixon's paper mill
business records and other small deposits.

Access: Researchers may use the collection only on the
premises, and preferably by appointment. Inquiries should be
directed to the Archivist. Search Room facilities are available

in the Local History Collection Room of the Reference Library.
The hours are Monday to Friday, 9:30 A.M. to 8:00 P.M.;
Saturday, 9:00 A.M. to 5:00 P.M.

Publications: None.

Duplication: Full-size copying facilities are available.

Services: None of the material is available on loan, but telephone and postal inquiries are answered.

GUERNSEY

66 Institution   The Greffe
    Address   The Royal Court House, Guernsey, Channel Islands
    Telephone   0481-25277
    Holdings   100, 000 documents

Subject Coverage: The Greffe is a working archive in daily use
by members of the Guernsey bar and other authorized persons.
It contains contemporary copies of charters granted to the baili-
wick from 1394; judicial records of the Royal Court of Guernsey
from 1526; legislative records from 1553; records of land con-
veyances from 1576; records of the states of Guernsey from
1605; registers of births, marriages, and deaths from 1840.
Virtually all records prior to 1948 are in French.

Access: Written application should be addressed to Her Majesty's Greffier. A letter of introduction is recommended. The
Greffe is open Monday to Friday, 9:00 A.M. to 1:00 P.M.,
2:00 P.M. to 4:00 P.M.

Publications: The List and Index Society of London has published List of Records in the Greffe, vol. 2 in the Society's
Special Series (1969). A partial catalogue of single documents
exists in transcript and may be consulted at the Greffe.

Duplication: Full-size copying facilities are available.

Services: Material is not loaned, but telephone or written inquiries are answered, as resources permit.

GUILDFORD

67 Institution   Surrey Record Office, Guildford Muniment Room
    Address   Castle Arch, Guildford GU1 3SX
    Telephone   0483-66551
    Holdings   printed records; manuscripts; maps

Subject Coverage: The collection includes official records of
Guildford Borough; family and estate papers (including manorial

records); business papers (including Wey and Godalming Navigations); Anglican parish registers for the Diocese of Guildford; and some non-conformist church records.

Access: The record office is open to the public. Seating space is limited in the Search Room, and shortage of staff may sometimes make it impossible to produce documents without notice. An appointment in advance is, therefore, desirable for weekday visits and essential for Saturday visits. Documents needed on Saturday must be ordered in advance. Inquiries should be directed to the County Archivist. The hours are Tuesday to Friday, 9:30 A.M. to 12:30 P.M., 1:45 P.M. to 4:45 P.M.; first and third Saturday in the month, 9:30 A.M. to 12:30 P.M. (by appointment only).

Publications: None.

Duplication: Full-size copying is available, but the cost is high.

Services: Telephone and postal inquiries of a specific nature will be answered. Records may be consulted in the Search Room only.

HAVERFORDWEST

68 Institution   Pembrokeshire Record Office
   Address   The Castle, Haverfordwest, Dyfed SA61 1QZ
   Telephone   0437-3707
                   See also: CARMARTHEN, Dyfed Archive Service
                   (Reference No. 32)
   Holdings   books; pamphlets; periodicals; records; newspapers

Subject Coverage: In addition to being the official archive repository of the County Council and Quarter Sessions, the record office contains privately-owned documents relating to Pembrokeshire. It has some parish and non-conformist records. It holds local newspapers among which are Western Telegraph, West Wales Guardian, The County Echo, Tenby and West Wales Weekly Observer, Narberth Whitland Weekly News, Pembroke and Pembroke Dock Weekly News.

Access: Researchers are permitted to use the records for reference purposes only. Inquiries should be addressed to the Archivist. A letter of introduction is recommended. The hours are Monday to Thursday, 9:15 A.M. to 1:00 P.M., 2:00 P.M. to 4:30 P.M.; Friday, 9:15 A.M. to 1:00 P.M., 2:00 P.M. to 4:00 P.M.

Publications: Record guides are issued by the office.

Duplication: Full-size and micro-copying facilities are available. The cost of full-size copying is moderate. Processing takes three days.

Services: The collection does not circulate.

HAWARDEN   See: DEESIDE

HEREFORD

69 Institution   County Council of Hereford and Worcester Record
                   Office
    Address   The Old Barracks, Harold Street, Hereford HR1
                   2QX
    Telephone   0432-65441
    Holdings   manuscripts

Subject Coverage: The collection contains manuscript material
on the diocesan, political, economic, and social history of Herefordshire; resources on the Midlands iron works (16th to 18th
centuries); and high farming in the 19th century.

Access: Visiting scholars are permitted to use the records.
This permission covers practically all documents more than
one hundred years old. Some classes of documents of more
recent date have restricted access. Application should be made
to the Archivist in Charge. A letter of introduction is recommended. The hours are Monday to Friday, 9:15 A.M. to 4:45
P.M.

Publications: The record office issues catalogues which are
available for consultation in the office. These are not at present
published in a form which could be widely available.

Duplication: Full-size copying facilities are available.

Services: The collection does not circulate.

HEREFORD

70 Institution   Hereford Cathedral Library
    Address   The Cathedral, Hereford HR1 2NG
    Telephone   0432-3537
    Holdings   11,000 books; 227 volumes of manuscripts; 30,000
                   archives; 800 negatives

Subject Coverage: The main emphasis of the collection is on
religion and ecclesiastical history. The special collections include manuscripts from the 8th to 15th centuries, early printed
books (many of which are chained), incunabula, 18th and 19th
century manuscript and printed music and archives of the Dean
and Chapter of Hereford Cathedral from Anglo-Saxon times.

Access: Visiting scholars and students must have an appoint-

ment to use the collections. There is no charge. Subscribers
have the use of a key to the modern lending library. During
the summer months, the chained library in the upper transept
room is open as a place of interest Monday to Saturday, 10:30
A.M. to 12:30 P.M., 2:00 P.M. to 4:00 P.M. unless the Cathedral is closed for services. An appointment must be made at
other times. All inquiries should be directed to the Hon. Librarian.

Publications: Hereford Cathedral: A Short Account of the
Chained Library, rev. by F. C. and P. E. Morgan; Hereford
Cathedral Libraries (Including the Chained Library and the
Vicars Choral Library) and Muniments, by F. C. and P. E.
Morgan, 2d ed. Both are illustrated pamphlets.

Duplication: No duplication facilities exist on the premises, but
arrangements can be made elsewhere in Hereford for copying
suitable items. Positive microfilm copies of manuscript volumes
can be supplied on request. Photographic prints can be made
from negatives.

Services: Only modern books circulate.

HERTFORD

71	Institution	Hertfordshire Record Office
	Address	County Hall, Hertford, Hertfordshire SG13 8DE
	Telephone	32-54242
	Holdings	books; pamphlets; periodicals; printed records; manuscripts; prints; photographs; drawings

Subject Coverage: The collection includes official and semi-
official records, including records of the County Council, from
1888; Quarter Sessions, 1588-1971; Sheriffs, 1742-1932; Turnpike Trusts, 1725-1877; Highway Boards, 1868-1899; School
Boards, 1876-1903; individual and grouped schools, 19th and
20th centuries; Boards of Guardians, 1834-1929; Local Boards
of Health, 1849-1898; records of water, gas, and electricity
undertakings; non-medical and administrative records of hos-
pitals and Joint Hospital Boards, 1826-1948; records of the
Borough of Hertford, from 1226.

The collection contains ecclesiastical records, including records
of the Diocese of St. Albans, 19th and 20th centuries; Archdeaconry of St. Albans, including probate records, 15th to 19th
centuries; Archdeaconry of Hunts, Hitchin division, including
probate records, 16th to 19th centuries; rural deaneries, 19th
to 20th centuries; parish records, including registers of baptisms, marriages, and burials from 1538, vestry minutes,
churchwardens', overseers', constables', and surveyors' records; some non-conformist records, including Quaker records,
1658-1879.

The record office holds deposited non-official records, including
manorial records, title deeds, estate papers, personal correspondence and diaries, farm and business records. It also contains printed and manuscript maps, including estate, tithe and
enclosure maps, and Ordnance Survey maps; books, pamphlets,
and periodicals relating to local people and the history of the
county and individual parishes; County Directories, 1826-1937;
and appropriate works of reference.

Access: The record office is open to the public. Inquiries
should be addressed to the County Archivist. The hours are
Monday to Thursday, 9:15 A.M. to 5:15 P.M.; Friday, 9:15
A.M. to 4:30 P.M.

Publications: Guide to the Hertfordshire Record Office, pt. I,
ed. by William Le Hardy; Hertfordshire County Records--
Calendars to Sessions Rolls, Books, Etc., ed. by William Le
Hardy; Catalogue of Manuscript Maps, ed. by Peter Walne
(1969); Industrial Monuments in Hertfordshire, by W. Branch
Johnson (1967); Genealogical Sources, by R. A. Bowden.

Duplication: Full-size and micro-copying facilities are available.

Services: Inquiries which do not require prolonged research are
answered by mail or telephone.

HIGH WYCOMBE

72 Institution   The Disraeli Museum
    Address   Hughenden Manor, High Wycombe, Buckinghamshire
                   HP14 4LA
    Telephone   0494-28051
    Holdings   manuscripts

Subject Coverage: The collection consists of a part of the
papers of Benjamin Disraeli.

Access: The resources are available to bona fide researchers,
but permission must be acquired and an appointment is necessary. Inquiries should be directed, by letter, to the Area
Agent. A letter of introduction is recommended.

Publications: The museum issues a handlist of papers.

Duplication: Micro-copying facilities are available and require
about three weeks for completion.

Services: The material may only be used on the premises.

HOVE

73 Institution   East Sussex County Library, Hove Area Library
   Address   Church Road, Hove, Sussex BN3 2EG
   Telephone   0273-70472
   Holdings   95,000 books; 150 periodicals; microforms; news-
                  papers; 3,000 photographs; 4,000 transparencies;
                  1,400 film strips

Subject Coverage: The library holds a collection of over 5,000
books on local history of Hove, Brighton, and the surrounding
area within East Sussex. This collection includes some original
records, photographs, and newspapers dating from 1749. Papers of the family of Lord Wolseley (1833-1913), Commander-
in-Chief of the British Army, include his autograph collection
(with letters from many politicians and dignitaries of the time),
scrapbooks and personal family letters. His daughter, Lady
Frances Garnet Wolseley, has contributed a collection of manuscript notes on Sussex villages and histories of local manor
houses as well as notes on agricultural and horticultural activities in the first quarter of the 20th century.

Access: The library is open to the public. Inquiries should be
addressed to the Librarian. The hours are Monday to Friday,
10:00 A.M. to 6:30 P.M.; Saturday, 9:30 A.M. to 4:00 P.M.

Publications: The library issues catalogues of its special collections on rare books.

Duplication: Full-size copying facilities are available at high
cost. Processing is generally available on demand.

Services: Books may be borrowed by ticket holders, and books
are easily available to visitors.

HULL   See: KINGSTON UPON HULL

HUNTINGDON

74 Institution   County Record Office, Huntingdon
   Address   Grammar School Walk, Huntingdon, Cambridgeshire
                  PE18 6LF
   Telephone   0480-52181, ext. 42
   Holdings   books; records

Subject Coverage: The collection contains the following records:
local government, Clerk of the Peace, probate, ecclesiastical,
statutory authorities, estate, and family.

Access: The office is open to the public. A letter of introduction is recommended. Inquiries should be directed to the Senior

Archivist. The Search Room is open Monday to Friday, 9:00
A.M. to 5:00 P.M.; Saturday morning (by appointment).

Publications: None.

Duplication: Full-size copying facilities are available. Processing may be completed immediately, and the cost is moderate. Photostats are made by order, and the cost varies according to size.

Services: Records may be used on the premises only. Group
talks and demonstrations of records will be given at the office
if arrangements have been made in advance.

ISLE OF MAN   See: DOUGLAS (Reference No. 41)

KENDAL

    Institution   The Record Office
                   See: CARLISLE, Cumbria County Council Archives
                   Department (Reference No. 31)

KING'S LYNN

    Institution   Norfolk Western Divisional Library
                   See: NORWICH, Norfolk County Library (Reference
                   No. 187)

KINGSTON UPON HULL

75 Institution   Hull Division Libraries
    Address   Central Library, Albion Street, Hull, North Hum-
                   berside HU1 3TF
    Telephone   0482-223344
    Holdings   144,000 books and pamphlets; 450 periodicals;
                   2,183 microforms; 487 manuscripts; 9,997 maps
                   and plans

Subject Coverage: The library includes a separate Local History
Library which contains important special collections. Among
these are Civil War tracts; resources on William Wilberforce,
whaling, Winifred Holtby, Andrew Marvell, Napoleon; books published between 1740 and 1759.

Access: The library is open to the public. Inquiries should be
directed to the Divisional Librarian. The hours are Monday to
Friday, 9:00 A.M. to 10:00 P.M.; Saturday, 9:00 A.M. to 5:30
P.M.

Publications: Parliamentary Index; Monitor; Medical Library
Contents List; Humberside Diary of Local Events; Civic Index;
Books in the Lending Library; Commercial and Technical Bulletin; Reference Library Review; Local History (quarterly); In-
terlock.

Duplication: Limited photocopying facilities are available.

Services: An information service is conducted which draws upon
the resources of the library and maintains several indexes.
Books circulate to those who hold library tickets. Tickets of
other library authorities are accepted.

KINGSTON UPON HULL

76 Institution   Kingston upon Hull Record Office
    Address   Guildhall, Kingston upon Hull HU1 2AA
    Telephone   0482-223111, ext. 407
    Holdings   books; pamphlets; periodicals; records

Subject Coverage: The collection contains records of the City
Council and all previous local authorities within the city from
1299; Quarter Session records from c.1620; deposited records
of local businesses, churches, organizations, and individuals
from c.1920; all aspects of local government, the administration of justice, manufacturing, commerce, transport, religion,
genealogy and biography, topography, agriculture, architecture,
and warfare. The collection also includes a small library
dealing with archival matters, local history, and a general
background to the holdings.

Access: The Search Room is open to the public. First-time
visitors are asked to make an appointment. Inquiries should
be directed to the Town Clerk. The hours are Monday to Friday, 8:30 A.M. to 12:45 P.M., 2:15 P.M. to 5:15 P.M.

Publications: Charters and Letters Patent Granted in Kingston
upon Hull (the texts of the charters in English), by J. R.
Boyle; Calendar of the Ancient Records, Letters, Miscellaneous
Old Documents, etc. in the Archives of the Corporation of
Kingston upon Hull ... 1300-1800, by L. M. Stanewell; Exhibi-
tion Catalogue: Hull at War.

Duplication: Full-size copying facilities are available.

Services: The collection may only be used on the premises.

KINGSTON UPON THAMES

    Institution   Surrey Record Office and Kingston Borough Muni-
                     ment Room

See: LONDON, Surrey Record Office and Kingston
Borough Muniment Room (Reference No. 156)

LAMPETER

77 Institution   St. David's University College Library
    Address   Lampeter, Dyfed SA48 7ED
    Telephone   0570-422351
    Holdings   92,000 books and pamphlets; 500 periodicals;
                   microforms; manuscripts

Subject Coverage: The Main Library has holdings in the
classics, geography, history, philosophy, theology, Welsh,
English, French, and German.

The Old Library holds pre-1850 material (some 20,000 vols.,
general in scope), including the Library of Bishop Burgess.
Among the special collections are the Tract Collection (chiefly
17th to 18th centuries); early Welsh periodicals; Welsh Bibles,
prayer-books, hymnals, catechisms, and ballads; manuscripts
(including 15th century Books of Hours and service books); incunabula. Much of the pamphlet collection was built up over
the years by the Bowdler family and presented to the college
by Thomas Bowdler. It is of major importance.

Access: Reference facilities are granted to the public during
normal library hours. Inquiries should be directed to the Li-
brarian. Visiting scholars are recommended to make prior
written application in order that their individual requirements
may more readily be met. During the academic year, the
Main Library hours are Monday to Friday, 9:00 A.M. to 10:00
P.M.; Saturday, 9:00 A.M. to 1:00 P.M., 2:00 P.M. to 5:00
P.M. During vacation, the hours are Monday to Friday, 9:00
A.M. to 5:00 P.M.; Saturday, 9:00 A.M. to 12 noon (closed
Saturday in the summer vacation). The Old Library is open
Monday to Friday, 2:00 P.M. to 5:00 P.M. during the aca-
demic year only.

Publications: The library issues fortnightly accessions lists
and a type-script Notes for Readers. A Catalogue of the Tract
Collection is scheduled for publication.

Duplication: Full-size copying facilities are available at low
cost. Whenever possible, requests from visiting scholars,
whether made by post or in person, are processed immediately.

Services: Information requests by telephone or mail will be
answered. The library is a member of the regional library
bureau.

LEEDS

78 Institution   Leeds City Libraries
    Address   Central Library, Municipal Buildings, Leeds
                    LS1 3AB
    Telephone   0532-31301
                    (Note: some material of interest to social sci-
                    entists is in the stock of other departments, such
                    as the Library of Commerce, Science and Tech-
                    nology, and the Art Library. These have the same
                    opening hours.)
    Holdings   273,000 books and pamphlets; 600 periodicals;
    (Reference   3,500 microforms
    Library)

Subject Coverage: The Reference Library contains a strong
local history collection; the Gascoigne Collection (military and
naval history); Porton Collection (Judaica); all HMSO publications; UN official records. It is a depository for UNESCO publications. The Archives Department (Sheepscar Library, Chapel-
town Road, Leeds LS7 3AP; telephone: 0532-628339) contains
older official records of the city of Leeds; diocesan, probate,
estate, and business archives.

Access: The library is open to the public. Inquiries should
be directed to the Librarian (for Archives Department to the
Archivist). The hours are Monday to Friday, 9:00 A.M. to
9:00 P.M.; Saturday, 9:00 A.M. to 4:00 P.M.

Publications: None.

Duplication: Facilities for full-size copying, microprints, and
microfilm are available. Time necessary for processing is one
day for full-size copies and microprint and several weeks for
microfilm.

Services: Books are not normally borrowed from the Reference
Library, but are freely available for use there. Proof of identity will be needed before certain books are issued.

LEEDS

79 Institution   University of Leeds, The Brotherton Library
    Address   University of Leeds, Leeds LS2 9JT
    Telephone   0532-31751, ext. 6556
    Holdings   643,177 books; 199,731 pamphlets; 6,500 periodicals;
                    108,765 microforms; 2,882 manuscripts; 37,241 let-
                    ters; 4,116 deeds

Subject Coverage: The library resources, supporting the faculties of the university, include bibliography, modern Chinese
studies, Slavonic and Russian studies, history, economics, ge-

ography, politics, sociology, and linguistics. There are several
departmental and sectional libraries within the university containing separate collections. Those with important social science holdings are the Law Library (ext. 6398) and the Institute
of Education Library (ext. 6102). The resources of the Law
Library (27,794 books; 1,515 pamphlets; 217 periodicals) cover
English, American, Commonwealth, European and international
law and jurisprudence. Law reports of England, Scotland, Ireland, the Commonwealth, and the United States are collected.
The Law Library is a Documentation Centre for publications of
the European Communities. The Institute of Education Library
(49,215 books and pamphlets; 320 periodicals) covers education,
sociology, psychology, and linguistics. The Alf Mattison Collection, which is part of the Brotherton Collection, comprises
books, periodicals, and manuscripts relating to the early history of socialism in Britain. Business records from approximately fifty Yorkshire textile companies are also held. Other
special collections are the Romany Collection and the Ripon
Cathedral Archives.

Access: Visiting scholars must make application to use the
collection. Inquiries should be directed to the Librarian. A
letter of introduction is recommended. During the academic
year, the library is open Monday to Friday, 9:00 A.M. to
10:00 P.M.; Saturday, 9:00 A.M. to 1:00 P.M.; Sunday, 2:00
P.M. to 7:00 P.M. During summer vacation, the hours are
Monday to Friday, 9:00 A.M. to 5:00 P.M.; Saturday, 9:00
A.M. to 12:30 P.M. During other vacations, the hours are
Monday to Friday, 9:00 A.M. to 9:00 P.M.; Saturday, 9:00
A.M. to 1:00 P.M. The hours for the Parkinson Building Li-
brary during the academic year are Monday to Friday, 9:00
A.M. to 9:00 P.M.

Publications: The library issues catalogues of special collections.

Duplication: Full-size copying facilities are available (self-
service) at moderate cost. Microfilming is also provided at
moderate cost, but processing takes three weeks.

Services: A full interlibrary loan system is available. The
collection circulates to members of the university only.

LEICESTER

80 Institution   Leicestershire Record Office
    Address   57 New Walk, Leicester LE1 7JB
    Telephone   0533-539111
    Holdings   several thousand books; several hundred pamphlets;
                   periodicals; microforms; records; tapes

Subject Coverage: The record office holds works on the history of Leicestershire and Rutland. It contains official records of the two counties and the city of Leicester; parish records; records of the Leicester Archdeaconry; family and estate papers; maps.

Access: The record office is open to the public. Inquiries should be directed to the Archivist. The hours are Monday to Thursday, 9:15 A.M. to 5:00 P.M.; Friday, 9:15 A.M. to 4:45 P.M.; Saturday, 10:00 A.M. to 12 noon.

Publications: Triennial reports (old County Record Office); annual reports (old Museum Archives Department); various sectional lists.

Duplication: Full-size and micro-copying facilities are available. Photographic service is also provided. Photography and microfilm must be ordered, but full-size copying can be done immediately.

Services: Postal and telephone inquiries are answered. An information service is provided.

LEICESTER

81 Institution   Leicester University Library
    Address   University Road, Leicester LE1 7RH
    Telephone   0553-50000
    Holdings   430,000 books and pamphlets; 6,000 periodicals;
                   microforms

Subject Coverage: The library contains general social science material and several special collections, including the Hatton Collection of English and Welsh topography, and the Fairclough Collection on 17th century studies. The library also has holdings in transport history, English local history, and Victoriana.

Access: Visiting American scholars may apply to the Librarian to use the collection. The library is open Monday to Friday, 9:00 A.M. to 10:00 P.M.; Saturday, 9:00 A.M. to 12:30 P.M. during the academic year. At other times, the library is open Monday to Friday, 9:00 A.M. to 5:30 P.M.; Saturday, 9:00 A.M. to 12:30 P.M.

Publications: The library publishes an Annual Report. Library guides and other bibliographical aids are issued from time to time.

Duplication: Two self-service coin-operated photocopying machines are available at low cost. Some micro-copying facilities are also provided.

Services: Books circulate to all individuals who use the library.

The library is a member of the British Library Lending Division and the East Midlands Regional Library Bureau.

LEWES

82 Institution   East Sussex Record Office
    Address   Pelham House, St. Andrews Lane, Lewes, Sussex
                   BN7 1UN
    Telephone   07916-5400, ext. 580
    Holdings   books; records

Subject Coverage: The records include Quarter Sessions, County Council and other official records, family and estate papers, parish registers, and the maps and wills of the Archdeaconry of Lewes. There is also a small reference library for use of staff and researchers.

Access: The record office is open to the public. Inquiries should be made to the County Record Officer. The office is open Monday to Thursday, 8:45 A.M. to 4:45 P.M.; Friday, 8:45 A.M. to 4:15 P.M.

Publications: A Descriptive Report on the Quarter Sessions. Other Official and Ecclesiastical Records in the Custody of the County Councils of East and West Sussex (1954); A Catalogue of the Shiffner Archives, ed. by Francis W. Steer (1959); Records of the Corporation of Seaford, ed. by Francis W. Steer (1959); The Records of Rye Corporation, ed. by Richard F. Dell (1962); A Catalogue of Sussex Estate and Tithe Award Maps, ed. by Francis W. Steer (1962); Winchelsea Corporation Records, ed. by Richard F. Dell (1963); The Glynde Place Archives, ed. by Richard F. Dell (1964); The Danny Archives, ed. by Judith A. Wooldridge (1966); The History of a Parish or Locality, by Judith A. Brent (1970); Catalogue of the Frewen Archives, by Heather M. Warne (1972).

Duplication: Full-size copying facilities are available. The cost is moderate.

Services: Limited telephone and mail inquiries are answered.

LICHFIELD

83 Institution   Lichfield Joint Record Office
    Address   Bird Street, Lichfield, Staffordshire WS13 6PN
    Telephone   05432-22177
    Holdings   microforms; records

Subject Coverage: The record office contains Probate Records of the Diocese of Lichfield (250,000 documents from 1472-1858) and historical records of the Diocese (from 1298). Among these

are found records of the Dean and Chapter of Lichfield from
the 13th to the 19th centuries; administrative records (presentation deeds, papers relating to convocation, financial records of
the registrars and the courts); Ecclesiastical Court records
(court books, marriage allegations and bonds, cause papers);
visitation records (visitation books, excommunication books,
penances and absolutions); wills (250,000); diocesan boundaries;
peculiar jurisdictions.

Access: Visiting academics are welcome to use the records.
Inquiries should be directed to the Archivist. The record office is open Monday, Tuesday, Thursday, Friday, 10:00 A.M.
to 5:15 P.M.; Wednesday, 10:00 A.M. to 4:45 P.M.; Saturday,
9:30 A.M. to 12:30 P.M. Documents to be used on Saturday
must be requested in advance.

Publications: Guide to Diocesan Records; Cumulative Handlist,
pt. I: Lichfield Joint Record Office (Diocesan, Probate and
Church Commissioner's Records) (1970).

Duplication: Full-size copying facilities are available at moderate cost. Arrangements can be made for micro-copies.

Services: Information concerning the scope of the records in
the record office is provided, but in-depth searches must be
undertaken by the inquirer.

LICHFIELD

84 Institution   Lichfield Library
                    (Area Library of Staffordshire County Library
                    Service)
    Address   Bird Street, Lichfield, Staffordshire WS13 6PN
    Telephone   05432-22177
    Holdings   2,000,000 books (in the county system); 50 peri-
                    odicals; 18 microforms; newspapers; 430 maps

Subject Coverage: The library houses the Lichfield Joint Record
Office. There are resources relating to local history, material
to aid searches in the county records, and a collection of books
on Samuel Johnson.

Access: The library is open to the public. Inquiries should be
directed to the Librarian. The hours are Monday, Tuesday,
Thursday, Friday, 10:00 A.M. to 6:30 P.M.; Wednesday, Saturday, 10:00 A.M. to 5:00 P.M.

Publications: None.

Duplication: Full-size copying facilities are available at moderate cost, and arrangements can be made for micro-copies.

Services: Most of the collection circulates and ticket holders
are allowed to borrow books. Tickets from other libraries are
accepted. The library cooperates with the British Library
Lending Division.

LINCOLN

85 Institution   Lincolnshire Archives Office
   Address   The Castle, Lincoln LN1 3HT
   Telephone   Lincoln 25158
   Holdings   20, 000 books; 3, 000 pamphlets; 18 periodicals;
                  microforms; 14, 000 linear feet of records

Subject Coverage: The collection includes County Council and
Quarter Session records (Lindsey, Resteven, and Holland from
1625); diocesan and Dean and Chapter records of Lincoln (from
the 12th century); wills (from 1320); numerous family estate and
business collections. A reference library and several special
collections of printed books are also included.

Access: The office is open to the public. An advance appointment is advisable. Inquiries should be directed to the Archivist. The hours are Monday to Friday, 9:30 A.M. to 5:00
P.M.; most Saturdays, 10:00 A.M. to 12:45 P.M.

Publications: Handlist of the Records of the Bishop of Lincoln
and Archdeacons of Lincoln and Stow (1953); Annual Reports.

Duplication: Full-size and micro-copying facilities are available.

Services: Telephone and mail inquiries are answered, but the
staff is not able to undertake detailed searches. Records and
books can be used only under supervision in the record office.

LIVERPOOL

86 Institution   Liverpool Central Libraries
   Address   William Brown Street, Liverpool L3 8EW
   Telephone   051-207 2147
   Holdings   1, 200, 000 books; pamphlets; 2, 765 periodicals;
                  113, 523 microforms; manuscripts

Subject Coverage: The library is divided into several departments, by subject. Those of most interest to the social scientist are:

          Picton Reference Library: Bibliographical Unit,
          philosophy and religion library.

          Hornby Library: rare books, incunabula, first

editions, fine bindings, prints, and autographs.

Commercial and Social Sciences Library: business
training, law, government, commerce, government
publications, statistics, trade catalogues, commercial newspapers, tariffs, directories.

Commonwealth Library: history and topography of
the British Commonwealth and the United Kingdom,
arranged by country.

International Library: literature, history, and
topography of countries outside the British Commonwealth and the United States.

American Library: literature, history, and topography of the United States.

Record Office: Liverpool Corporation Archives,
records of firms, societies, individuals, and corporate bodies including manuscripts and documents
of national importance.

Local History Library: printed material on the
history of Liverpool, Lancashire, and Cheshire.

Access: The library is open to the public. Inquiries should
be directed to the City Librarian. Most of the library departments are open Monday to Friday, 9:00 A.M. to 9:00 P.M.;
Saturday, 9:00 A.M. to 5:00 P.M.

Publications: New Books and Announcements (monthly);
LADSIRLAC Technical Bulletin (monthly); LADSIRLAC Commercial Bulletin (monthly); Liverpool, 1207-1957; Liverpool Under
James I; Liverpool Under Charles I; Liverpool Bulletin; Catalogue of Non-fiction (1952-55, 1956-59, 1960-63, 1964-66).

Duplication: Full-size and micro-copying facilities are available at moderate cost. Xerox copies can be obtained immediately, photostats require about two days, and microfilm takes
several weeks.

Services: A subject specialist is provided in each of the library's departments. A translation advisory service is maintained in the International Library. Ticket holders and individuals who can produce identification are permitted to borrow books. The library cooperates with the British Library
Lending Division.

LIVERPOOL

87 Institution   University of Liverpool, Harold Cohen Library;

Sidney Jones Library
Address   The University, Liverpool
Telephone   051-709 6022
                 (Note: a new library is under construction which
                 is expected to open in 1976. It will be known as
                 the Sidney Jones Library. The Harold Cohen Li-
                 brary, which holds social science collections, will
                 then contain resources in the pure and applied sci-
                 ences. The information below refers to the new
                 Sidney Jones Library.)
Holdings   500,000 books; 75,000 pamphlets; 6,000 periodicals;
                 microforms

Subject Coverage: The library contains resources in business
management, commerce, economics, and history of science.
The special collections include early printed books; manuscripts; fine press books; English pamphlets (1685-1727); gypsy
folklore and the Rathbone Papers. The Campbell Brown Collection (books on chemistry and alchemy from the 16th to 19th centuries) will remain in the Harold Cohen Library. There are
separate departmental libraries for law and education.

Access: Visiting scholars are permitted to use the resources.
Inquiries should be directed to the University Librarian. To
use the special collections, a letter of introduction is required,
and the Curator of Special Collections determines what material can be made available. The hours are Monday to Friday,
9:00 A.M. to 9:30 P.M.; Saturday, 9:00 A.M. to 1:00 P.M.
during the academic year. During Easter vacation, the hours
are Monday to Friday, 9:00 A.M. to 6:00 P.M.; Saturday,
9:00 A.M. to 1:00 P.M. During other vacations, the library
is open, Monday to Friday, 9:00 A.M. to 5:00 P.M.

Publications: British Government Publications Concerning Education, by J. E. Vaughan and M. Argles, 3d ed. (1969); A
Guide to the Literature of Special Education, by D. J. Thomas
(1968); Guide to the Manuscript Collection in the Liverpool University Library (1962); Guide to Special Collections in the Harold Cohen Library (1971).

Duplication: Facilities for full-size copying are available at low
cost. There are no micro-copying facilities at the library, but
arrangements can usually be made through the university.

Services: The collection circulates only to members of the university. The library cooperates with the British Library Lending Division.

LLANGEFNI

88 Institution   Llangefni Area Record Office
    Address   Shire Hall, Llangefni, Gwynedd

Telephone   0248-723262
Holdings   books; records

Subject Coverage: The collection includes the official records
of the county; shipping records; private papers; tithe maps;
Anglesey Calvinistic Methodists Chapel records; Eisteddfodau
Papers.

Access: The collection is open to the public. The hours are
Monday to Friday, 9:00 A.M. to 5:00 P.M.

Publications: Gwynedd Archives Service Bulletin (annual).

Duplication: Full-size copies are available at moderate cost.
Photographic prints are provided. Transparencies can be made
by arrangement.

Services: None of the material is available on loan. Telephone
and mail inquiries are answered.

LONDON

89 Institution   Aslib (Association of Special Libraries and In-
                   formation Bureaux)
    Address   3 Belgrave Square, London SW1X 8PL
    Telephone   01-235 5050
    Underground   Hyde Park Corner
    Holdings   25,000 books, pamphlets, and reports; 370 peri-
                   odicals

Subject Coverage: Aslib Library contains material on all aspects of library and information science and documentation.
The collection includes material on information storage and re-
trieval, indexing classification, mechanization in the context of
documentation sciences, and abstracting techniques.

Access: The library may be used by individuals whose organizations are members. Membership is available to libraries,
documentation centers, and industrial and commercial organizations. The library is open Monday to Friday, 9:00 A.M. to
5:15 P.M. Inquiries should be directed to the Librarian for information science and documentation and to the Information Officer for all other subjects. Inquiries can be made by telephone,
letter, or telex.

Publications: Aslib publications include Aslib Proceedings
(monthly); Aslib Booklist (monthly); Aslib Information (monthly);
Forthcoming International Scientific and Technical Conferences
(quarterly); Technical Translation Bulletin (three times a year);
Journal of Documentation (quarterly); Program: News of Computers in Libraries (quarterly); Index to Theses Accepted for
Higher Degrees in the Universities of Great Britain and Ireland

(annual); Aslib Directory, 2 vols., 3d ed. (1968-1970); Aslib Handbook of Special Librarianship and Information Work, ed. by W. Ashworth, 3d ed. (1967); Faceted Classification, by B. C. Vickery (1968); Periodicals and Serials, Their Treatment in Special Libraries, by D. Grenfell, 2d ed. (1965); Use of Mechanized Methods in Documentation Work, by H. Coblans (1966); Guide to Foreign-language Printed Patents and Applications, by I. F. Finlay (1969); An Evaluation of British Scientific Journals, by J. Martyn and A. Gilchrist (1968); Use Made of Technical Libraries, by M. Slater and P. Fisher (1969); The Use of Bibliographic Records in Libraries, by P. A. Thomas and H. East (1969).

Duplication: Full-size copying facilities are available at moderate cost.

Services: Aslib is important not so much because of its library, but rather because of the services it provides. Aslib furnishes the following aids which may be of interest to social scientists: referral and inquiry, bibliographical checking and locating resources, document reproduction, and translation service.

The referral and inquiry service will accept inquiries on any subject and in any depth, the only limitation being that the question is not one which the researcher can be expected to answer from his own resources. It is essential that the researcher be as specific as possible in his inquiry, and it is helpful if he states the sources he has unsuccessfully tried. Printed inquiry forms are available, but requests will be accepted by letter, telephone, or telex and should be addressed to the Information Officer. This service is free to members unless the inquiry is complicated and likely to take several weeks.

The bibliographical checking and locating services provide for tracing details of publications and identifying references. Researchers should give as much detail as possible. Inquiry forms and procedures are similar to those specified in the referral and inquiry service.

A document reproduction service is available to identify, locate, and obtain microfilm or paper copies of articles. This is primarily a locating service intended to handle difficult references not easily supplied from normal sources. The service, consequently, is slow and costly. Requests for this service must be made on special requisition forms. These may be obtained in advance, and incorporate the usual copyright declaration which must be signed. These forms must be purchased either singly or in books of ten. Forms can be obtained from the Information Office.

The translation service provides a central index to translations which have already been made. The researcher may consult

this index before engaging in the expensive and time-consuming
process of having a document translated. If, however, no
translation exists, this service provides a register of specialist
translators available to Aslib members only. This list contains
the names of over 250 translators with both subject and linguis-
tic qualifications. Fees for translations are a matter for negotiation between employer and translator.

LONDON

90 Institution   Bank of England Library
    Address   Threadneedle Street, London EC2R 8AH
    Telephone   01-601 4846
    Underground   Bank
    Holdings   50,000 books; 4,000 periodicals

Subject Coverage: The library contains works dealing primarily
with banking and finance. Among its holdings are central bank
reports; trade statistics; economic tracts (17th to 19th centuries); Acts of Parliament (both public and private from 1693);
London Gazette (from 1665); Finance Accounts of the United
Kingdom (from 1702); Course of the Exchange (Castaing Sher-
gold, Lutyens and Wetenhall, 1698-1898).

Access: The library is open to visiting scholars by prior appointment with the Librarian. The hours are Monday to Friday,
9:30 A.M. to 5:00 P.M.

Publications: Bank of England Quarterly Bulletin and Bank of
England Annual Report.

Duplication: Facilities for full-size copying are available at
moderate cost. Duplication can usually be accomplished at
once.

Services: Library material is available for consultation only
on the premises.

LONDON

    Institution   Bedford College Library
                   See: LONDON, University of London, Bedford Col-
                   lege Library (Reference No. 161)

LONDON

    Institution   Bexley Library Service
                   See: LONDON, London Borough of Bexley, Bexley
                   Library Service (Reference No. 133)

LONDON

    Institution   Birkbeck College Library
                     See: LONDON, University of London, Birkbeck
                     College Library (Reference No. 162)

LONDON

91 Institution   Bishopsgate Institute Library
    Address   230 Bishopsgate, London EC2M 4QH
    Telephone   01-247 6844
    Underground   Liverpool Street
                 See also: MANCHESTER, Co-operative Union
                 Library (Reference No. 176)
    Holdings   70, 500 books and pamphlets; 400 periodicals;
                 microforms; 150 manuscripts; 2, 000 maps;
                 15, 000 pictures, prints, and drawings

Subject Coverage: The library has good general resources and
many fine collections. Notable among these are the London
Collection (history and topography of the inner London area
with emphasis on the City); George Howell Library (economics,
early labor movement and history of trade unionism, Howell's
diaries and correspondence, International Working Men's Association Minutes, 1850-1900, Ernest Jones' Diaries); George
Jacob Holyoake Collection (early co-operative movement, including muster roll of Garibaldi's British Legion, diaries, log-
books, and correspondence, 1840-1890; but most of the correspondence is at the Co-operative Union Library, Manchester).
The Archaeological Society Library is presently housed at the
institute. A move to the Museum of London in Barbican is
anticipated about 1977.

Access: The Reference Library is open to the public. Re-
searchers would be allowed to use the London and Middlesex
Archaeological Society collection on request. The Lending
Division forms a part of the City of London Lending Library
Service. The library is open Monday to Friday, 9:30 A.M. to
5:30 P.M.

Publications: The library has published a Catalog of the London
Collection (1974); Catalog of the Lending Library (1901); First
Supplement (1911); Index to the Correspondence in the Howell
Collection, 1844-1910, 2d ed. (1975); various exhibition cata-
logs, pamphlets, and monographs.

Duplication: Full-size copying facilities are available at moderately high cost. Small orders are completed at once; large
orders take four to five days.

Services: The reference works must be used at the library,
but the Lending Division maintains a small collection of recent

books for circulation. The London and Middlesex Archaeological Society collection is available for loan to accredited researchers and libraries.

LONDON

92 Institution   Board of Inland Revenue Library
    Address   New Wing, Somerset House, Strand, London
                     WC2R 1LB
    Telephone   01-438 6325
    Underground   Temple
    Holdings   45,000 books; 5,000 pamphlets; 350 periodicals

Subject Coverage: The library collection includes publications on economics, financial statistics, direct taxation, and law. There is a special collection of translations of foreign direct tax legislation. A collection of cuttings on fiscal subjects is maintained.

Access: Visiting scholars are welcome to use the library, but only with written permission of the Librarian. Inquiries should be directed, by letter, to the Librarian. The library is open Monday to Friday, 9:00 A.M. to 5:30 P.M.

Publications: Monthly Accessions Lists; Income Taxes Outside the United Kingdom (annual, HMSO); Double Taxation Agreements of the United Kingdom, 2 vols. (HMSO); Overseas Tax Development Circulars.

Duplication: Full-size and micro-copying facilities at moderately high cost are available.

Services: The collection does not circulate.

LONDON

    Institution   Board of Trade, Civil Aviation Department,
                     Aeronautical Information Service
                     See: LONDON, Civil Aviation Authority, Aero-
                     nautical Information Service (Reference No. 99)

LONDON

93 Institution   British Broadcasting Corporation Reference Li-
                     brary
    Address   The Langham, Portland Place, London W1A 1AA
    Telephone   01-580 4468
    Underground   Oxford Circus
    Holdings   140,000 books; 1,500 periodicals; 3,100 micro-
                     forms; 500 newspapers; 4,200 maps and town

plans; 400, 000 illustrations

Subject Coverage: The British Broadcasting Corporation has
several library systems, including Reference Library, Film
Library, Music Library, and Gramophone Library. The Reference Library contains resources on all subjects, with special
collections on broadcasting, music, and drama. The branch in
the Television Centre at Shepherd's Bush (Wood Lane, London
W12 7RJ; telephone: 01-743 8000) holds an extensive collection of illustrations on all subjects. The BBC Film Library
(Windmill Road, Brentford, Middlesex TW8 9NF; telephone:
01-567 6655) contains film recordings, news films, and material shot by the BBC for use in television programs. There
are 250, 000 film cans with all types of film material located
here.

Access: Visiting researchers are permitted to use the resources in the Reference Library. The scale of charges can
be obtained from the Librarian. A letter of introduction is required. All of the Reference Libraries are intended principally
for internal use; an appointment is, therefore, necessary. The
hours are Monday to Friday, 9:30 A.M. to 8:00 P.M.; Saturday, 9:30 A.M. to 5:30 P.M.

Publications: British Broadcasting: A Select Bibliography,
1922-1972 (1972).

Duplication: Full-size and micro-copying facilities are available. Cost and information about the time necessary for processing are available on request.

Services: The staff of the Reference Library maintains specialist indexes to short stories, poetry, music and dance, and
drama film. The Reference Library cooperates with the British
Library Lending Division and various other interlibrary loan
schemes. News films and stock shots are available for sale
through Film Library Sales (a division of BBC-TV Enterprises,
Windmill Road, Brentford, Middlesex TW8 9NF).

LONDON

94 Institution   The British Library (Library Association Library)
    Address   7 Ridgmount Street, London WC1E 7AE
    Telephone   01-636 7543
    Underground   Goodge Street
                   See also: The Library Association, p. 236
    Holdings   40, 000 books; 850 periodicals; 5, 000 microforms;
                   30 films

Subject Coverage: The collection includes works on library
methods, documentation, bibliographical methods, information
services, library equipment, and library education. There is

also current and historical information on particular libraries
in Britain and overseas.

Access: The Library Association Library is now administered
as part of the British Library. Visiting scholars should have
an appointment to use the collection, as advance notice of arrival is appreciated. Inquiries should be addressed to the Librarian and Information Officer. A letter of introduction is
recommended. The hours are Monday, Wednesday, Friday,
9:00 A.M. to 6:00 P.M.; Tuesday, Thursday, 9:00 A.M. to
8:00 P.M. except during the summer months. From mid-July
to mid-September, the hours are Monday to Friday, 9:00 A.M.
to 6:00 P.M.

Publications: British Technology Index (monthly); British Humanities Index (quarterly); Library and Information Science Abstracts (six times a year); Library Association Record (monthly); RADIALS Bulletin (three times a year); Catalogue of the Library (1958); Public Library Conference Proceedings; monographs (on library subjects) and subject bibliographies.

Duplication: Full-size copying facilities are available at moderate cost. Duplication is completed on demand as far as possible.

Services: The collection is available on loan to members of
the association and through the British Library Lending Division.

LONDON

Institution   British Library of Political and Economic Science
                   See: LONDON, London School of Economics and
                   Political Science, British Library of Political and
                   Economic Science (Reference No. 138)

LONDON

95 Institution   The British Library (Reference Division) (formerly
                   the British Museum Library)
   Address   Great Russell Street, London WC1B 3DG
   Telephone   01-636 1555
   Underground   Russell Square, Tottenham Court Road, Goodge
                   Street, Holborn
   Holdings   8,500,000 books; 80,000 periodicals; microforms;
                   150,000 volumes of manuscripts; 500,000 volumes
                   in Newspaper Library (located at 130 Colindale
                   Ave., London NW9 5HE; telephone: 01-205 6039;
                   underground stop: Colindale); 1,000,000 maps

Subject Coverage: The British Library, comprised of Reference
Division, Lending Division, and Bibliographic Services Division,

contains books in all subjects and all languages. The emphasis
is, not surprisingly, on English works. The Reference Division is responsible for the departments of the former British
Museum Library (Printed Books, including the Science Reference Library; Manuscripts; Oriental Printed Books and Manuscripts). The collection is, regrettably, not centralized, although by far the largest part is located in the familiar British
Museum Library Building. None of this material circulates.
The Newspaper Collection is at 130 Colindale Avenue (see above).
Eighteenth-century provincial newspapers are also kept at that
address, but 18th century London newspapers are found with the
main collection.

The Lending Division is located at Boston Spa in Yorkshire.
This collection comprises the resources of the former National
Central Library and the National Lending Library for Science
and Technology. There are over 2,250,000 books and 43,000
periodicals available for borrowing. This division is the national center for interlibrary loan and has access to millions
of books in the United Kingdom for this purpose. It is efficient
and prides itself on the rapid handling and high degree of success in processing requests. The division generally fulfills requests for material within twenty-four hours and boasts a ninety-
four per cent success rate. It does not undertake bibliographical searches; therefore, requests must be specific and have ac-
curate bibliographical citations. It acts as a clearinghouse for
interlending between British libraries and foreign countries.
(Ordinarily, these resources are available only to other libraries
or corporate organizations in the United Kingdom, but a photocopy service is maintained for organizations and individuals in
both the United Kingdom and overseas.) It includes, in addition, a British National Book Centre for the distribution of
duplicate books from other collections.

The Bibliographic Services Division incorporates the former
British National Bibliography, Ltd. and the Copyright Receipt
Office. This division is located in Store Street, London WC1E
7DG; telephone: 01-636 0755. The Official Publications Library, located with the main collection, contains many bibliographies in the social sciences easily available on open shelves.

Access: Admission to the Reference Division is by ticket, obtainable from the Admissions Office. Proof of identity is required. It is necessary to inform the librarian what materials
one expects to use in the library. Since space is so limited in
the Reading Room, the librarians are interested in evaluating
whether or not the publications needed may be found elsewhere.
The tickets may be applied for in advance. The library is
open Monday, Friday, Saturday, 9:00 A.M. to 5:00 P.M.;
Tuesday, Wednesday, Thursday, 9:00 A.M. to 9:00 P.M. It
is closed Good Friday, December 24, 25, 26, New Year's Day,
and the week beginning the first Monday in May.

Publications: The General Catalogue of Printed Books, photo-
lithographic edition to 1955, 263 vols. (1959-66) with its supplements: Ten-year Supplement, 1956-65, 50 vols. (1968);
Five-year Supplement, 1966-1970 (1971-) and the Subject Index (1881-   ) are among the major publications of the library.
Catalogs of special collections are also available--notably the
Catalogue of Maps, 15 vols. (1967-68) and the catalog of newspapers which is arranged by countries and towns and has an
index on cards in alphabetical order of titles. This is not published, but there are copies available at the Newspaper Library
and in the Reading Room in the British Museum Building. In
addition to the published catalogs of the Department of Manuscripts, there is the Class Catalogue, a comprehensive index
to the manuscripts in Western languages, which is maintained
in the Manuscripts Students Room. Monographs on special subjects, guides to the museum (The British Museum: A Guide to
Its Public Services), guides to the exhibitions, popular handbooks, and postcards are prominent among the publications.
The British Museum Quarterly no longer pertains to the library,
but the British Library Journal began publication in 1975. A
complete list of current publications is available on application
to The Press Office, The British Library, Store Street, London
WC1E 7DG.

Duplication: Facilities for full-size copying and microfilming
are available. Microfilming can take as long as four months
in busy periods. Xeroxing is expensive, but an expedited service is available for a limited number of copies to those who
apply in person with the item in hand they wish copied. No
manuscripts or pre-1800 printed books are accepted for Xeroxing.

Services: General reference service is available if the inquiries
do not involve a great deal of research. Typing and microfilm
facilities are limited. Desk or shelf space for long-term users
is also extremely scarce. It is possible to prepare ahead by
writing to request that books (up to twelve) be held on reserve.
In addition to the author and title reference, the shelf mark
(number) must be given. This information is obtainable from
the General Catalogue of Printed Books, available in major libraries in the United States. Books (again, up to twelve) being
used in the library may also be held on reserve, but will be
returned to the shelves on the third day if unused for two days.

LONDON

    Institution   British Museum
                     See: LONDON, The British Library (Reference
                     Division) (Reference No. 95)

LONDON

96 Institution   Business Archives Council Library
    Address   Dominion House, 37-45 Tooley Street, London
                      SE1 2QF
    Telephone   01-407 6110
    Underground   London Bridge
    Holdings   3, 000 items; films (deposited with National Film
                      Archive)

Subject Coverage: The council contains information about the
history of business in general and about industrial companies
in particular; records management; archive administration.

Access: The library is available to researchers. Inquiries
should be directed to the Secretary. The library is open Tuesday to Friday, 10:00 A.M. to 3:00 P.M.

Publications: Business Archives (annual); Occasional Newslet-
ters; Letters of a West African Trader: Edward Grace 1767-
70, with an introduction by T. S. Ashton (1950); The Walker
Family: Iron Founders and Lead Manufacturers 1741-1893, ed.
by A. H. John (1951); The First Five Hundred: A Duplicated
List of Chronicles and House Histories of Companies and Organizations in the BAC Library (1959); The Management and
Control of Business Records (1966); A Survey of the Records
of the Shipping Industry (1971).

Duplication: Copying facilities are not available.

Services: The council provides advice to researchers about the
location and availability of business records and maintains a
register of business archives.

LONDON

    Institution   Cabinet Office Library
                      See: LONDON, Treasury and Cabinet Office Li-
                      brary (Reference No. 159)

LONDON

97 Institution   Canning House Library, The Hispanic and Luso-
                      Brazilian Council
    Address   2 Belgrave Square, London SW1X 8PJ
    Telephone   01-235 2303/7
    Underground   Hyde Park Corner
    Holdings   50, 000 books; 200 periodicals; maps; photographs

Subject Coverage: The library contains resources on Latin
America, the West Indies, Spain, and Portugal. Special collec-

tions include George Canning, R. B. Cunninghame Graham, Portuguese and Brazilian Economics Studies, and the Hudson Collection of books on Argentina, Paraguay, and Uruguay.

Access: Visiting scholars are free to use the collection, but a letter of introduction is required. Inquiries should be addressed to the Librarian. The library is open Monday to Friday, 9:30 A. M. to 1:00 P. M. , 2:00 P. M. to 5:30 P. M.

Publications: British Bulletin of Publications (semi-annual); Canning Library. Luso-Brazilian Council. London. Author Catalogue and Subject Catalogue (Boston: G. K. Hall, 1967); Canning House Library. Hispanic Council. London. Author Catalogue and Subject Catalogue (Boston: G. K. Hall, 1967). These are kept up to date by supplements.

Duplication: No copying facilities are available.

Services: Books are loaned only to authorized borrowers. Canning House is the headquarters of the Hispanic and Luso-Brazilian Council and the Economic Affairs Council and is a center for activities concerning Spanish- and Portuguese-speaking countries. The library cooperates with the British Library Lending Division.

LONDON

98 Institution   Central Office of Information
    Address   Hercules Road, London SE1 7DU
    Telephone   01-928 2345
    Underground   Lambeth North
    Holdings   50, 000 books; 400 periodicals; maps; 200, 000
                    photographs; 50, 000 color transparencies; films

Subject Coverage: The library contains information on Britain, the Commonwealth, and international affairs; technical aspects of research for social scientists; old engravings and woodcuts; contemporary Britain; and photographs of British and Commonwealth cultural scenes. The reference material is generally available at other libraries.

Access: The library is primarily for the staff of the Central Office of Information. It is arranged along divisional lines: Reference, Social Survey, Photographs and Films, and Television. Most of the material is available for sale at HMSO and Government Bookshops. Statistical information may be found at the Office of Population Censuses and Surveys (see Reference No. 145). The only section of the library open to visitors is the Photographs Division (telephone: ext. 707), containing photographs and color transparencies, primarily concerned with the British way of life. The public can purchase Crown Copyright photographs at commercial rates. The hours are Monday to

Friday, 10:00 A. M. to 4:00 P. M.

Publications: Britain: An Official Handbook (annual); Survey (fortnightly); reference pamphlets on various topics.

Duplication: Copying facilities are not available, but photographs can be purchased.

Services: Some of the reports derived from the Social Survey Division are publicly available. A catalogue of these is obtainable from the Librarian.

LONDON

99 Institution   Civil Aviation Authority, Aeronautical Information
                      Service
    Address   Tolcarne Drive, Pinner, Middlesex HA5 2DU
    Telephone   01-866 8781
    Holdings   periodicals; reports; circulars

Subject Coverage: The resources include aeronautical information from most countries of the world (exceptions are Albania, People's Republic of China, and Eastern Russia). Included in the collection are Aeronautical Information Publications (AIP); Notices to Airmen (NOTAM); Aeronautical Information Circulars (AIC); and miscellaneous official and privately produced aeronautical information. These are kept up to date by means of amendment lists.

Access: Researchers are permitted to use the collection. Inquiries should be made to the Aeronautical Information Service. A letter of introduction is recommended. The office is open Monday to Friday, 8:00 A. M. to 5:00 P. M. ("skeleton" staff twenty-four hours a day).

Publications: United Kingdom Aeronautical Information Publications; Notices to Airmen; pre-flight bulletins; information circulars.

Duplication: Full-size copying facilities are available.

Services: The collection may be used only on the premises. Route information and advice are given on request. Current aeronautical information about the United Kingdom and overseas territories is collected, recorded, and distributed within the United Kingdom.

LONDON

    Institution   Colonial Office Library
                      See: LONDON, Foreign and Commonwealth Office,

Library and Records Department (Reference
No. 109)

LONDON

100	Institution	Commonwealth Institute Library and Resource Centre
	Address	Kensington High Street, London W8 6NQ
	Telephone	01-602 3252
	Underground	Kensington High Street
	Holdings	40,000 books and pamphlets; 600 periodicals; press clippings

Subject Coverage: The library is not oriented toward advanced research. It contains material on all aspects of the Commonwealth, including many books and journals published in Commonwealth countries and not readily available in other British libraries. News cuttings about Commonwealth affairs taken from leading British dailies and from some other newspapers are included in the collection.

Access: The library is open to the public Monday to Saturday, 10:00 A.M. to 5:30 P.M. Inquiries should be directed to the Librarian.

Publications: The library publishes leaflets describing services of the institute, bibliographies, and several selected reading lists.

Duplication: Full-size copying facilities are available at moderate cost. Duplication can usually be completed the same day.

Services: Loan service is provided to all United Kingdom citizens either at the centre or through the mail.

LONDON

	Institution	Commonwealth Relations Office Library
		See: LONDON, Foreign and Commonwealth Office, Library and Records Department (Reference No. 109)

LONDON

101	Institution	Confederation of British Industry
	Address	21 Tothill Street, London SW1H 9LP
	Telephone	01-930 6711, ext. 312
	Underground	St. James's Park
	Holdings	5,000 books; 6,000 pamphlets and government

publications; 200 periodicals

Subject Coverage: The library contains information of interest
to industry, including legislation, economics, industrial relations, corporate taxation, education and training, and overseas
trade.   It also includes collections of material relating to the
predecessors of the CBI (Federation of British Industry, British Employer's Confederation, and National Association of
British Manufacturers).

Access: The library is primarily for the use of CBI secre-
tariat and members.   American social scientists, however, can
apply to the Librarian for permission to use the library.   A
researcher should possess a letter of introduction from his
home institution.   The library is open Monday to Friday, 9:30
A. M. to 5:30 P. M.

Publications: The CBI publishes CBI Review (quarterly); CBI
Overseas Reports (monthly); CBI Industrial Trends Survey
(quarterly); Members Bulletin (including Industrial Relations
Supplement and Overseas Supplement); Educational, Training
and Technical Bulletin (quarterly); Annual Report; specialist
monographs, e. g. , Taxation in Western Europe and West
European Living Costs; pamphlets.

Duplication: Photocopying equipment is available in the building.   Duplication can be provided quickly and at moderate cost.

Services: The collection is non-circulating.   CBI publications,
which contain much current British economic information, are
offered for sale.

LONDON

102 Institution   Conservative Research Department Library (Con-
                      servative Party)
     Address   24 Old Queen Street, London SW1H 9HX
     Telephone   01-930 1471
     Underground   St. James's Park
                      See also: Conservative Party, p. 230
     Holdings   books; periodicals; manuscripts; press clippings;
                      archives

Subject Coverage: The library holds most of the printed material of the Conservative Party, including party periodicals
from 1893; a nearly complete set of all the printed pamphlets
and leaflets issued by the party since 1868; and the campaign
guides which appeared before general elections since 1892.
Special collections include a set of candidates' by-election and
general election addresses since 1922; and a set of the Ashridge Journal from 1930 to 1948.   The library has only a few
manuscript collections.   Some older, non-printed papers are

held at Swinton College (Ripon, Yorkshire). The party's press
cutting collection is held at Central Office (32 Smith Square,
London SW1P 3HH). The National Union, a federation of Conservative constituency associations, holds reports of party conferences and annual reports from 1867. The National Union is
located at the same address as Central Office.

The Conservative Central Office contains mostly post-World
War II material. Its collection is primarily organizational.
It does, however, hold documents of the Junior Movement from
1905, the Conservative Women's Conferences from 1921 to 1952,
the Conservative Agents' Journal from 1902, and the Conservative Clubs Gazette from 1895 to 1941.

Access: Access to the library is restricted. Because of the
limited facilities, the library makes it a condition that research work must be for a book, article, or thesis which will
eventually be available for other scholars to consult. Inquiries
should be directed to the Librarian. Use of the library is by
appointment only.

Publications: Reports and pamphlets.

Duplication: Full-size copying facilities are available.

Services: The collection does not circulate.

LONDON

103   Institution   Corporation of London Records Office
      Address   P. O. Box 270, Guildhall, London EC2P 2EJ
      Telephone   01-606 3030
      Underground   St. Paul's, Bank, Moorgate
      Holdings   microforms; manuscripts

Subject Coverage: The office contains the official records of
the Corporation of the City of London. The collection includes
royal charters, records of rentals and deeds both in London
and outside the City, judicial records and financial records
(ledgers, accounts, assessments for the levying of taxes).
There are also medieval compilations of City laws and customs and administrative records. The archives include material of national as well as local interest and range in date
from the 11th century.

Access: Visiting scholars can use the collection. Inquiries
should be directed to the Deputy Keeper of the Records. The
office is open Monday to Friday, 9:30 A. M. to 5:00 P. M.

Publications: The Corporation of London Records Office has
published A Guide to the Records at Guildhall, London, by P.
E. Jones and R. Smith (1951); Calendars of Letter Books

A-L, 1275-1498, by R. R. Sharpe, 11 vols. (1899-1912);
Calendar of Wills, Court of Husting, London, 1258-1688, by
R. R. Sharpe, 2 vols. (1889); Calendar of Letters, City of
London, 1350-70, by R. R. Sharpe (1885); Calendar of Coro-
ners' Rolls of the City of London, 1300-78, by R. R. Sharpe
(1913); Munimenta Gildhallae Londoniensis, Liber Albus, Liber
Custumarum, et Liber Horn (Liber Horn not covered), by H.
T. Riley, 3 vols. in 4 (1859-62); Liber Albus (translation), by
H. T. Riley (1861); Memorials of London and London Life,
1276-1419, by H. T. Riley (1868); Liber de Antiquis Legibus,
by T. Stapleton (London: Camden Society, 1846); Chronicles of
Old London, by H. T. Riley (1863); The Historical Charters and
Constitutional Documents of the City of London, by W. de G.
Birch (1884 and 1887); Calendar of Early Mayors Court Rolls,
1298-1307, by A. H. Thomas (Cambridge, 1924); Calendars of
Plea and Memoranda Rolls, 1323-1437, by A. H. Thomas, 4
vols. (Cambridge, 1926, 1929, 1932, 1943); Calendars of Plea
and Memoranda Rolls, 1437-82, by P. E. Jones, 2 vols. (Cambridge, 1954, 1961); The Fire Court, Calendars to the De-
crees, 1667-68, by P. E. Jones, 2 vols. (1966, 1970); Analytical Index to the Remembrancia, 1579-1664, by W. H. and
H. C. Overall (1878).

The London Record Society has published London Possessory
Assizes: A Calendar (Calendar Rolls AA-FF, 1340-1451), by
H. M. Chew, vol. 1 (1965); London Inhabitants Within the
Walls, 1695, by D. V. Glass, L. R. S. vol. 2 (1966); The Lon-
don Eyre of 1244, by H. M. Chew and M. Weinbaum, L. R. S.
vol. 6 (1970); London Assize of Nuissance, 1301-1431, by
H. M. Chew and W. Kellaway, L. R. S. vol. 10 (1973). The
London Topographical Society has published The Public Markets
of the City of London Surveyed by William Leybourn in 1677,
by B. R. Masters, L. T. S. Publication No. 117 (1974).

The Catholic Record Society has published London Sessions
Records, 1605-85, by Dom. H. Bowler (1934); A List of Emigrants from England to America, 1682-92, by M. Ghirelli
(Baltimore, 1968); A List of Emigrants from England to America, 1718-59, by J. and M. Kaminkow (Baltimore, 1964).

Duplication: Limited full-size and micro-copying facilities are
available. The service is expensive and takes from one to
two weeks for completion.

Services: The collection can be used only on the premises.
Ultraviolet lamps are available to aid reading manuscripts.

LONDON

104   Institution   Department of Employment Library
      Address   12 St. James's Square, London SW1Y 4LL
      Telephone   01-214 8265 (Deputy Librarian)

Underground   Piccadilly Circus
Holdings   80,000 books; 400 periodicals

Subject Coverage: The library contains resources on all aspects of industrial relations, trade unions, safety, health,
management, and women in industry.

Access: Visiting researchers must make application to use
the collection. A letter of introduction is recommended. Inquiries should be directed to the Librarian. The hours are
Monday to Friday, 9:30 A.M. to 5:00 P.M.

Publications: Library Bulletin; List of Selected Articles from
Periodicals; subject bibliographies and contents pages from
periodicals.

Duplication: Full-size copying facilities are available. Service is usually immediate.

Services: The collection is available on loan to members of
the Department of Employment and to other libraries.

LONDON

105   Institution   Department of Health and Social Security Library
      Address   Alexander Fleming House, Elephant and Castle,
                       London SE1 6BY
      Telephone   01-407 5522
      Underground   Elephant and Castle
      Holdings   140,000 books and pamphlets; 1,300 periodicals

Subject Coverage: The library holds publications covering
health and medical services, food hygiene, welfare services
and international health. The Social Security Library (10
John Adam Street, London WC2; underground stop: Strand;
telephone: 01-930 9066) contains material covering all aspects of social security including national insurance, war injury pensions, industrial injury pensions, and family allowances. The main library (Alexander Fleming House) receives
the publications of the U.S. Public Health Service, is a depository for World Health Organization publications, and maintains reports of officers of health in England and Wales.

Access: The library is open to researchers who cannot locate
needed material elsewhere. A letter of introduction should be
sent to the Librarian. The library is open Monday to Friday,
9:00 A.M. to 5:00 P.M.

Publications: The library publishes a Library Bulletin (monthly) and is responsible for Hospital Abstracts (monthly) which
is a primary source of information in this field. A complete
list is found in HMSO Sectional List no. 11. The publications

of the Social Security Library are found in HMSO Sectional
List no. 49.

Duplication: Full-size copying facilities at moderate cost are
available without delay.

Services: The library offers a photocopy service for subscribers to Hospital Abstracts. It also cooperates with the
British Library Lending Division.

LONDON

Institution	Department of Industry, Statistics and Market Intelligence Library
	See: LONDON, Statistics and Market Intelligence Library (Reference No. 155)

LONDON

106 | Institution | Department of the Environment, Property Services Agency Library |
|---|---|
| Address | Lambeth Bridge House, London SE1 7SB |
| Telephone | 01-211 7236 |
| Underground | Westminster, St. James's Park |
| Holdings | 80, 000 books; 1, 000 periodicals; photographs |

Subject Coverage: The library contains works on architecture,
engineering, surveying, and other aspects of the construction
industry. It includes British legislation on the construction industry, both main and subsidiary. There is a collection covering furniture and furnishing office buildings; research and development; post office building; army works; naval and air
force works; supplies; training. A special collection of photographs covering ancient monuments and the construction industry is kept at Hannibal House, and a second collection
covering Scotland at Argyle House, Edinburgh.

Access: Visiting researchers are permitted to use the library
when the material they require is not readily available elsewhere. Inquiries should be directed to the Chief Librarian.
The library is open Monday to Friday, 9:30 A. M. to 5:00 P. M.

Publications: Current Information in the Construction Industry
(fortnightly); Construction References (semi-annual); Current
Information on Maintenance (issued in six parts and updated
annually); Bibliography on the Application of Computers in the
Construction Industry (every four years); Bibliography on Data
Co-ordination (every three years); Landscaping Office Build-
ings (irregular); Energy Conservation (updated as appropriate);
PSA Publications (annual).

Duplication: Full-size and micro-copying facilities are available, but are expensive. Copies are available on demand.

Services: The library cooperates with the British Library Lending Division and with other cooperative library services in the United Kingdom.

LONDON

107 Institution   Department of the Environment Headquarters Library
     Address   2 Marsham Street, London SW1P 3EB
     Telephone   01-212 4847
     Underground   St. James's Park, Westminster
     Holdings   250,000 books; 2,500 periodicals; 12,500 microforms; maps (located at The Map Library, Prince Consort House, 27-29 Albert Embankment, London SE1 7TF; telephone: 01-582 8366; underground stop: Vauxhall)

Subject Coverage: The library contains works on housing; local government; regional planning; town and country planning; new and expanded towns; roads; traffic; transport (ports, roads, rail, inland waterways, etc.); environmental pollution (clean air, coastal waters, noise, refuse, radio-activity, water); water supply; sewage; countryside; sport and recreation. The library is a depository for U.S. Census and Environmental Protection Agency publications. The Map Library is administered by the department's Cartographic Services (see above).

Access: The main purpose of the library is to serve the needs of the staff of the department. Accredited researchers must make written application to the Chief Librarian and obtain an appointment to use the collection. A letter of introduction is recommended. The hours are Monday to Friday, 10:30 A.M. to 4:30 P.M.

Publications: DOE Library Bulletin (fortnightly); DOE Annual List of Publications (annual); DOE Register of Research (annual); Index of Current Government and Government Supported Research in Environmental Pollution in Great Britain; Bibliography Series; Information Series; Occasional Papers Series.

Duplication: Photo-copying facilities are available at moderate cost.

Services: The collection can be used only on the premises, but interlibrary loan through other libraries is possible. If the searcher knows the kind of material he wishes to consult, he can write ahead and it will be collected and ready for his use when he arrives.

LONDON

    Institution   Department of Trade and Industry Central Library
                   See: LONDON, Statistics and Market Intelli-
                   gence Library (Reference No. 155)

LONDON

108 Institution   Financial Times/SVP, Business Information Ser-
                   vice
    Address   Bracken House, Cannon Street, London EC4P
                   4BY
    Telephone   01-248 8000
    Underground Bank
    Holdings   books; periodicals; microforms; newspapers

Subject Coverage: The resources of the Business Information
Service include detailed data about individual companies, industries, marketing, countries, law and tax, personalities,
scientific and technical matters, general reference, and translation.

Access: The service is a private information resource, available only to subscribers. Subscription rates are high, and the
cost depends on the use made of the service by the subscriber.
Subscribers generally are institutional rather than personal.
Inquiries are accepted by telephone, telex, or letter. A reading room is open to subscribers, but access is arranged by
negotiation.

Publications: Business and financial reports.

Duplication: Extensive full-size and micro-copying facilities
are available in many forms.

Services: A wide variety of professional research services
is provided.

LONDON

    Institution   Foreign and Commonwealth Office
                   See also: LONDON, India Office Library and
                   India Office Records (Reference Nos. 124 and
                   125)

LONDON

109 Institution   Foreign and Commonwealth Office, Library and
                   Records Department
    Address   Main Library, 3 Sanctuary Buildings, 20 Great

                         Smith Street, London SW1P 3BZ
Telephone   01-212 0663/6568/0732
Underground   St. James's Park, Westminster
Holdings   750,000 books and pamphlets; 2,500 periodicals;
                 microforms; 200 newspapers; 150,000 maps

Subject Coverage: The library resources include material on
international relations, treaties, diplomacy, politics, history,
and economics of foreign and Commonwealth countries, overseas development, and technical assistance.   The library also
holds official publications of Commonwealth countries.   When
a country leaves the Commonwealth, the collection for that
country becomes less complete.   The library contains material
from the 17th century.   Certain categories of Commonwealth
official publications are transferred to the Public Record Office after about fifteen years.   Official Foreign and Commonwealth Office files are also transferred but are not available
to the public for thirty years.

Access: The library is open to the public.   A letter of introduction is recommended.   Inquiries should be directed to the
Librarian at the appropriate address (see below).   The present library has evolved from the merging of the Foreign Office and Commonwealth Office, whereupon the Library and
Records Department was established.   Jointly administered is
the Library of the Ministry of Overseas Development.   The library combines the Colonial Office Library, the Commonwealth
Relations Office Library, and the Foreign Office Printed Library.

This is a joint library system which operates in four locations: the Main Library on Great Smith Street (books, pamphlets, and periodicals dealing with foreign and Commonwealth
countries); Downing Street (Commonwealth legislation; publications on foreign, domestic, and international law; and statistical material), London SW1A 2AL; telephone: 01-930 2323,
ext. 1271; underground stop: Westminster; Cornwall House
(maps), Stamford Street, London SE1 9NF; telephone: 01-928
7511, ext. 7; underground stop: Waterloo; Ministry of Overseas Development, Eland House (resources on developing countries), Stag Place, London SW1E 5DH; telephone: 01-834 2377,
ext. 510; underground stop: Victoria.   The hours are Monday
to Friday, 9:30 A.M. to 5:30 P.M. for all branches.

Publications: Technical Co-operation (monthly bibliography of
Commonwealth official publications); Public Administration: A
Select Bibliography (with supplements); Catalogue of the Co-
lonial Office Library, 15 vols. (Boston: G. K. Hall, 1964);
First Supplement (1967); Second Supplement (1972); Catalogue
of the Foreign Office Library, 1962-1968, 8 vols. (Boston:
G. K. Hall, 1971).

Duplication: Limited copying facilities are available at moderate cost.   The time necessary for duplication is one day.

Services: Library material does not circulate.

LONDON

    Institution   Foreign Office Printed Library
                 See: LONDON, Foreign and Commonwealth Of-
                 fice Library and Records Department (Reference
                 No. 109)

LONDON

    Institution   General Register Office
                 See: LONDON, Office of Population Censuses
                 and Surveys (Reference No. 145)

LONDON

    Institution   Gladstone Library
                 See: LONDON, National Liberal Club, Gladstone
                 Library (Reference No. 142)

LONDON

    Institution   Government Social Survey
                 See: LONDON, Office of Population Censuses
                 and Surveys (Reference No. 145)

LONDON

110   Institution   Gray's Inn Library
      Address   5 South Square, Gray's Inn, London WC1R 5EU
      Telephone   01-242 8592
      Underground Chancery Lane
      Holdings   40,000 books; periodicals

Subject Coverage: The library is a private reference source
for members of Gray's Inn.   Special collections include 12th
to 14th century manuscripts and material on Bacon.

Access: Visiting academics are admitted on application to the
Librarian.   A letter of introduction is required.

Publications: None.

Duplication: Full-size copying facilities are available.

Services: The collection may be used only on the premises.

LONDON

111 Institution   Greater London Council (Maps, Prints and Photo-
                    graphs)
     Address   The County Hall, Room B66, London SE1 7PB
     Telephones   01-633 7193 (maps and prints); 01-633 3255
                    (photographs)
     Underground   Waterloo, Westminster
     Holdings   10,000 maps and plans; 30,000 prints and draw-
                    ings; 200,000 photographs; slides

Subject Coverage: The collection includes extensive holdings
of maps, prints, and photographs. The map collection contains detailed material indicating the growth of London, street
by street and district by district. Maps dating from the 16th
century are found here. It is one of the most comprehensive
map collections of its kind. Ordnance Survey plans are particularly well represented.

The prints and drawings collection constitutes a valuable topographical record. It includes illustrations of the London scene,
including portraits, cartoons, and ephemera; and many original watercolors and drawings. Most of the material is arranged topographically.

The photograph holdings provide a visual record of the changing
character of London and of the services of the Greater London
Council and the former London County Council. It is based
upon photographs taken for official purposes from 1900, although some date from the 19th century. Others have been
specially commissioned. Among the photographs are illustrations of housing estates, schools, parks, bridges and streets,
public buildings and dwelling houses both palatial and slum.
Photographs of people at work and play are included.

Access: The collection is open to the public Monday to Friday, 9:15 A.M. to 5:00 P.M.

Publications: The council has published a series of fine-line
lithographic reproductions of historical maps and prints of the
London area, including Braun and Hogenberg's map of 1572
and Visscher's Panoramic View of 1616. Some color reproductions, including Norden's map of Middlesex, 1593, are also
available. Artist and subject indexes for the prints and drawings collection are in process of compilation.

Duplication: Full-size copying facilities are available.

Services: Copies of photographs from the original negatives
can be ordered in the majority of cases. The council holds

the copyright of most of the photographs; therefore, written permission must be obtained before publication. A reproduction fee may be charged.

LONDON

112 Institution   Greater London Council (Members') Library
    Address   Room 114, The County Hall, London SE1 7PB
    Telephone   01-633 6759/7132
    Underground   Waterloo, Westminster
    Holdings   90,000 books; 400 periodicals

Subject Coverage: The library contains information on history, topography, local government of Greater London, and subjects related to the work of past and current local authorities in the area. It holds the John Burns Collection of books on London.

Access: The library is open to the public for reference. Inquiries should be addressed to the Librarian. The hours are Monday to Friday, 9:15 A.M. to 5:00 P.M. Library material can also be made available on Tuesday until 7:30 P.M. by appointment.

Publications: Members' Library Catalogue: London History and Topography (1939); The Council's Library and Record Office Accessions List (quarterly); Greater London Record Office and Library Report (annual).

Duplication: Depending on the nature and format of the original, photocopies and Xerox copies can usually be purchased.

Services: The library is an institutional member of Aslib and the London Library and is authorized to borrow from the British Library Lending Division.

LONDON

113 Institution   Greater London Record Office (London Section)
    Address   The County Hall, London SE1 7PB
    Telephone   01-633 6851/5464
    Underground   Waterloo, Westminster
    Holdings   records

Subject Coverage: The London Section of the Greater London Record Office has inherited the records of many predecessors of the London County Council and the Greater London Council. The London Section contains official records; ecclesiastical records; and manorial, family, estate, business, and other private records.

Among the records preserved in the record office are those

of Commissioners of Sewers (1570-1847), Metropolitan Commission of Sewers (1847-1855), Metropolitan Buildings Office (1845-1855), Metropolitan Board of Works (1855-1889), London County Council (1889-1965), School Board for London (1870-1904), Technical Education Board (1893-1904), Board of Guardians (1834-1930), and Metropolitan Asylums Board (1867-1930). Among deposits under the Public Records Act, 1958, are the records of Westminster Hospital and St. Thomas' Hospital Group (13th to 20th centuries), including those of the Nightingale Training School and the Nightingale Collection. Other official records include those of the Middlesex Deeds Registry (registers, 1709-1938).

The record office is the Diocesan Record Office for parish records of the Dioceses of London and Southwark. (The London Section was approved for this purpose for the area within the dioceses administered by the former London County Council, excluding the pre-1965 City of Westminster; the City of London is also excluded.) The record office holds archives from more than 250 parishes. Diocesan archives include Bishop's Transcripts; records of the Consistory Court of London (1467-1858); the Commissary Court of the Bishop of Winchester in Surrey (1662-1858) and the Archdeaconry Court of Surrey (1480-1858), dealing with judicial, testamentary, and matrimonial business; and certain office papers of the Dioceses of Southwark (from 1905) and Rochester (southeast London only, 1867-1905). Some tithe awards and plans for the Diocese of London are also held. Congregational Church records include registers, minutes of church meetings, and trust deeds from the 17th century for more than sixty churches, as well as records of the London Congregational Union. Among Methodist archives received are circuit and mission minutes, chapel deeds, and registers.

The manorial, family, estate, business, and other private records relating primarily to the area of the former London County Council have been accepted as gifts or on deposit since at least 1946. They include those of the manors of Stepney, Barnsbury, and Rotherhithe and the three Hackney manors. Court rolls of the manor of Tooting Bec (1394-1843) were inherited from the Metropolitan Board of Works. Among records of important estates are those of St. Pancras estates of Lord Camden and Lord Southampton, the Islington and Clerkenwell estates of the Marquess of Northampton, the Bedford estates in Covent Garden and south London, the Maryon-Wilson estates in Hampstead and Charlton, and the De Beauvoir property chiefly in Hackney and Shoreditch. The office contains strong archival collections of charities, societies, and schools, such as the Foundling Hospital, the Surrey Dispensary, the Corporation of the Sons of the Clergy, the Royal Standard Benefit Society, the Liberation Society, and the Bacon Free School, Bermondsey. Business records include those of gas companies (predecessors of the North Thames Gas Board), breweries, makers of chemicals, sweets, boots, hats, baskets, eye ointment and gin.

Access: The London Section is open to the public. The Search Room (B21) is open Monday, Wednesday to Friday, 9:45 A. M. to 4:45 P. M.; Tuesday, 9:45 A. M. to 7:45 P. M. Readers using the Search Room after 4:45 P. M. on Tuesday must give prior notice of their requirements.

Publications: Guide to the Records in the London County Record Office, pt. I: Records of the Predecessors of the London County Council, Except the Boards of Guardians (1962); A Survey of the Parish Registers of the Diocese of London, Inner London Area (1968); A Survey of the Parish Registers of the Diocese of Southwark, Inner London Area (1970); Court Minutes of the Surrey and Kent Sewer Commission, 1569/70-1579 (1909); Court Rolls of Tooting Bec Manor, 1394-1422 (1909).

Duplication: Full-size copies can normally be obtained. Written permission must be given before publication or further reproduction.

Services: The material does not circulate.

LONDON

114 Institution   Greater London Record Office (Middlesex Section)
     Address   1 Queen Anne's Gate Buildings, Dartmouth Street,
                    London SW1H 9BS
     Telephone   01-633 4431
     Underground   St. James's Park
     Holdings   maps; prints, drawings, watercolors; photo-
                    graphs; archives

Subject Coverage: The Middlesex Section contains official records; ecclesiastical records; manorial, family, estate, business, and other private records; maps and illustrations. The Middlesex Sessions records (beginning in 1549), together with the records of the Gaol Delivery of Newgate for the County of Middlesex (Old Bailey records, 1549-1834) and the Westminster Sessions records (1620-1844), deal with judicial functions and administrative matters affecting highways, the poor, wages and trading practices, and places of worship. They include the many series of records deposited with the Clerk of the Peace-- inclosure awards, plans of railways and other public utilities, hearth tax and land tax returns, registers of papists' estates, lists of persons qualified to serve on juries or to vote in parliamentary elections, etc. Except for the post-1888 records, these relate to the historical County of Middlesex (i. e., they include the whole of London north of the Thames except the City). Also contained in the official records are those of Middlesex Deeds Registry (enrolled memorials, 1709-1837);

Metropolis Roads Commission (1826-1872); Turnpike Trusts
(1726-c. 1870); Petty Sessions (most divisions from c. 1880,
Edmonton and Uxbridge earlier); Middlesex County Council
(1889-1965).

The record office is the Diocesan Record Office for parochial
records of the Middlesex area of the Diocese of London. It
has received parish records (including in many cases registers)
from nearly half of the old Middlesex parishes. It holds the
Bishop's Transcripts for the same area (1800-1903), the probate records of the Middlesex Division of the Archdeaconry of
Middlesex (1609-1810), tithe awards and plans (over thirty
parishes), and certain other series.

The records office holds the records of nearly sixty manors
(the most important being those of the two Harrow manors,
virtually complete from 1315 to 1913). They include also the
records of the Northwick Park estate of the late Lord Northwick, the Osterley estate of the Earl of Jersey (with much
family material), the Middlesex and other estates of the Marquess of Anglesey, the Harefield estate of F. H. M. Fitzroy
Newdegate, the Middlesex and other widely scattered estates
of the Hawtrey Dean family and the Littleton Park estate.
Business archives contain the records of Howards and Sons,
Ltd., manufacturing chemists, of several breweries, and of
constituent companies of the North Thames and Eastern Gas
Boards; and in the field of education, the archives of the National Society's Training College for Domestic Subjects (Ber-
ridge House, Hampstead) and of the Royal Pinner School
Foundation (the Commercial Travellers' School).

The Middlesex Section also contains large collections of
printed maps of Middlesex and of prints, drawings, watercolors, and photographs, principally topographical.

Access: The Search Room is open to the public Monday to
Wednesday, Friday, 9:30 A. M. to 5:00 P. M.; Thursday, 9:30
A. M. to 7:30 P. M. Readers using the Search Room after
5:00 P. M. on Thursday are asked to give prior notice of their
requirements.

Publications: Guide to the Middlesex Sessions Records, 1549-
1889 (1965); Middlesex County Records, 1549-1688 (old series),
ed. by J. Cordy Jeaffreson, vols. 1-4 (1886-1892); Middlesex
County Records: Calendar of the Sessions Books, 1689-1709,
ed. by W. J. Hardy (1905); Middlesex County Records: Reports, 1902-1928 (being reports by W. J. Hardy and W. Le
Hardy on the contents of unpublished Calendars of the Sessions Records (1928); Middlesex Sessions Records, 1612-1618
(new series), ed. by W. Le Hardy, vols. 1-4 (1935-1941).

Duplication: Full-size copies can normally be obtained. Written permission must be granted before publication or further
reproduction.

Services: The material does not circulate.

LONDON

115 Institution   Guildhall Library
     Address   Alder Manbury, London EC2P 2EJ
     Telephone   01-606 3030 (general inquiries, ext. 277 and
                     279)
     Underground   Bank, Moorgate
     Holdings   150, 000 books; 69, 000 manuscripts (archival
                     units); 30, 000 maps; 30, 000 prints

Subject Coverage: The library contains a major collection on
all aspects of London history. The Manuscripts Collection includes London parochial records, records of the majority of
the City Livery Companies, and London diocesan records.
The library also contains provincial directories and poll books;
British Government publications; extensive films of historical
and commercial periodicals (including the proceedings of local
societies); Lock Collection on Sir Thomas More; and publications of international organizations.

Access: Admission is open to the public. Inquiries should be
directed to the Librarian preferably by letter. The library is
open Monday to Saturday, 9:30 A. M. to 5:00 P. M.

Publications: Guildhall Studies in London History (semi-annual); Parish Registers, a Handlist, pt. I: Registers of
Church of England Parishes Within the City of London, 3d ed.,
rev. and enl. (1972); pt. II: Register of Church of England
Parishes Outside the City of London, Non-parochial Registers
and Registers of Foreign Denominations, Burial Ground Records (1970); pt. III: Provisional to "Foreign Registers"
(1967); Vestry Minutes of Parishes Within the City of London,
a Handlist, 2d ed. (1964); London Rate Assessments and Inhabitants Lists in Guildhall Library and in the Corporation of
London Records Office, a Handlist, 2d ed., rev. and enl.
(1968); London Business House Histories, a Handlist (1964);
A List of Books Printed in the British Isles and of English
Books Printed Abroad Before 1701 in Guildhall Library (1966-
1967); Selected Prints and Drawings in Guildhall Library (1964-
1969).

Duplication: Full-size copying facilities are available, but the
cost is high. The time necessary for duplication depends on
the work in hand. Arrangements for micro-copying are made
commercially.

Services: Library material can be made available on loan
through the regional schemes. Photocopies of periodical
articles are provided.

LONDON

Institution	The Hispanic and Luso-Brazilian Council
	See: LONDON, Canning House Library (Reference No. 97)

LONDON

Institution	Historical Manuscripts Commission
	See: LONDON, Royal Commission on Historical Manuscripts (Reference No. 150)

LONDON

116	Institution	Home Office Library
	Address	Romney House, Marsham Street, London SW1P 3DY
	Telephone	01-212 5945
	Underground	Westminster, St. James's Park
	Holdings	50,000 books and pamphlets; 700 periodicals

Subject Coverage: The library collection reflects the responsibilities of the Home Office and the Northern Ireland Office. It includes administration of justice, criminology, penology, community relations, Northern Ireland, and immigration.

Access: The library is available to researchers, but only by prior arrangement with the Librarian. A letter of introduction is advisable. The library is open Monday to Friday, 9:30 A.M. to 5:15 P.M.

Publications: A Brief Guide to the Home Office Library.

Duplication: Facilities for full-size copying are available, but the service is expensive and takes from one to three days.

Services: The collection does not circulate.

LONDON

117	Institution	The Honourable Society of Lincoln's Inn
	Address	Holborn, London WC2A 3TN
	Telephone	01-242 4371
	Underground	Chancery Lane
	Holdings	100,000 books; 66 periodicals; 2,000 volumes of manuscripts; House of Lords Appeals and Privy Council Cases

Subject Coverage: The library contains information on law books; the Inns of Court; a comprehensive collection of the laws and law reports of the British Commonwealth; works on history; Parliamentary Papers; parish registers; biographical details of members. Special collections include the Sir Matthew Hale Collection of manuscripts.

Access: Visiting scholars must receive permission to use the library's resources. Inquiries should be directed to the Librarian by letter. The hours are Monday to Friday, 9:30 A. M. to 7:00 P. M. except September when the library is open Monday to Friday, 10:00 A. M. to 4:00 P. M.

Publications: Catalogue of the Library, 1859 (1890); Catalogue of Pamphlets, 1506-1700; Records of the Society, 1422-1914; Guide to Commonwealth Collection in Lincoln's Inn (1974).

Duplication: Limited full-size copying service is available and is expensive. Arrangements can be made for microfilming.

Services: The collection does not circulate.

LONDON

118   Institution   Honourable Society of the Inner Temple, The
                          Inner Temple Library
      Address   The Inner Temple, London EC4Y 7DA
      Telephone   01-353 2959
      Underground   Temple
      Holdings   87, 000 books and pamphlets; 350 periodicals;
                          10, 000 manuscripts

Subject Coverage: The library resources include legislation, law reports, journals, and treatises relating to English, Commonwealth, and international law; heraldry; genealogy; and London topography. Among the special collections are Inner Temple Records, Mitford Legal Manuscripts, and Petyt and Barrington Manuscripts.

Access: Visiting academics can use the collection only with permission of the Librarian. A letter of introduction is required. The library is open Monday to Friday, 10:00 A. M. to 6:00 P. M. except in August and September when the hours are Monday to Friday, 10:00 A. M. to 4:00 P. M. Manuscript material is not available during these two months.

Publications: Catalog of Manuscripts in the Library of the Inner Temple, ed. by J. Conway Davies, 3 vols. (1972).

Duplication: Full-size copying facilities are available for use by the reader. Manuscript material may be duplicated only by overhead camera supplied by an outside agency and upon special application.

Services: Bibliographical and legal information is provided.
The collection does not circulate.

LONDON

119 Institution   The Honourable Society of the Middle Temple
     Address   Middle Temple Lane, London EC4Y 9BT
     Telephone   01-353 4303
     Underground   Temple
     Holdings   125,000 books; periodicals

Subject Coverage: The collection is strongest in legal resources, which cover all parts of the world. The emphasis
is on Great Britain, European Communities, the Commonwealth,
and the United States. The special collections include books
from Donne's Library (works on religious controversy, apolo-
getics, philosophy, and magic); Phillimore Collection (international law); Lord Chancellor Eldon (law books); and the Ashley
Collection (geography, astronomy, and history).

Access: The library is available to scholars on application to
the Librarian and Keeper of the Records. A letter of introduction is recommended. The library is open Monday to Friday, 9:30 A.M. to 7:00 P.M., but keeps fewer hours during
the summer vacation.

Publications: A complete list of publications is available on
request. Among the most notable of these is Middle Temple
Admission Register, 1501-1944, 3 vols.; and Middle Temple
Library Catalogue, 1914-1925, 4 vols.

Duplication: Full-size copying facilities are available at moderate cost.

Services: The Middle Temple Library Collection does not
circulate.

LONDON

120 Institution   House of Commons Library
     Address   Westminster, London SW1A 0AA
     Telephone   01-219 3666
     Underground   Westminster
     Holdings   125,000 volumes; 1,500 periodicals; newspapers;
                     press clippings

Subject Coverage: The library contains the publications of
Parliament, HMSO, European Communities, the UN, and other
inter-governmental agencies. It also has works in social science and statistics.

Access: The library is a private library for Members of
Parliament. When the House of Commons is not in session,
it is possible for visiting scholars to use the resources with
special permission of the Librarian. It is necessary to write
ahead for an appointment. A letter of introduction is usually
required from the home institution. The library contains two
divisions: Parliamentary and Research (with the main library
resources held by the Parliamentary Division). When the
House is sitting, the library is open 9:30 A. M. until adjourn-
ment. At other times, the hours are 10:00 A. M. to 5:00 P. M.

Publications: Publications include House of Commons Library
Documents Series which is published occasionally through
HMSO.

Duplication: Duplication facilities are not available.

Services: The library will answer written inquiries for Parliamentary information not readily obtainable elsewhere. Library
resources circulate only to Members of Parliament. There is
close cooperation with the House of Lords Library for reference and loan facilities.

LONDON

121   Institution   House of Lords Library
      Address   Old Palace Yard, Westminster, London SW1A
                       0PW
      Telephone   01-219 5242
      Underground   Westminster
      Holdings   85, 000 books and pamphlets; 200 periodicals

Subject Coverage: The library contains resources on law and
Parliament, peerage cases, genealogy, heraldry, and British
topography. It also holds Lord Truro's Law Library and
manuscript notebooks donated by Lady Truro, Lords and Commons Sessional Papers, Parliamentary Papers and Debates,
publications of learned societies, history, classics, and English
and French literature.

Access: Admission is obtained with the permission of the Librarian. The library is primarily for members of the House
of Lords and House of Commons, but others may use the facilities if the material they seek is not readily obtainable elsewhere. An appointment must be made in advance. When the
House of Lords is in session, the hours are 10:30 A. M. to
1:00 P. M. At other times, the hours are 10:30 A. M. to 4:30
P. M.

Publications: The library has issued A Short Guide (1972) and
A Short History (1972).

Duplication: Full-size copying can be done at the Librarian's discretion. The cost is moderate.

Services: The collection can be used only on the premises.

LONDON

122 Institution   House of Lords Record Office
     Address   House of Lords, London SW1A 0AA
     Telephone   01-930 6240
     Underground   Westminster
     Holdings   books; periodicals; microforms; 3,000,000 records; press clippings; photographs

Subject Coverage: The office contains the records and archives of Parliament (House of Lords from 1497, House of Commons from 1835); journals of the House of Commons from 1547; other records relating to the Palace of Westminster. Among the private papers held are the Brand Papers (diaries of Mr. Speaker Brand, later 1st Viscount Hampden); Braye Manuscripts (papers of John Browne, Clerk of the Parliaments, 1638-1691); Lloyd George Papers and 1st Viscount Samuel Papers. There are also papers placed by Ministers for the use of members (mostly post-1920). The press cuttings books preserved include those of D. M. Mason, Sir Stuart Samuel, and Sir Frank Sanderson.

Access: Visiting academics are welcome to use the collection on the premises. If the search is for business or legal purposes, a small fee is charged. An advance appointment is preferable and a letter of introduction is recommended. Inquiries should be directed to the Clerk of the Records. The hours are Monday to Friday, 9:30 A.M. to 5:30 P.M.

Publications: Among the publications issued by the office are memoranda concerning the records, calendars of the records, facsimile reproductions, and catalogs of exhibitions. HMSO has issued Guide to the Records of Parliament, by M. F. Bond (1971).

Duplication: Efficient full-size and micro-copying facilities are provided. Photographic services are also available.

Services: The collection does not circulate. Brief telephone and postal inquiries will be answered, but no extensive research will be undertaken.

LONDON

     Institution   Imperial Institute Library

See: LONDON, Commonwealth Institute Library
(Reference No. 100)

LONDON

123 Institution   Imperial War Museum Libraries and Archives
    Address   Lambeth Road, London SE1 6HZ
    Telephone   01-735 8922
    Underground   Lambeth North, Elephant and Castle
    Holdings   100,000 books; 25,000 pamphlets; 350 periodicals;
                  2,000 shelf feet of documents; press clippings;
                  15,000 maps and technical drawings; 4,000,000
                  prints and negatives; 9,000 war paintings, draw-
                  ings, and sculptures; sound records and tapes;
                  30,000,000 feet of film

Subject Coverage: The library contains materials relating to
all aspects of the two world wars and other (military, political,
economic, and social) activities of Britain and the Commonwealth since 1914. Specifically included are histories of service units, technical literature, and wartime periodicals of
both British and foreign origin.

The Department of Documents is a repository for documentary
records of all types relating to warfare in the 20th century.
It also collects and disseminates information on the documentary holdings of European and American archives and research
institutes. The main documentary collections contain captured
German material and British private papers.

The German collection consists almost entirely of photocopies.
It contains campaign files for the Western, Norwegian, and
Eastern campaigns in World War II, the plans for the Austrian
and Czechoslovakian invasions, and a number of high-level
military intelligence documents. The collection of High Command files contains material on the organization of the German
armed forces in the pre-war period and includes copies of the
war diaries of OKW, OKH, and the Operations Division of
OKM. The two largest microfilm collections of German official files contain material from the Reich Ministry of Arma-
ments and War Production (the Speer Ministry) and from the
Reich Air Ministry. The Speer Ministry records include the
ministerial papers of Speer himself, the minutes of the Central
Planning Committee, and records of the Planungsamt and the
Rohstoffamt. The German collections also contain material
from the Reich Air Ministry, the Reich Ministry of Economics,
the records of major German industrial firms, and the various
War Crimes Trials.

The Italian material held by the museum includes largely the
records of the Italian Ministry of War Production from 1940 to
1943.

The Department of Documents also contains the private papers of British citizens. Among these are the letters and diaries of Field Marshal Sir Henry Wilson and the papers of Marshal of the Royal Air Force Lord Douglas of Kirtleside, Major-General G. P. Dawnay, Admiral Sir Dudley de Chair, Major-General L. O. Lyne, General Sir Ivor Maxse, Admiral Sir Edward Parry, and Air Commodore C. R. Samson.

The Department of Printed Books contains detailed coverage of the two world wars, but also includes works on other 20th century wars. The library has strong holdings of British, French, German, and American unit histories. There is an important collection of technical manuals and handbooks; examples of wartime propaganda, ration books, enlistment cards, and army forms; news cuttings; trench maps and situation and order of battle maps.

The Department of Photographs is responsible for administering the national photographic collection of war in the 20th century.

The Department of Film contains film records of the two world wars including captured German, Japanese, and Italian films. In addition, propaganda and industrial films are included in the collection. The department has promoted specialized historical film conferences and seminars.

The Department of Sound Records is a national archive which collects, preserves, and makes available recordings which have a bearing on the understanding of warfare in the 20th century. The department operates an oral history program.

Access: Admission is available for visiting American academics. Letters should be addressed to the individual in charge of each section, i. e., Film Librarian, Keeper of Art, Head of Document Section, or Head of the Photographic Section. To use the libraries and archives, an appointment must be made either by telephone at least twenty-four hours in advance, or by mail. Upon appearing on the premises for the first time, the researcher should have some identification or letter of introduction. The library is open Monday to Friday, 10:00 A. M. to 5:00 P. M. The Department of Printed Books and the Department of Documents are closed the last two full weeks in October.

Publications: The publications of the Imperial War Museum Libraries and Archives include bibliographies on campaigns and other selected subjects; A Concise Catalogue of Paintings, Drawings and Sculpture of the First World War, 1914-1918, 2d ed. (1963); A Concise Catalogue of Paintings, Drawings and Sculpture of the Second World War, 1939-1945, 2d ed. (1964); Provisional Reports on archives which include repositories in the United Kingdom, the German Federal Republic, Italy, the German Democratic Republic, and Poland; monthly accessions lists.

Duplication: Full-size copying and other photographic reproduction processes are available. In some cases, a period of
up to three months may be necessary to complete a copying
order.

Services: General reference service is available. Seating
space is limited, thus, there is a necessity for making an appointment in advance.

LONDON

124   Institution   India Office Library, Foreign and Commonwealth
                       Office
      Address   197 Blackfriars Road, London SE1 8NG
      Telephone   01-928 9531
      Underground   Waterloo, Blackfriars
      Holdings   300, 000 books; 680 periodicals; 4, 110 micro-
                       forms; 40, 000 manuscripts; 120, 000 photographs;
                       25, 000 drawings and paintings

Subject Coverage: The library contains material on all aspects of South Asian studies. Much of the collection is in
Oriental languages.

Access: A letter of recommendation from a recognized authority is required to use the collection. The library is open
Monday to Friday, 9:30 A. M. to 6:00 P. M.; Saturday, 9:30
A. M. to 1:00 P. M. Inquiries should be addressed to the Director.

Publications: Publications include A Guide to the India Office
Library, by S. C. Sutton, 2d ed. (1967); The India Office Library: An Historical Sketch, by A. J. Arberry (1967); library
catalogs of drawings and of Oriental printed books and manuscripts; Annual Report.

Duplication: Full-size and micro-copying facilities are available but are expensive.

Services: Library material does not circulate. Queries will
be answered by telephone or mail. The library contributes
to the Union Catalogue of Asian Publications at the School of
Oriental and African Studies, University of London.

LONDON

125   Institution   India Office Records, Foreign and Common-
                       wealth Office
      Address   197 Blackfriars Road, London SE1 8NG
      Telephone   01-928 9531
      Underground   Waterloo, Blackfriars

Holdings   20, 000 maps; 200, 000 volumes and files of
archival material; 100, 000 official publications

Subject Coverage: The record office holds the archives of the
East India Company (1600-1858), the Board of Control (1784-
1858), the India Office (1858-1947), and the Burma Office
(1937-1948). These relate primarily to the British role in
South Asia from 1600 to 1948 but also include some material
on areas ranging from St. Helena to Japan.

Access: A letter of recommendation from a recognized authority is required to use the collection. The office is open
Monday to Friday, 9:30 A. M. to 6:00 P. M.; Saturday, 9:30
A. M. to 1:00 P. M. Inquiries should be addressed to the Director.

Publications: A Guide to the India Office Records, 1600-1858,
by Sir William Foster (1919, reprinted 1966); The India Of-
fice Records (Archives, ix, 130-41, 1970); Catalogue of the
Home Miscellaneous Series, by S. C. Hill (1927); The Court
Minutes of the East India Company, 1602-1617 (1896-1908);
The English Factories in India, 1684 (1906-1955).

Duplication: Full-size and micro-copying facilities are available but are expensive.

Services: Record office material does not circulate. Inquiries
by telephone or mail will be answered.

LONDON

Institution   The Inner Temple Library
See: LONDON, Honourable Society of the Inner
Temple (Reference No. 118)

LONDON

Institution   Institute of Advanced Legal Studies
See: LONDON, University of London, Institute
of Advanced Legal Studies (Reference No. 163)

LONDON

126 Institution   Institute of Classical Studies and Joint Library
of the Hellenic and Roman Studies
Address   31/34 Gordon Square, London WC1H 0PY
Telephone   01-387 7697
Underground   Euston Square, Euston, Russell Square, Goodge
Street
Holdings   45, 000 books; 400 periodicals

Subject Coverage: The library contains works on Greek and Roman antiquity, including language, history, papyrology, epigraphy, archaeology, philosophy, and language.

Access: Visiting scholars must obtain permission to use the collection. Inquiries should be directed to the Librarian. A letter of introduction is recommended. The hours are Monday to Friday, 9:30 A.M. to 6:00 P.M.; Saturday, 10:00 A.M. to 5:00 P.M. The library is closed on Saturday during August.

Publications: Bulletin of the Institute of Classical Studies (issued with supplements); Journal of Hellenic Studies; Journal of Roman Studies; Britannia (annual); Studies in Mycenaean Inscriptions and Dialect (annual).

Duplication: Copying facilities are not available.

Services: The collection circulates only to members of the Hellenic and Roman Society.

LONDON

127 Institution   Institute of Contemporary History and Wiener
                    Library
     Address   4 Devonshire Street, London W1N 2BH
     Telephone   01-636 7247
     Underground   Regent's Park, Great Portland Street
     Holdings   80,000 books and pamphlets; 150 periodicals;
                    2,000,000 press clippings; photographs; 40,000
                    Nuremberg documents

Subject Coverage: The library, a leading resource for the study of totalitarianism, contains works on Nazism, fascism, anti-Semitism, history of Germany since 1914, history of German nationalism, Middle East history in the 20th century (emphasis on Israel, Palestine, Zionism), the Nuremberg Trials Collection, classified collection of photographs, eyewitness reports of survivors of Nazi persecution, press cuttings from international sources.

Access: The library is available to accredited researchers who may become members on payment of a moderate fee. The library is open Monday to Friday, 10:30 A.M. to 5:30 P.M. Inquiries should be sent to the Librarian.

Publications: Wiener Library Catalogue Series, 5 vols., ed. by I. Wolff and H. Kehr (1949-1964), includes revised editions of vols. 1 and 2; The Wiener Library Bulletin (quarterly); Catalog of Nuremberg Documents (1961); First-Third Supplements (1962-63); Journal of Contemporary History (quarterly).

Duplication: Full-size duplication resources are available for
immediate use.

Services: Only members may borrow books.

LONDON

       Institution   Institute of Historical Research
                      See: LONDON, University of London, Institute
                      of Historical Research (Reference No. 164)

LONDON

128   Institution   International Institute for Strategic Studies
       Address   18 Adam Street, London WC2N 6AL
       Telephone   01-930 3757/1102
       Underground Trafalgar Square, Charing Cross Embankment
       Holdings   3,000 books; 180 periodicals; press clippings

Subject Coverage: The library contains a small but select col-
lection--mostly of recently published books--which deals with
strategic matters affecting the nations of the world.   News
clippings are collected from ten newspapers (four British, two
American, two French, one West German, and one Swiss).

Access: Admission is with the discretion of the Librarian.
Members of the IISS are permitted free access to the collection.   Non-members may use the library on payment of a small
fee.   The library is open Monday to Friday, 10:00 A. M. to
6:00 P. M.

Publications: The publications issued by the institute are Sur-
vival (bi-monthly); Military Balance (annual); Strategic Survey
(annual); Adelphi Papers (irregular); Studies in International
Security; a catalog of the library (which may be purchased in-
expensively) listing all the books in the collection and giving
publication information.

Duplication: Duplication facilities are available at moderate
cost.

Services: Reference service is available to aid the researcher
in locating his material.   Books circulate only to members.
Newspaper clipping files, among the most important assets of
the library, can be used only on the premises.   Accessions
lists are sent annually without charge to purchasers of the catalog.

LONDON

    Institution   King's College Library
                    See: LONDON, University of London, King's
                    College Library (Reference No. 165)

LONDON

129   Institution   Labour Party Library
      Address   Transport House, Smith Square, London SW1P
                    2JA
      Telephone   01-834 9434, ext. 31
      Underground Westminster, St. James's Park
                    See also: Labour Party, p. 235
      Holdings   8,000 books; 30,000 pamphlets; 300 periodicals;
                    600,000 press clippings; 10,000 photographs

Subject Coverage: The library contains resources covering
socialism in Britain and the world; economics and industry;
social services; education; and political campaign literature.
Press cuttings (some dating from 1918) are from all national
and most provincial British newspapers.

Access: Visiting scholars may use the collection.   Inquiries
should be directed to the Librarian.   The hours are Monday
to Friday, 9:30 A.M. to 5:00 P.M.

Publications: Bibliographies of publications by the Labour
Party and associated organizations; Labour Party pamphlets.

Duplication: Facilities for full-size copying are available at
moderate cost.

Services: The collection is not normally available on loan.

LONDON

130   Institution   Lambeth Palace Library
      Address   London SE1 7JU
      Telephone   01-928 6222
      Underground Westminster
      Holdings   150,000 books; 137 periodicals; 3,000 volumes
                    of manuscripts

Subject Coverage: The library contains work in ecclesiastical
history, canon law, liturgy, inter-church relations, and theology.   It also holds archives of the Archbishops of Canterbury, Court of Arches, Faculty Office, Vicar General Office;
Parliamentary Surveys; Papers of Bacon, Carew, Shrewsbury,
and Selborne; and many incunabula.

Access: The resources of the library may be used by researchers upon presentation of a letter of introduction.   Inquiries should be directed to the Librarian and Archivist.
The library is open Monday to Friday, 10:00 A. M. to 5:00
P. M.

Publications: A Catalogue of the Archiepiscopal Manuscripts
in the Library at Lambeth Palace, by Henry J. Todd (1812,
reprinted by Gregg International Publishers, 1965); A Descriptive Catalogue of the Manuscripts in the Library of Lambeth
Palace: The Medieval Manuscripts, by M. R. James (Cambridge University Press, 1932); A Catalogue of Lambeth Manuscripts 889 to 901 (Carte Antique et Miscellanée), by Dorothy
M. Owen (1968); Original Papal Documents in the Lambeth
Palace Library: A Catalogue, by Jane Sayers (in: Bulletin
of the Institute of Historical Research, Special Supplement no.
6 [1967]); Estate Documents at Lambeth Palace Library: A
Short Catalogue, by Jane Sayers (Leicester University Press,
1965); Faculty Office Registers, 1534-1549: A Calendar, by
D. S. Chambers (Oxford University Press, 1966); A Calendar
of the Shrewsbury and Talbot Papers in Lambeth Palace Li-
brary and the College of Arms, vol. 1: Shrewsbury MSS. in
L. P. L. MSS. 694-710, by Catherine Jamison, rev. by E. G.
W. Bill (HMSO, 1966); Catalogue of Ecclesiastical Records of
the Commonwealth, 1643-1660, in the Lambeth Palace Library,
by Jane Houston (Gregg International Publishers, 1968); The
Fulham Papers in the Lambeth Palace Library: American and
Colonial Section, Calendar and Indexes, by W. W. Manross
(Oxford University Press, 1965); A Catalogue of the Papers of
Roundell Palmer (1812-1895) First Earl Selborne, by E. G. W.
Bill; A Catalogue of Manuscripts in Lambeth Palace Library:
MSS. 1222-1860, by E. G. W. Bill (Oxford University Press,
1972); Index of Cases in the Records of the Court of Arches
at Lambeth Palace Library, 1660-1913, ed. by Jane Houston
(1972); Index to the Papers of Anthony Bacon in Lambeth Pal-
ace Library (1974).

Duplication: Full-size and micro-copying facilities are available.

Services: Books do not circulate.   The library cooperates
with the Association of British Theological and Philosophical
Libraries.

LONDON

131	Institution	The Law Society Library
	Address	113 Chancery Lane, London WC2A 1PL
	Telephone	01-242 1222
	Underground	Chancery Lane, Temple
	Holdings	65,000 books; 300 periodicals

Subject Coverage: The library collection is comprehensive in all branches of English law and includes legal treatises, professional journals, law reports, and Acts of Parliament. The holdings are selective for other jurisdictions (e. g. , Scottish, Irish, European Economic Community).

Access: The library is a private reference library for members of the society. Inquiries should be directed, by letter, to the Librarian. The library is open to members, Monday to Friday, 9:00 A. M. to 5:00 P. M.

Publications: Law Society Gazette (weekly).

Duplication: Full-size copying facilities are available for members.

Services: The collection is for reference only and does not circulate.

LONDON

      Institution   Library Association Library
                     See: LONDON, The British Library (Library Association Library) (Reference No. 94)

LONDON

      Institution   Lincoln's Inn Library
                     See: LONDON, The Honourable Society of Lincoln's Inn (Reference No. 117)

LONDON

132   Institution   Lloyd's Register of Shipping Library
       Address   71 Fenchurch Street, London EC3M 4BS
       Telephone   01-709 9166
       Underground Tower Hill
       Holdings   1, 000 books; 240 periodicals; records

Subject Coverage: The library contains information about shipping, registration of ships, and statistical matters.

Access: The collection is available to visiting scholars by appointment only. Inquiries should be directed to the Librarian. The hours are Monday to Friday, 9:00 A. M. to 5:00 P. M.

Publications: Lloyd's Register Book; Lloyd's Register of Yachts; rules and regulations covering survey and construction of ships and their machinery and materials.

Duplication: No copying facilities are available.

Services: Inquiries concerning registration and statistics are handled by the Shipping Information Services. The collection does not ordinarily circulate.

LONDON

133 Institution   London Borough of Bexley, Bexley Library
                       Service
     Address   Central Administrative Offices, Hall Place,
                       Bourne Road, Bexley, Kent DA5 1PQ
     Telephone   29-26574
     Holdings   404,151 books; 515 periodicals; 1,240 micro-
                      forms; photographs

Subject Coverage: The library has resources on Bible history and commentary, church history, including primitive and Oriental churches. There is also information on legislation, elections, and suffrage, together with the All England Law Reports from 1555, and a complete set of the London Bibliography of the Social Sciences. The Local Studies Collection contains books, archives, and museum material relating to the Borough of Bexley, including all surviving rate books and local authority minutes from 1880. There is a strong collection relating to the County of Kent. The library also includes a general illustrations collection containing 5,000 items and another collection of 7,500 photographs of the Borough of Bexley.

Access: The library is open to the public, and books may be borrowed by anyone who lives, works, or studies in the Borough of Bexley. The hours are Monday to Friday, 9:30 A.M. to 8:00 P.M.; Saturday, 9:30 A.M. to 5:00 P.M.

Publications: Medieval Bexley, by F. R. H. DuBoulay; Hall Place, Bexley, by P. E. Morris; Belvedere and Bostall: A Brief History, by J. A. Prichard; Bexley Village, by P. J. Tester; From Footscray to the Thames: A Portfolio of Prints; Statistical Report; subject lists; guides to the services.

Duplication: Full-size copying facilities are available at high cost.

Services: SEAL (South East Area Libraries Information Service), an information service for commerce and industry, covers the boroughs of Bexley, Dartford, Greenwich, and Lewisham.

LONDON

134 Institution   London Borough of Bromley Public Libraries

Address	Central Library, Tweedy Road, Bromley BR1 1EX
Telephone	01-460 9955
Holdings	808,117 books, pamphlets, and reports; 350 periodicals

Subject Coverage: The library includes publications on the description and history of Central and Southern Africa, commercial law, and history. Local history information on Bromley and Kent and special collections on H. G. Wells, the Crystal Palace, and Walter de la Mare are included in the holdings.

Access: The library is open to the public for reference. A ticket is necessary to borrow material. Inquiries should be addressed to the Borough Librarian. The library is open Monday, Thursday, 9:15 A.M. to 8:00 P.M.; Tuesday, Wednesday, Friday, 9:15 A.M. to 6:00 P.M.; Saturday, 9:15 A.M. to 5:00 P.M.

Publications: A Bibliography of Printed Materials Relating to Bromley, Hayes and Keston, in the County of Kent, by B. Burch (1964); The Catalogue of the H. G. Wells Collection in the Bromley Public Libraries, ed. by A. H. Watkins (1974); The Manor and Town of Bromley AD 862-1934, by A. H. Watkins (1972); Portfolio of Views of the London Borough of Bromley (in the 18th and 19th Centuries) (1972); Introduction to the History of Orpington, comp. by Peter Heinecke (1975); History of Bromley, by A. H. Watkins (in preparation).

Duplication: Full-size copying facilities are available and can be provided immediately, but the cost is high.

Services: The library is a member of Aslib.

LONDON

135	Institution	London Borough of Ealing Library Services
	Address	Central Library, Walpole Park, London W5 5EQ
	Telephone	01-567 3656 (Central Reference Library)
	Underground	Ealing Broadway
		(Note: there are also three district and nine branch libraries.)
	Holdings	624,111 books and pamphlets; 698 periodicals;
	(Social Science only)	65,600 microforms; 6,500 maps

Subject Coverage: There are thirteen libraries in the borough which have a general stock, including the social sciences and humanities. Notable items at the Central Library are a collection of British State Papers, a selection from the British National Archives and the Historical Manuscripts Commission, and a complete collection of the List and Index Society. At

Southall Library, there is a collection on immigrants and immigration.   For social sciences, the principal libraries are
Central, Southall, and Acton.

Access: The libraries are open to the public.   Inquiries should
be addressed to the Borough Librarian.   Hours of opening for
the Central Library are Monday, Thursday, Friday, 9:00 A.M.
to 7:00 P.M.; Tuesday, 9:00 A.M. to 8:00 P.M.; Wednesday,
9:00 A.M. to 1:00 P.M.; Saturday, 9:00 A.M. to 6:00 P.M.

Publications: None.

Duplication: Full-size copying facilities are available on
demand at Central, Acton, and Southall Libraries.   The cost
is high.   Microfilming and full-size reproduction from microprint can be arranged, but delay may be up to fourteen days.

Services: Interlending through LASER (London and South
Eastern Region) and British Library Lending Division is available.   The library is a member of CICRIS West London Industrial Information Service.

LONDON

136   Institution   London Borough of Tower Hamlets Libraries De-
                          partment
      Address   Central Library, Bancroft Road, London E1 4DQ
      Telephone   01-980 4366
      Underground   Mile End, Stepney Green
      Holdings   423, 224 books; 250 periodicals; press clippings;
                          photographs

Subject Coverage: The Local History Department at the Central Library contains 6, 684 books; 3, 617 pamphlets; 673 maps;
and 232 reels of microfilm relating to Tower Hamlets.   A
Shipping Collection covers the history of shipping up to the
First World War, with special reference to Tower Hamlets.
It includes the Bolt Collection of notes, cuttings, and photographs of ships.

Access: The library is open to the public.   Inquiries should
be directed to the Librarian.   The hours are Monday to Friday, 9:00 A.M. to 8:00 P.M.; Saturday, 9:00 A.M. to 5:00
P.M.

Publications: Bygone Tower Hamlets, 2d series (portfolios of
six local prints).

Duplication: Full-size copying facilities are available at high
cost.   Other photographic copying can be arranged at commercial prices.

Services: Limited local history research is provided.

LONDON

137 Institution   London Library
     Address   14 St. James's Square, London SW1Y 4LG
     Telephone   01-930 7705
     Underground   Piccadilly Circus
     Holdings   850,000 books; 4,000 volumes of pamphlets; 380
                      periodicals

Subject Coverage: The library contains works in many fields--
particularly history, politics, travel, biography, and religion.
These resources are in all European languages.

Access: This is a private subscription library with special
membership facilities for scholars from overseas. The collection is available to members only. To become a member,
one must apply to the Librarian.

Publications: Author Catalogue, 5 vols. (to 1950); Subject
Index, 4 vols. (to 1953).

Duplication: Full-size copying facilities are available at moderate cost. Several days are required to process copying
orders.

Services: Books circulate to members. The library has open
stacks and a Reading Room.

LONDON

138 Institution   London School of Economics and Political Sci-
                      ence, British Library of Political and Economic
                      Science
     Address   Houghton Street, Aldwych, London WC2A 2AE
     Telephone   01-405 7686
     Underground   Holborn, Temple
     Holdings   660,000 books; 450,000 pamphlets; 24,000 peri-
                      odicals; microforms; manuscripts

Subject Coverage: The British Library of Political and Economic Science (BLPES), a major social science resource, contains literature on all aspects of the subject in all Western
languages. It includes works in history, politics, economics,
statistics, law, British socialism, public administration, business, and publishing and the book trade. A carefully considered acquisitions policy assures comprehensive coverage of
the history of major European nations and the United States
for the past 250 years and of the history of developing countries in the post-World War II period. It is a depository for

publications of the United States Federal Government; the UN
and its specialized agencies; European Communities; Organization of African States; and is a selective depository for Canadi-
an Federal Government publications.   It also contains extensive
collections of publications from the Organization for Economic
Cooperation and Development, the International Labor Organization, and other international bodies.   Through an exchange
agreement with the National Library of Nigeria, all Nigerian
Federal Government documents are received.   It has a comprehensive collection of United Kingdom Government publications
and documents of some local authorities.

The BLPES is a vast storehouse of manuscripts, particularly
in the 19th and 20th centuries.   Among its important personal
papers are those of John Stuart Mill, the Webbs, Ramsay Mac-
Donald, Lord Beveridge, and Hugh Dalton.   Among the academic and public papers are those of Sir Charles Webster and
Bronislaw Malinowski; account books of a corporate bank; and
correspondence and minutes of political parties and interest
groups.

Access: Non-members of the London School of Economics and
Political Science can be given special permits to use the library for advanced research.   These permits might be issued
for a long term or for a few days.   A letter of introduction is
recommended.   Inquiries should be directed to the Librarian
by letter or to the Enquiry Desk by telephone or in person.
The library is open Monday to Friday, 10:00 A. M. to 9:20
P. M. ; Saturday, 10:00 A. M. to 5:00 P. M.   In July and August,
the library is closed on Saturday.

Publications: Notes for Readers; A London Bibliography of the
Social Sciences; A Classified Catalogue of a Collection of Works
on Publishing and Bookselling in the British Library of Political
and Economic Science; Monthly List of Additions (temporarily
suspended in 1975); Interim Checklist of the Publications of
Sidney and Beatrice Webb; Outline of the Resources of the Library.

Duplication: Staff-operated electrostatic copying services during office hours, Monday to Friday, are available.   Coin-
operated machines can also be used whenever the library is
open.   Micro-copying facilities are not available, although arrangements can sometimes be made for material to be copied.

Services: Books do not circulate to non-members.   A professional staff is available to aid researchers in their efforts.   A
cafeteria and coffee shop in the main building are open to permit holders.

LONDON

139   Institution   Marx Memorial Library
      Address   37a Clerkenwell Green, London EC1R 0DU
      Telephone   01-253 1485
      Underground   Farringdon
                        See also: Communist Party, p. 230
      Holdings   16,000 books; 28,000 pamphlets; 500 periodicals;
                        microforms; newspapers

Subject Coverage: The library resources include political science, political theory, economics, and labor history (mainly,
but not exclusively, British).   There is a significant collection
of the works of Marx, Engels, Lenin, and Stalin (including
editions of the collected works of Marx and Engels in German
and Russian and all available English editions).   There are
several important special collections including the J. T. Ber-
nal Peace Library (peace movement material); John William-
son American Library (rare pamphlets of the early American
labor movement); publications of the First, Second, and Third
Internationals; memoirs and autobiographies of labor and socialist leaders and a wide variety of trade union histories.   The
unusual pamphlet collection includes material of the Social-
Democratic Federation, Socialist Labour Party, Workers' Socialist Federation, Communist Party, and Independent Labour
Party.   A large group of works on the International Brigade
in the Spanish Civil War constitutes an almost unique collection.   This material covers the battalions of Great Britain and
other countries.

Access: A visiting scholar must become a full member of the
library to use the resources for research purposes.   A small
entrance fee and a moderate annual subscription are required.
Members have borrowing privileges and may use the reference
material on the premises.   Organizations may become affiliated
members, and those who wish access only to the lending library and current periodicals may become associate members.
Inquiries should be directed to the Librarian.   The hours are
Monday to Friday,   4:00 P. M. to 9:00 P. M.; Saturday, 11:00
A. M. to 1:00 P. M.

Publications: A Quarterly Bulletin is published (which members receive without charge), and catalogs of book holdings
are issued.

Duplication: There are no copying facilities at the library,
but arrangements can be made for full-size copying.   The
cost is high and processing takes about half a day.   In some
circumstances, arrangements can also be made for micro-
copying.

Services: Limited telephone and postal inquiries will be answered, but no extensive research will be undertaken.   Ma-

terial will be loaned to affiliated institutions. Classes, discussions, seminars, and exhibitions are arranged.

LONDON

> Institution   Marylebone Library
>   See: LONDON, Westminster City Libraries
>   (Reference No. 174)

LONDON

140 Institution   Ministry of Defence, Royal United Services In-
>   stitute Library
>   Address   Royal United Services Institute Building, White-
>   hall, London SW1A 2ET
>   Telephone   01-218 5062
>   Underground   Trafalgar Square
>   Holdings   100,000 books; 100 periodicals

Subject Coverage: The library contains resources on the history of British armed services (especially 19th century material), current international affairs, and management. The
special collections include works on modern military strategy
and defense studies and regimental histories.

Access: Visiting scholars are permitted to use the collection.
Inquiries should be directed to the Librarian. A letter of in-
troduction is recommended. The library is open Monday to
Friday, 9:00 A. M. to 5:30 P. M.

Publications: Royal United Services Institute Journal (quarterly); Seminar Reports; Defence Studies (irregular); list of periodical holdings.

Duplication: Full-size copying facilities are available at moderate cost with little delay.

Services: The collection circulates only to members of the
Royal United Services Institute and Ministry of Defence.

LONDON

141 Institution   Ministry of Defence Library, Whitehall Library
>   Address   Old War Office Building, Whitehall, London
>   SW1A 2EU
>   Telephone   01-218 0015
>   Underground   Westminster, Trafalgar Square
>   Holdings   600,000 books, pamphlets, and reports; 1,500
>   periodicals

Subject Coverage: The library is comprised primarily of books on military subjects, including historical, scientific, technical, and administrative aspects. The emphasis is on British and other Commonwealth armies. Drill books and manuals from the 16th century are included. The library also contains British, Indian, and other Commonwealth regimental histories and works on contemporary military affairs in many countries. It holds no original papers.

Access: A letter of introduction is required. Prior application by mail or telephone should be directed to the Chief Librarian. The hours are Monday to Friday, 9:30 A.M. to 5:00 P.M.

Publications: Weekly Selected Accessions; Book List Index (annual with supplements); Technical Books List Index (semiannual); Periodicals List.

Duplication: Full-size copying facilities are available, but restricted. Processing is completed on demand.

Services: The library has both closed and open stacks. The staff will furnish prepared selective lists of books and articles to the scholar when he describes his subject interest. The staff will answer written inquiries about the history of the British Army. Books do not circulate directly, but loans may be requested through public and university libraries and the libraries of learned societies. The library cooperates with the British Library Lending Division.

LONDON

    Institution   Ministry of Health Library
                       See: LONDON, Department of Health and Social Security Library (Reference No. 105)

LONDON

    Institution   Ministry of Housing and Local Government
                       See: LONDON, Department of the Environment Headquarters Library (Reference No. 107)

LONDON

    Institution   Ministry of Labour Library
                       See: LONDON, Department of Employment Library (Reference No. 104)

LONDON

    Institution   Ministry of Overseas Development Library
                     See: LONDON, Foreign and Commonwealth Office Library and Records Department (Reference No. 109)

LONDON

    Institution   Ministry of Overseas Development, Directorate of Overseas Surveys
                     See: SURBITON, Ministry of Overseas Development, Directorate of Overseas Surveys (Reference No. 213)

LONDON

    Institution   Ministry of Public Buildings and Works
                     See: LONDON, Department of the Environment, Property Services Agency Library (Reference No. 106)

LONDON

    Institution   Ministry of Social Security Library
                     See: LONDON, Department of Health and Social Security Library (Reference No. 105)

LONDON

    Institution   Ministry of Transport
                     See: LONDON, Department of the Environment Headquarters Library (Reference No. 107)

LONDON

    Institution   Mocatta Library and Museum
                     See: LONDON, University College London Library (Reference No. 160)

LONDON

    Institution   National Central Library
                     See: LONDON, The British Library (Reference Division) (Reference No. 95)

LONDON

>   Institution   National Lending Library
>   See: LONDON, The British Library (Reference
>   Division) (Reference No. 95)

LONDON

142   Institution   National Liberal Club, Gladstone Library
      Address   Whitehall Place, London SW1A 2HE
      Telephone   01-930 9871
      Underground   Charing Cross Embankment
      Holdings   35, 000 books; 40, 000 pamphlets

Subject Coverage: The library is strong in liberal politics,
with most of the material dating from the last half of the 19th
century.   Much of the pamphlet collection is on permanent
loan to St. Deiniol's Library, Hawarden, Deeside, Flintshire.
The special collections include the Charles Bradlaugh Collection and election addresses of candidates in general elections
from 1892.

Access: Visiting scholars must have a recommendation or permission of the Librarian or a club member to use the collection.   A letter of introduction is advisable.   The hours are
Monday to Saturday, 10:00 A. M. to 10:00 P. M.   (Staff is
available Monday to Friday, 10:00 A. M. to 6:00 P. M. ; Saturday, 10:00 A. M. to 1:00 P. M.)

Publications: Early Railway Pamphlets, 1825 to 1900 (1938);
Gladstone Library Pamphlet Collection.

Duplication: No copying facilities are available in the library.
There are, however, commercial facilities nearby which visiting scholars can use.   Replies to requests received through the
mail might be delayed.

Services: The collection does not circulate.   The library cooperates with the British Library Lending Division.

LONDON

143   Institution   National Maritime Museum Library
      Address   Romney Road, Greenwich, London SE10 9NF
      Telephone   01-858 4422
      Holdings   50, 000 books; 125, 000 pamphlets; 200 periodicals;
                        microforms; press clippings

Subject Coverage: The library contains works on all aspects
of British maritime history in war and peace, but also includes resources about other countries--particularly in cartog-

raphy, navigation, naval history, and merchant shipping. It
holds some rare items, e.g., atlases, signal books, and navi-
gational works. Among the special collections are Lloyd's
Register of Shipping from 1768 and the Styring Collection of
illustrated data on the flags and funnels of British and foreign
ship-owners, the Reynolds Polar Library, the Philip Gosse
Pirate Library, and the Bowen Collection of nautical press
cuttings.

Access: Admission is by ticket. Inquiries should be directed
to the Secretary. A letter of introduction is recommended.
The hours are Monday to Friday, 10:00 A.M. to 1:00 P.M.,
2:00 P.M. to 5:00 P.M. On Saturday, the library is open at
the same time, but a previous appointment is necessary.

Publications: Analytical Printed Catalogue of the Library (in
four parts: Voyages and Travels, Biography, Atlases and
Cartography, and Piracy and Privateering); guides, picture
booklets, color reproductions, and color transparencies.

Duplication: Full-size and micro-copying facilities are available. Photographic copies can also be made, but for color
transparencies and microfilm, a negative must already exist.
Orders for negatives will not be accepted. The cost is moderate, and there is some delay in processing.

Services: The collection can be used only on the premises.
An information index, classified by ships' names, places,
persons, and events in date order, is maintained. This file
contains information not available elsewhere, and serves as a
guide to information in the library.

LONDON

144 Institution   National Monuments Record
     Address   Fortress House, 23 Savile Row, London W1X
                    1AB
     Telephone   01-734 6010
     Underground   Oxford Circus
     Holdings   800,000 photographs; 600,000 photographic nega-
                    tives

Subject Coverage: The resources in the National Monuments
Record consist of photographs and drawings of historic architecture in England. Reproductions of ecclesiastical, domestic,
and civic buildings are included. Information about monuments and buildings from earliest times to 1850 is maintained.
The official lists of buildings of special architectural or historic interest are available for reference.

Access: The National Monuments Record (administered by the
Royal Commission on Historical Monuments, England) is open

to the public. Inquiries should be directed to the Curator.
The hours are Monday to Friday, 10:00 A. M. to 5:30 P. M.

Publications: None.

Duplication: Copies of photographs can be provided when negatives are available.

Services: An index of architectural records in public and
private possession is maintained. The National Monuments
Record cooperates with the British National Book Centre.

LONDON

145 Institution   Office of Population Censuses and Surveys
                     (formerly General Register Office and Govern-
                     ment Social Survey)
     Address   St. Catherines House, 10 Kingsway, London
                     WC2B 6JP
     Telephone   01-242 0262
     Underground   Holborn
     Holdings   Library: 20,000 books; 270 periodicals; Office:
                     records

Subject Coverage: The library holds sets of population census
and vital statistics reports which are complete for the United
Kingdom and comprehensive for Commonwealth and many foreign countries (especially for Europe and the United States).
Other resources include social survey reports; material relating to law, demography, statistical methods, and administration of births, deaths, and marriage registration.

The office contains a central record of all births, deaths, and
marriages registered in England and Wales since 1837. An
index to these records, arranged in alphabetical order within
each quarter of each year, gives in all cases the surname,
forename, place, year, and quarter for each event. In the
case of births, the mother's maiden name is given and in the
case of marriage, the name of both persons being married is
given.

Specific information in the Census of Population (held every
ten years) is kept secret for one hundred years, then deposited
in the Public Record Office. Published census statistics are
available in the library as noted above. Unpublished statistics
may be acquired from Customer Service (Segensworth Road,
Titchfield, Fareham, Hampshire PO15 5RR; telephone: 03294-
42511).

Access: Visiting scholars are permitted to use the library
collection on the premises by arrangement with the Librarian.
The hours for the office Search Room are Monday to Friday,

9:30 A. M. to 4:30 P. M.

The indexes held by the office are available to the public, but
the records themselves are not.   Anyone can, however, acquire a copy of any record he wishes to see.   If he appears
in person, a small fee is charged.   If a postal inquiry is
made, the fee is somewhat higher.   For copies of certificates,
inquiries should be addressed to the Registrar General.   Because of the arrangement of the indexes, specific dates are
needed, and genealogical research is difficult.

Publications: Statistics of population, births, deaths, marriages, divorces, migration, infectious diseases, and morbidity
are published.   Some of these are weekly publications, some
quarterly, and some annual.   A complete list of publications
is found in HMSO Sectional List no. 56.

Duplication: Full-size copying facilities are available.   Service can usually be provided at once, but costs are high.

Services: Inquiries for specific records are handled for a fee.
No extensive searches are undertaken, so a reasonable amount
of information is necessary.   The library will lend material
to other libraries.

LONDON

Institution	The Polish Institute
	See: LONDON, The Polish Library (Reference No. 146)

LONDON

146   Institution   The Polish Library
      Address   9 Princes Garden, London SW7 1QL
      Telephone   01-589 2154
      Underground   South Kensington
                    (Note: the library plans to move to 238-246
                    King Street, London W6 0RF in May, 1976.)
      Holdings   85, 000 books; 10, 000 pamphlets; 400 periodicals;
                    500 manuscripts; maps; 38, 000 photographs;
                    11, 000 bookplates

Subject Coverage: The library contains works in Polish and
other languages and resources on all aspects of Polish affairs.
Some of these were published in Poland.   Among the special
collections are Polish emigré publications and the Lanckoronski
Collection (old Polish books and prints).

The library of the Polish Institute (26/28 Pont Street, London
SW1X 0AB; telephone: 01-584 7399) is separately adminis-

tered and contains a large collection relating to Polish history,
politics, and law.   The Record Department of the institute (20
Princes Gate, London SW7 1PT; telephone: 01-589-9249) contains diplomatic documents relating to the outbreak of World
War II, resources concerning the 1939 September Campaign,
Polish national life in exile, and archival material.   The Sikorski Museum is also located at 20 Princes Gate.

Access: The library is open to the public.   The hours are
Monday, Thursday, 10:00 A. M. to 5:00 P. M. ; Tuesday, Fri-
day, 10:00 A. M. to 8:00 P. M. ; Wednesday, Saturday, 10:00
A. M. to 1:00 P. M.

Publications: Quarterly Books in Polish or Relating to Poland
(list of new acquisitions); Bibliography of Books in Polish or
Relating to Poland, Published Outside Poland Since September,
1939, vols. 1-3 (1953-1966); vols. 4-5 (in preparation); Catalog of Periodicals in Polish or Relating to Poland and Other
Slavonic Countries, Published Outside Poland Since September,
1939, comp. by Maria Danilewiczowa and Barbara Jabłońska,
2d ed. (1971).

Duplication: Facilities for full-size copying are available, but
the cost is high.   Duplication takes a week.

Services: The library cooperates with the British Library
Lending Division.

LONDON

	Institution	Property Services Agency Library
		See: LONDON, Department of the Environment, Property Services Agency Library (Reference No. 106)

LONDON

147	Institution	Public Record Office
	Address	Chancery Lane, London WC2A 1LR
	Telephone	01-405 0741
	Underground	Chancery Lane
		(Note: by 1977, a greater part of the Public Record Office will have been moved to a new building at Ruskin Avenue, Kew, Surrey)
	Holdings	The Public Record Office (PRO) contains millions of documents which presently occupy nearly 400,000 feet of shelves.

Subject Coverage: The documents in the PRO relate to the
actions of the central government and the courts of law of
England and Wales from the Norman Conquest, of Great Brit-

ain from 1707, and of the United Kingdom from 1801.

Access: Admission is by a reader's ticket, valid for five
years. The ticket is issued upon a recommendation from
someone of recognized position to whom the applicant is known
personally, or from a recognized institution (e.g., government
agency, embassy, university). Corporate tickets to representatives of firms or businesses can be made through special
arrangements. Applicants may write ahead for the necessary
forms.

The Search Rooms--consisting of the Round Room, the Rolls
Room, the Long Room, the Census Room, the North Room,
the West Room, and the East Room, and the British Transport
Historical Records at Porchester Road, Paddington--are open
Monday to Friday, 9:30 A.M. to 5:00 P.M. On Saturday, the
Round Room and the Census Room are open 9:30 A.M. to 1:00
P.M. Documents seen in the Round Room must be ordered in
advance if they are to be examined on Saturday. Advance
notice of closing days is given in the Search Rooms. Written
communication should be addressed to the Enquiries Desk
(Requisitions).

Publications: Guide to the Contents of the Public Record Office, which is kept up to date by supplements, is among the
most important of the PRO publications. A list and description
of other publications can be found in HMSO Sectional List no.
24, British National Archives.

Duplication: The Photographic Section of the PRO furnishes
copies of documents by microfilm, Xerox, electro-static prints
from microfilm, and photographic processes. Xerox processing, which is expensive, may take up to one week, depending
upon current demand. The cheapest form of reproduction is
microfilm, but the processing time varies. Three months or
more is the anticipated waiting time for those documents which
have already been microfilmed; six months or more for those
which have not. In addition, the researcher must allow for
transport time.

Services: First-time visitors should go to the Enquiries Desk,
where they will be directed to the appropriate Search Room.
The staff will assist them in a procedure for ordering documents. Requisition forms are provided for this purpose, and
no more than three documents may be ordered at a time without special arrangements. Once these three documents are
delivered, three more may be ordered.

A requisition must be presented before 3:30 P.M. to use a
document on the same day. Requests for Saturday must be
presented before 3:30 P.M. on Friday. A notable exception
is that the PRO records held at the Provincial Repository at
Ashridge require three full days' notice to be received at

Chancery Lane.   Work may be done at Ashridge by prior arrangement.   The time needed for acquiring a record depends
on its location and the pressure for applications.   Under normal circumstances, the waiting time is about one hour.

Delays may be avoided by making requisitions for documents
through the mail.   These requisitions, however, are accepted
only from applicants with a reader's ticket.   Precise references must be quoted.   A maximum of three documents may
be reserved, but only for a few days.   Only pencils may be
used for note-taking.

Not all official records are located at the PRO, since some
have been placed in local repositories.   Some government departments keep their own records which are available for
examination, in particular the Principal Probate Registry,
Somerset House, London WC2R 1LT (which contains registra-
tions of wills) and the Foreign and Commonwealth Office
(which holds the records of the former India Office, including
those of the East India Company and those relating to the Indian Army, now at 197 Blackfriars Road, London SE1 8NG).

Other official documents are held in the following locations:

House of Lords Record Office, London SW1A 0PW (records of
Parliament).

The Scottish Record Office, HM General Register House, Edinburgh EH1 3YY (records of the Kingdom of Scotland to 1707;
legal registers, including testaments; records of the Scottish
courts and departments; records of the Church of Scotland;
certain local records and collections of family muniments).

The General Register Office of Births, Deaths and Marriages
(Scotland), New Register House, Edinburgh EH1 3YT.

The Public Record Office of Northern Ireland, Law Courts
Building, May Street, Belfast (the records of the Northern
Ireland courts and departments, and collections of privately
deposited papers).

The Registrar-General's Office for Northern Ireland, Fer-
managh House, Ormeau Avenue, Belfast (birth, death, and
marriage certificates).

LONDON

      Institution   Queen Mary College Library
                      See: LONDON, University of London, Queen
                      Mary College Library (Reference No. 166)

LONDON

148   Institution   Royal Air Force Museum
      Address   RAF Hendon, Aerodrome Road, London NW9
                       5JA
      Telephone   01-205 2266
      Underground   Colindale
      Holdings   70,000 books; 1,000 pamphlets; 300 periodicals;
                       100,000 photographs; 100,000 archives; films,
                       recordings

Subject Coverage: The library contains works on the history
of British flying services and of British aviation.   The collection includes plans, photographs, films, and recordings.

Access: Visiting scholars are permitted to use the collection
by appointment only.   Inquiries should be addressed to the Director.   A letter of introduction is recommended.   The library
is open Monday to Friday, 10:00 A.M. to 5:00 P.M.

Publications: Occasional Publications are issued by the museum.

Duplication: Full-size and micro-copying facilities are available.   Time necessary for duplication varies.

Services: The collection may only be used on the premises.

LONDON

149   Institution   Royal Anthropological Institute of Great Britain
                       and Ireland
      Address   6 Burlington Gardens, London W1X 2EX
      Telephone   01-734 6370
      Underground   Piccadilly Circus
      Holdings   65,000 books and pamphlets; 678 periodicals

Subject Coverage: The library contains one of the best collections of anthropological literature in the world.   The coverage
is comprehensive.   A notable special collection is the library
of Sir Richard Burton.

Access: The library is open to non-members on the recommendation of a Fellow of the Institute.   A visiting scholar
could then use the library for reference purposes.   The library
is open Monday to Friday, 10:00 A.M. to 4:45 P.M.

Publications: Man, the Journal of the Royal Anthropological Institute (quarterly); Anthropological Index to Current Periodicals
in the Library of the Institute (quarterly index by regions and
subjects); Rain (newsletter); Occasional Papers.

Duplication: Full-size copying facilities are available. The cost is high for non-Fellows.

Services: The library provides no information service. It does, however, cooperate with the British Library Lending Division.

LONDON

150 Institution   Royal Commission on Historical Manuscripts
    Address   Quality House, Quality Court, Chancery Lane,
                    London WC2A 1HP
    Telephone   01-242 1198
    Underground   Chancery Lane
    Holdings   19,000 lists of private archives

Subject Coverage: The purpose of the commission is to advise researchers in history and social science concerning the location of primary sources, other than public records. The commission is probably the most valuable starting point for a scholar who has either a specific group of papers or subject matter to research.

Access: Visiting academics are welcome to use the resources and take advantage of the services of the commission. A letter of introduction is recommended. Written inquiries should be directed to the Secretary. The Search Room is open Monday to Friday, 9:30 A.M. to 5:00 P.M.

Publications: The commission has issued Quinquennial Reports to the Crown by the Commission; Annual Reports of the Secretary to the Commissioners; Lists of Accessions to Repositories; Record Repositories in Great Britain, 5th ed. (1973), and printed reports consisting of lists, calendars, and edited texts. A complete list of publications is found in HMSO Sectional List no. 17.

Duplication: Copying facilities are not available.

Services: The commission determines the location of manuscripts and papers in private hands and of other records of historical importance.

LONDON

    Institution   Royal Holloway College Library
                    See: EGHAM, University of London, Royal Hol-
                    loway College Library (Reference No. 56)

LONDON

151   Institution   Royal Institute of International Affairs Library
      Address   Chatham House, 10 St. James's Square, London
                         SW1 4LE
      Telephone   01-930 2233
      Underground   Piccadilly Circus
                         See also: Royal Institute of International Affairs,
                         p. 240
      Holdings   140,000 books and pamphlets; 645 periodicals;
                         18,000 box files of press clippings

Subject Coverage: The library contains works (in English and
other European languages) on international affairs, concen-
trating on the period since 1945 but with some material for
1918-1945. The Press Library consists of a large archive
of closely classified and cross-referenced newspaper clippings,
taken from a wide range of the world's press in major West
European languages and dealing with most aspects of international affairs. The archive has been maintained since 1924.

Access: The library and Press Library are separate divisions.
Admission to both is by reader's ticket for which a charge is
made. Visiting academics should have some identification and
letter of introduction for admission. The libraries are open
Monday to Friday, 10:00 A.M. to 6:00 P.M. except for the
month of August when they are closed.

Publications: International Affairs (quarterly); World Today
(monthly); British Yearbook of International Law (annual);
monographs.

Duplication: Full-size copying facilities are available.

Services: The library cooperates with the British Library
Lending Division.

LONDON

      Institution   Royal United Services Institute Library
                         See: LONDON, Ministry of Defence (Reference
                         No. 140)

LONDON

      Institution   School of Oriental and African Studies Library
                         See: LONDON, University of London, School of
                         Oriental and African Studies Library (Reference
                         No. 167)

LONDON

Institution   School of Slavonic and East European Studies Library
See: LONDON, University of London, School of Slavonic and East European Studies Library (Reference No. 168)

LONDON

Institution   Senate House Library
See: LONDON, University of London Library (Reference No. 171)

LONDON

Institution   Sikorski Museum
See: LONDON, The Polish Library (Reference No. 146)

LONDON

152 Institution   Sion College Library
     Address   Victoria Embankment, London EC4Y 0DN
     Telephone   01-353 7983
     Underground   Blackfriars
     Holdings   100,000 books and pamphlets; 45 periodicals; 40 manuscripts

Subject Coverage: The library contains resources in the humanities and is strong in Anglican Church history and theology. The special collections include the Port Royal Library and the pamphlet collections of Rev. J. Russell, Rev. W. Scott, and Dr. William Goode.

Access: Visiting scholars are permitted to use the library only for reference purposes. A letter of introduction is recommended. Inquiries should be directed to the Librarian. The library is open Monday to Friday, 10:00 A.M. to 5:00 P.M.

Publications: None.

Duplication: Copying facilities are not available.

Services: The library cooperates with the Association of British Theological and Philosophical Libraries. The collection circulates only to subscribing members.

LONDON

153 Institution   Society of Antiquaries of London Library
     Address   Burlington House, Piccadilly, London W1V 0HS
     Telephones   01-734 0193, 01-437 9954
     Underground   Piccadilly Circus
     Holdings   130,000 books; 15,000 pamphlets; 550 periodicals;
                    300 manuscripts; prints, drawings

Subject Coverage: The library contains works on archaeology,
both British and foreign; resources in history, genealogy, and
heraldry.   There are special collections of manuscripts, early
printed books, broadsides, prints and drawings, and the transactions of British and foreign archaeological societies.   An extensive collection of works by and about William Morris is
held, but prior arrangement must be made to gain access.

Access: Researchers must have a letter of introduction, preferably by a Fellow, to use the collection.   Inquiries should be
directed to the Librarian.   The hours are Monday to Friday,
10:00 A.M. to 5:00 P.M.; Saturday, 10:00 A.M. to 1:00 P.M.

Publications: Archaeologia; Antiquaries Journal; Research Reports.   A list of publications which includes off-prints from
Archaeologia and Antiquaries Journal is available upon request
from the society.

Duplication: Full-size copying facilities are available.   The
cost is high, but duplication service is provided without delay.

Services: The collection does not circulate.   The library cooperates with the British Library Lending Division.

LONDON

     Institution   The Social Security Library
                    See: LONDON, Department of Health and Social
                    Security Library (Reference No. 105)

LONDON

154 Institution   Society of Genealogists
     Address   37 Harrington Gardens, London SW7 4JX
     Telephone   01-373 7054
     Underground   Gloucester Road
     Holdings   books; periodicals; manuscripts; registers

Subject Coverage: The society has the largest collection of
Parish Register copies in the United Kingdom (over 4,000),
including an almost complete series of all that have ever been
printed, besides hundreds in manuscript and typescript which

have been specially copied for the society.   There is a collection of poll books, directories, topographical material, and publications of county records and archaeological societies arranged by counties.   There are other, smaller sections of works dealing with professions, schools and universities, the services, Inns of Court, religious denominations, the peerage and heraldry, and the standard genealogical periodicals.   Collections of material on English persons living abroad--in the Commonwealth and the United States--are also held.   The documents collections, arranged by families and places, fills 1,120 large box files, and there is a general card index of about three million references.   A marriage index of 531 volumes covers parts of sixteen counties, indexes about 2,600 parish registers, and contains about seven million names.

Access: The library is open to members of the society.   Nonmembers may use the library on payment of a search fee.   Inquiries should be addressed to the Librarian.   The hours are Tuesday, Friday, 10:00 A.M. to 6:00 P.M.; Wednesday, Thursday, 10:00 A.M. to 8:00 P.M.; Saturday, 10:00 A.M. to 5:00 P.M.

Publications: Genealogists' Magazine (quarterly).

Duplication: Full-size copying facilities are available at low cost.

Services: The society is able to undertake research for nonmembers for a moderate fee.

LONDON

155   Institution   Statistics and Market Intelligence Library, Department of Industry
      Address   Export House, 50 Ludgate Hill, London EC4M 7HU
      Telephone   01-248 5757, ext. 368
      Underground   Blackfriars, St. Paul's
      Holdings   6,500 statistical serials; 3,000 directories

Subject Coverage: The collection of material to facilitate preliminary desk research on overseas markets includes general statistical compilations and statistics of trade, production, distribution, population, and other economic topics for all countries of the world (retained for fifteen years); regional and international compilations of statistics (from 1946); trade and telephone directories for all countries (current editions only); market surveys; development plans; overseas manufacturers' catalogs.   The library also acts as a national reference library for United Kingdom statistics, and as a referral service to sources of information in the Government Statistical Service. United Kingdom statistics are retained from 1946.

Access: The library is open to the public. Inquiries should be directed to the Librarian. The hours are Monday to Friday, 9:00 A. M. to 5:30 P. M.

Publications: Sources of Statistics (a series of bibliographies); National Statistical Offices of Overseas Countries (a list of addresses).

Duplication: Full-size copying facilities are available at moderate cost. Service can be provided overnight or more rapidly in cases of urgency.

Services: The library maintains good accommodations for readers. Among the services are typing facilities, storage lockers, many foreign language dictionaries, and adequate working space. For those unable to visit the library, the department's Economics and Statistics Division will, whenever possible, extract figures on payment of the cost of the staff time involved.

LONDON

156 Institution   Surrey Record Office and Kingston Borough
                      Muniment Room
     Address   County Hall, Kingston upon Thames, Surrey
                      KT1 2DN
     Telephone   01-546 1050, ext. 3561 (Search Room); ext.
                      3562 (Muniment Room)
     Holdings   books; records; manuscripts; maps

Subject Coverage: The record office contains official records of county and other local administration; private, family, estate, and business papers; Anglican parish registers for the Diocese of Southwark in that part of the ancient county included within the administrative county from 1889 to 1965; some nonconformist church records; tithe maps for the whole county.

The muniment room holds archives of the Royal Borough of Kingston upon Thames.

Access: The record office and muniment room are open to the public. Inquiry should be directed to the County Archivist. The record office is open Monday to Wednesday, Friday, 9:30 A. M. to 4:45 P. M.; Thursday, 1:45 P. M. to 4:45 P. M.; second and fourth Saturday in the month, 9:30 A. M. to 12:30 P. M. (Saturday bookings must be arranged by 12:30 P. M. on the preceding Thursday.) Access to the muniment room is by appointment through the Surrey Record Office. Records required on weekdays should, if possible, be ordered at least one working day in advance. It may not be practicable to produce certain records without notice.

Publications: Royal Borough of Kingston upon Thames: Guide to the Borough Archives (1971).

Duplication: Full-size copying facilities at high cost are available. Photographic services can also be provided.

Services: Records may only be consulted on the premises. Telephone and postal inquiries of a specific nature will be answered.

LONDON

157	Institution	The Times (Archives)
	Address	P.O. Box 7, New Printing House Square, Gray's Inn Road, London WC1X 8EX
	Telephone	01-837 1234
	Underground	Russell Square
	Holdings	microforms; 500 boxes of papers

Subject Coverage: The collection includes information relating to the history of The Times in the context of British social and political life. Private papers, diaries of editors and correspondents, and letters from the Victorian period are included in the collection (dating from 1785). The holdings are strong in British socio-economic matters and in the history of overseas territories.

Access: The archives are open to scholars engaged in advanced research only. A letter of introduction from the home institution is required. A researcher should have knowledge of the history of The Times so that he has some idea of what kind of information the archives may contain. An appointment is required to use the archives, and the hours are Monday to Friday, 11:00 A.M. to 7:00 P.M. Inquiries should be directed to the Archivist.

Publications: None.

Duplication: Full-size copying facilities are available, and processing will be completed quickly. Microfilming can be arranged through a subsidiary company, but orders require up to ten weeks to complete.

Services: Material can be used only on the premises.

LONDON

	Institution	Tower Hamlets Library
		See: LONDON, London Borough of Tower Hamlets Libraries Department (Reference No. 136)

LONDON

158   Institution   Trades Union Congress Library
      Address   Congress House, Great Russell Street, London
                       WC1B 3LS
      Telephone   01-636 4030
      Underground   Tottenham Court Road
      Holdings   1,000 books; pamphlets; 800 periodicals; micro-
                       forms; newspapers

Subject Coverage: The library includes resources in the history of trade unions, economics, labor history, and trade
unionism. An important special collection is the Gertrude
Tuckwell Collection, which contains material relating to the
problems of women in trade unions and labor during the period
of World War I.

Access: Visiting academics are permitted to use the collection
on the premises. A letter of introduction is recommended, and
an advance appointment is essential. Inquiries should be directed to the Librarian. The hours are Monday to Friday,
9:30 A.M. to 5:15 P.M.

Publications: The TUC publishes an Annual Report, Annual
Congress Proceedings, monographs, and pamphlets.

Duplication: No copying facilities are available.

Services: The collection does not circulate. Only duplicate
material will be lent to other libraries. Telephone and postal
inquiries will be answered, but no extensive research will be
undertaken.

LONDON

159   Institution   Treasury and Cabinet Office Library
      Address   Parliament Street, London SW1P 3AG
      Telephone   01-930 1234
      Underground   Westminster
      Holdings   65,000 books and pamphlets; 250 periodicals;
                       prints

Subject Coverage: The library contains works in general
economics (including public and private finance, and trade and
industry), history of World War II, biographies of statesmen,
Parliamentary Papers from 1881, and the Lister Collection of
prints illustrating the history of Whitehall.

Access: Accredited researchers may use the library by advance appointment with the Librarian. The hours are Monday
to Friday, 9:30 A.M. to 5:30 P.M.

Publications: The library issues only accessions lists intended
for internal use.

Duplication: No copying facilities are available.

Services: The library is designed primarily to provide library
and information service for Treasury and Cabinet Office officials. It cooperates with Aslib and the British Library Lending Division.

LONDON

160   Institution   University College London Library
       Address   Gower Street, London WC1E 6BT
       Telephone   01-387 7050
       Underground   Warren Street
       Holdings   804,000 books; 8,150 periodicals

Subject Coverage: The working collections in American, Latin-
American, and London history; Egyptology; Roman law; and
Scandinavian studies are particularly strong. The major spe-
cial collections are Barlow Dante Library; Graves Early Sci-
ence Library; Johnston Lavis Vulcanology Library; Whitley
Stokes Celtic Library; Library of C. K. Ogden; Library of
Sir John Rotton; Hume Tracts; Lansdowne and Halifax Tracts;
James Joyce Collection; George Orwell Archive; Little Magazines Collection; Parliamentary Papers, 1735-1850. The
major manuscript collections are Jeremy Bentham; Henry
Peter, First Baron Brougham and Vaux; Sir Edwin Chadwick;
Moses Gaster; Latin-American Business Archives; Society for
the Diffusion of Useful Knowledge; manuscripts relating to University College and its members. The library is a depository
for the Bibliographical Society; Folklore Society; Gaelic Society of London; Geologists' Association; Hertfordshire Natural
History Society and Field Club; Huguenot Society; London
Mathematical Society; Malacological Society; Mocatta Library
of Anglo-Judaica; Norwegian Embassy; Royal Historical Society; Viking Society for Northern Research.

Access: The library is open to visiting scholars with permission of the Librarian. A letter of introduction is necessary. During the academic year, the library is open Monday
to Friday, 9:30 A. M. to 9:00 P. M.; Saturday, 9:30 A. M. to
12:30 P. M. During vacation, the hours are Monday to Friday, 9:30 A. M. to 5:00 P. M. The library is closed when
the college as a whole is closed. Applications to use the libraries of societies must be made to the societies.

Publications: Many of the learned societies whose collections
are housed in the University College Library issue publications. Among these are the following: Mocatta--Magna
Bibliotheca Anglo-Judaica, by C. Roth (1937); Nova Bibliothe-

ca Anglo-Judaica, by R. P. Lehmann (1961). Bibliographical
Society--The Library (quarterly) and annual monographs on
bibliographical subjects. Folklore Society--Folklore (quarterly)
and monographs on subjects in the field of folklore. Huguenot
Society--Proceedings and Quarto Series. Philological Society--
Transactions of the Philological Society (annual) and special
publications (irregular). For information regarding the publications of the Royal Historical Society, application should be
addressed to the Secretary of the society.

Duplication: Full-size and micro-copying facilities are available. Photographic processes are also provided.

Services: The library lends to members of University College,
members of the learned societies whose libraries are deposited
in the University College Library, and other persons who have
received permission from the Librarian.

LONDON

161 Institution   University of London, Bedford College Library
     Address   Regent's Park, London NW1 4NS
     Telephone   01-486 4400
     Underground   Baker Street
     Holdings   200,000 books and pamphlets; 1,000 periodicals

Subject Coverage: The library is strong in sociology and social
administration with some coverage of law, anthropology, and
economics. It has holdings in British medieval history and
politics; 18th and 19th century church history.

Access: Visiting scholars are welcome to use the collection
for reference purposes. Inquiries should be directed to the
Librarian. During the academic year, the library is open
Monday to Friday, 9:00 A.M. to 9:00 P.M.; Saturday, 9:00
A.M. to 1:00 P.M. During vacation, the hours are Monday
to Friday, 9:00 A.M. to 5:00 P.M.; Saturday, 9:00 A.M. to
1:00 P.M. The exceptions are the Easter vacation when it
remains open until 6:00 P.M. and August, when it is closed
on Saturday.

Publications: None.

Duplication: Full-size copying facilities are available at low
cost.

Services: The library cooperates with the British Library
Lending Division.

LONDON

162   Institution   University of London, Birkbeck College Library
     Address   Malet Street, London WC1E 7HX (Main Library)
     Telephone   01-580 6622, ext. 239
     Underground Goodge Street

     Address   7-15 Gresse Street, London W1P 1PA (Gresse
                      Street Library)
     Telephone   01-580 6622, ext. 492
     Underground Euston Square

     Address   Ormond, House, Boswell Street, Queen Square,
                      London WC1N 3JZ (Mathematics and Statistics
                      Library)
     Telephones   01-580 6622, ext. 740, 01-242 5816
     Underground Russell Square

     Holdings   152,000 books; 1,282 periodicals; microforms

Subject Coverage: The library has holdings in medieval English and European history; history of art; English shipping history in the 15th and 16th centuries; historical geography and cartography; 19th and 20th century social and economic history; economics; sociology; politics; geography; history; psychology; occupational psychology; statistics and philosophy.

Access: The library is open to qualified researchers with permission of the Librarian. Written application should be made in advance. The library collection is not held together as a unit, but is found in three locations (see above). Much of the social science material is at the Gresse Street address. During the academic year, the Main Library is open Monday to Friday, 10:00 A.M. to 10:30 P.M.; Saturday, 10:00 A.M. to 5:00 P.M. During Christmas and summer vacations, the hours are Monday to Friday, 10:00 A.M. to 8:00 P.M. and during Easter vacation, Monday to Friday, 10:00 A.M. to 9:00 P.M.; Saturday, 10:00 A.M. to 5:00 P.M. The hours of the Gresse Street Library are Monday to Friday, 10:00 A.M. to 9:30 P.M.; Saturday, 10:00 A.M. to 5:00 P.M. during the academic year. During Christmas and summer vacation, the hours are Monday to Friday, 10:00 A.M. to 8:00 P.M. During the Easter holiday, the hours are Monday to Friday, 10:00 A.M. to 8:00 P.M.; Saturday, 10:00 A.M. to 5:00 P.M. During the academic year, the Mathematics and Statistics Library is open Monday to Friday, 10:30 A.M. to 1:00 P.M., 2:00 P.M. to 9:00 P.M. During Christmas and summer vacations, the hours are Monday to Friday, 10:30 A.M. to 1:00 P.M., 2:00 P.M. to 5:00 P.M. During Easter vacation, the hours are Monday to Friday, 10:30 A.M. to 1:00 P.M., 2:00 P.M. to 7:00 P.M.

Publications: The library issues handlists of holdings on specific subjects.

Duplication: Full-size copying facilities are available at low cost.

Services: The library cooperates with the British Library Lending Division. Books do not circulate to non-members of the university.

LONDON

163	Institution	University of London, Institute of Advanced Legal Studies Library
	Address	25 Russell Square, London WC1B 5DR
	Telephone	01-580 4868
	Underground	Russell Square
	Holdings	120,000 books; 2,000 periodicals; microforms

Subject Coverage: The library holds a comprehensive collection of legal works, with special emphasis on English law, Commonwealth law, United States law, Latin American law, and West European law. It has holdings in comparative and international law, but is not strong in East European and Oriental law.

Access: Visitors undertaking advanced research are admitted with permission of the Director. A letter of introduction is recommended. The library is open Monday to Thursday, 10:00 A.M. to 8:00 P.M.; Friday, 10:00 A.M. to 5:30 P.M.; Saturday, 10:00 A.M. to 12:30 P.M.

Publications: List of Current Legal Research Topics (annual); List of Official Committees, Commissions and Other Bodies Concerned with the Reform of the Law (irregular); Union List of Legal Periodicals: A Location Guide to Holdings of Legal Periodicals in Libraries in the United Kingdom, 3d ed. (1968); Union List of Commonwealth and South African Law; Location Guide to Commonwealth and South African Legislation; Law Reports and Digests Held by Libraries in the United Kingdom at May 1963 (1963); Union List of United States Law Literature in Libraries in Oxford, Cambridge and London, 2d ed. (1967); Union List of West European Legal Literature: Publications Held by Libraries in Oxford, Cambridge and London (1966); Union List of Air and Space Law, 2d ed. (1975); A Manual of Legal Citations, pt. 1: The British Isles (1959); pt. 2: The Commonwealth (1960); A Bibliographical Guide to the Law of the United Kingdom, the Channel Islands and the Isle of Man, 2d ed. (1973); Index to Foreign Legal Periodicals (quarterly).

Duplication: Full-size copying facilities are available, but the costs are high.

Services: The library cooperates with the British Library Lending Division.

LONDON

164   Institution   University of London, Institute of Historical Re-
                        search
      Address   Senate House, London WC1E 7HU
      Telephone   01-636 0272/3
      Underground   Russell Square, Goodge Street
      Holdings   115,000 books and pamphlets; 650 periodicals

Subject Coverage: The institute is the University of London's center for post-graduate work in history. It consists of a series of seminar libraries with books containing or describing the main sources of medieval and modern history. The seminar libraries are principally concerned with the history of Europe, the Commonwealth, the Americas, international relations, and war. The collection is particularly rich in bibliographies, guides to archives, printed sources, reference works, and periodicals.

Access: Admission is available for visiting academics. Applicants may write ahead to the Secretary. A letter of introduction from an academic or research institution is required. The institute is normally open Monday to Friday, 9:00 A.M. to 9:00 P.M.; Saturday, 9:00 A.M. to 5:00 P.M. In August, the closing time is 7:00 P.M. (Saturday, 5:00 P.M.).

Publications: Bulletin of the Institute of Historical Research (bi-annual); Historical Research for University Degrees in the United Kingdom (annual); Teachers of History in the Universities of the United Kingdom (annual) constitute the serial publications of the institute. Two bibliographical series are published by the institute: Writings on British History (formerly published by Jonathan Cape for the Royal Historical Society) which lists exhaustively books and periodical articles, wherever published, on British history, and Bibliography of Historical Works Issued in the United Kingdom, which is published every five years and is not limited to British history but only includes books first published in the United Kingdom. Other series include Fasti Ecclesiae Anglicanae (Athlone Press for the institute) which lists, diocese by diocese, higher church dignitaries, and Office-Holders in Modern Britain (Athlone Press for the institute) which lists officials holding office in the departments of central government. By far the largest publication is Victoria History of the Counties of England (Oxford University Press for the institute) of which 160 volumes have so far appeared. Other publications include Victoria His-

tory of the Counties of England: Handbook for Editors and
Authors, 2d ed. rev., ed. by C. R. Elmington (1970) and
Registers of the Universities, Colleges and Schools of Great
Britain and Ireland: A List, by P. M. Jacobs (reprinted
from Bulletin, November, 1964).

Duplication: Photocopying facilities are available. The costs
are moderate, and processing is efficient.

Services: Books may be retrieved from the shelves by the researcher, hence little time is wasted in gathering material.
Books are never issued on loan and must be returned to the
shelves at the end of each day. Staff members are available
to show visitors around the institute. Typewriters may only
be used in the Upper Hall and the Asia Room on the third
floor. Coffee is available in the morning, and tea is served
in the Common Room between 4:00 and 5:15 P. M. every day
except Saturday.

LONDON

165 Institution   University of London, King's College Library
     Address   Strand, London WC2R 2LS
     Telephone   01-836 5454
     Underground   Temple, Aldwych
     Holdings   350,000 books; 12,750 pamphlets; 2,250 peri-
                       odicals; microforms; archives

Subject Coverage: The library covers all subjects taught in
the college, which has eight faculties including Arts, Education, Law, and Theology. It is especially strong in theology
and ecclesiastical history, imperial history, Byzantine and
Modern Greek studies, Portuguese (including Brazilian studies),
Spanish (including Spanish-American studies), and war studies.
It includes the Liddell Hart Centre for Military Archives (private papers relating to military affairs of the 20th century).
Among the special collections are Marsden (philology, travel,
etc.) and Prestage (Portuguese, especially Portuguese colonial
history).

Access: Visiting scholars will be admitted to the library with
permission of the Librarian. A letter of recommendation is
required. The library is open during the academic year Monday to Friday, 9:30 A. M. to 8:45 P. M. ; Saturday, 9:30 A. M.
to 12:45 P. M. During short vacations, it is open Monday to
Friday, 9:30 A. M. to 4:30 P. M. ; Saturday, 9:30 A. M. to
12:00 noon. During summer vacation, the library is closed
on Saturday.

Publications: None.

Duplication: Full-size copying facilities are available.

Services: The library cooperates with the British Library
Lending Division.

LONDON

166   Institution   University of London, Queen Mary College Li-
                       brary
      Address   Mile End Road, London E1 4NS
      Telephone   01-980 4811
      Underground   Mile End, Stepney Green
      Holdings   210,000 books; 2,100 periodicals; microforms

Subject Coverage: The library supports the faculties of the
college. It has works in history, economics, law, geography,
and a growing collection in credit law and European Community law. The library is a European Documentation Centre,
receiving all the European Communities publications and has a
background collection on the European Communities. The library holds the Webster Library of International History (a collection of 19th and 20th century diplomatic history and international relations which belonged to Sir Charles Webster).

Access: Visiting scholars will be permitted to use the collection with the permission of the Librarian. A letter of introduction is recommended. During the academic year, the library is open Monday to Friday, 9:15 A.M. to 9:30 P.M.;
Saturday, 10:00 A.M. to 6:00 P.M. During the Easter vacation, the hours are Monday to Friday, 9:15 A.M. to 9:30 P.M.
During Christmas and summer vacation, the hours are Monday
to Friday, 9:15 A.M. to 5:00 P.M.

Publications: The library issues regular accessions lists and
Guide to the Documentation Centre.

Duplication: Facilities for full-size copying are available.

Services: The library cooperates with the British Library
Lending Division.

LONDON

      Institution   University of London, Royal Holloway College
                       Library
                       See: EGHAM, University of London, Royal Hol-
                       loway College Library (Reference No. 56)

LONDON

167   Institution   University of London, School of Oriental and
                       African Studies Library

Address   Malet Street, London WC1E 7HP
Telephone   01-637 2388
Underground   Russell Square, Goodge Street
Holdings   420, 000 books and pamphlets; 2, 000 periodicals;
               40, 000 microforms; 2, 000 manuscripts

Subject Coverage: The library contains resources in all languages for humanities and social sciences relating to Asia and
Africa.

Access: The library is open to the public. Inquiries should
be directed to the Librarian. During the academic year, the
library is open Monday to Friday, 9:00 A. M. to 8:30 P. M. ;
Saturday, 9:30 A. M. to 12:30 P. M. During vacation, the library is open Monday to Friday, 9:00 A. M. to 5:00 P. M. ;
Saturday, 9:30 A. M. to 12:30 P. M.

Publications: Library Catalogue (1963); First Supplement
(1969); Second Supplement (1974); Library Guide, 2d ed.
(1972); List of Titles Added to the Catalogue (monthly).

Duplication: Full-size and micro-copying facilities are available.

Services: The library houses the Union Catalogue of Asian
publications. It acts as an interlending center for Asian material in the United Kingdom.

LONDON

168 Institution   University of London, School of Slavonic and
                      East European Studies Library
     Address   Senate House, Malet Street, London WC1E 7HU
     Telephone   01-637 4934/0
     Underground   Russell Square, Goodge Street
     Holdings   180, 000 books and pamphlets; 1, 000 periodicals

Subject Coverage: The library contains works on the history,
language, and literature of Russia, Finland, and the countries
of eastern and south-eastern Europe. Among the special collections are the Marsden, Barton, Gaster, and Iványi.

Access: Reading facilities are limited for non-members of the
university to evenings and Saturday mornings during the academic year. During vacation, the library is open to the public without restriction. The hours are Monday to Friday,
10:00 A. M. to 7:00 P. M. ; Saturday, 10:00 A. M. to 1:00 P. M.
during the academic year. During summer vacation, the library is open Monday to Friday, 10:00 A. M. to 6:00 P. M.
Inquiries should be directed to the Librarian.

Publications: Slavonic and East European Review; The Haps-

burg Monarchy, 1804-1918; Books and Pamphlets Published in
the United Kingdom Between 1818 and 1967: A Critical Bibliography, by F. R. Bridge (1967).

Duplication: Full-size copying facilities (self-service) are
available. Arrangements for other copying can be made with
the University of London Library.

Services: The collection does not circulate to non-members
of the school.

LONDON

169   Institution   University of London, Warburg Institute Library
      Address   Woburn Square, London WC1H 0AB
      Telephone   01-580 9663
      Underground   Russell Square, Euston Square
      Holdings   180,000 books; 1,000 periodicals; microforms

Subject Coverage: The library holds works concerned with the
history of the classical tradition.

Access: The library is open to non-members of the university
with special permission. Inquiries should be made to the Librarian. The library is open Monday to Friday, 10:00 A.M.
to 6:00 P.M.; Saturday, 10:00 A.M. to 1:00 P.M. (and is
closed on Saturday during August and September).

Publications: Warburg Institute Studies; Journal of the Warburg and Courtauld Institutes; Corpus Platonicum Medii Aevi;
Mediaeval and Renaissance Studies; Warburg Institute Surveys; Oxford-Warburg Studies.

Duplication: Limited full-size copying facilities are available
at moderately high cost. Micro-copying can be arranged at
moderate cost. The library reserves the right to refuse to
photocopy material which is easily available in other libraries.

Services: The library cooperates with the British Library
Lending Division.

LONDON

170   Institution   University of London, Westfield College Library
      Address   Kidderpore Avenue, London NW3 7ST
      Telephone   01-435 7141
      Underground   Finchley Road
      Holdings   113,000 books; 6,000 pamphlets; 700 periodicals

Subject Coverage: The library contains little of interest to the
social scientist. It does, however, hold the Lyttleton Letters

(19th and early 20th centuries).

Access: The library is open to the public. The hours are Monday to Friday, 9:00 A.M. to 9:00 P.M.; Saturday, 9:00 A.M. to 5:00 P.M. during the academic year. During vacations, the hours are Monday to Friday, 9:00 A.M. to 5:00 P.M.

Publications: Inaugural Lectures and Annual Reports of the college.

Duplication: Full-size and micro-copying facilities are available.

Services: The library cooperates with the British Library Lending Division.

LONDON

171 Institution   University of London Library
     Address   Senate House, Malet Street, London WC1E 7HU
     Telephone   01-636 4514
     Underground   Russell Square, Goodge Street, Tottenham Court Road
     Holdings   1,000,000 books and pamphlets; 6,000 periodicals; microforms; newspapers; 42,000 maps

Subject Coverage: The library contains resources covering economics, history, bibliography, politics, geography and maps, British Government publications, psychology, and archaeology. There are many special collections which render the library a valuable resource for social scientists. Among these are Goldsmiths' Library (early economic literature); Bromhead Library (books on London); United States Library; Belgian Library; Quick Memorial Library (early education); Fuller Collection (seals); and the Family Welfare Association Library.

Access: Full facilities are available to members of the university only. Visiting academics can use the reference facilities at the discretion of the Director of Central Library Services. At certain times of the year, visitors may find that they are permitted to use the library only after 5:30 P.M. and on Saturday. Inquiries should be addressed to the Director. A letter of introduction is recommended. During the academic year, the library is open Monday to Friday, 9:30 A.M. to 9:00 P.M.; Saturday and summer vacation, 9:30 A.M. to 5:30 P.M.

Publications: Catalogue of the Palaeography Collection (Boston: G. K. Hall, 1969); Union List of Periodicals in the Romance Languages and Literature (1964); List of Current

Periodicals in the Library; Catalogue of the Goldsmiths' Library (Cambridge University Press, vol. 1 [1970], vol. 2 [1975], vol. 3 [in preparation]); Annual Report; List of Theses and Dissertations (annual); Occasional Subject Lists of Periodicals and Special Collections.

Duplication: Full-size copying and micro-copying facilities are available. Self-service machines for full-size copying are provided at moderate cost.

Services: The library cooperates with the British Library Lending Division. Books do not normally circulate to non-members of the university.

LONDON

Institution   Victoria District Library
                     See: LONDON, Westminster City Libraries
                     (Reference No. 174)

LONDON

Institution   Warburg Institute Library
                     See: LONDON, University of London, Warburg
                     Institute Library (Reference No. 169)

LONDON

172   Institution   Wellcome Institute for the History of Medicine
                     Library
      Address   183 Euston Road, London NW1 2BP
      Telephone   01-387 4477
      Underground   Euston, Euston Square, Warren Street
      Holdings   350,000 books; pamphlets; 250 periodicals;
                     10,000 manuscripts

Subject Coverage: The library resources concentrate mainly on the history of medicine and allied sciences. The special collections include Western and Oriental manuscripts, Latin American Collection, and autograph letters.

Access: The library is open to bona fide students. Inquiries should be directed to the Librarian. The library is open Monday to Friday, 9:45 A.M. to 5:15 P.M.

Publications: Current Work in the History of Medicine (quarterly); Medical History (quarterly); Catalogue Series; Historical Monographs Series; Lecture Series; Exhibition Catalogues and postcards.

Duplication: Full-size and micro-copying facilities are available at moderate cost. Forms are provided and must be signed to obtain copies of material in the library.

Services: Duplicate reference books are lent to libraries or regional bureaus.

LONDON

Institution	Westfield College Library
	See: LONDON, University of London, Westfield College Library (Reference No. 170)

LONDON

173	Institution	Westminster Abbey, Muniment Room and Library
	Address	London SW1P 3PA
	Telephone	01-222 4233
	Underground	Westminster, St. James's Park
	Holdings	14,000 books; microforms; manuscripts

Subject Coverage: The library has works on the history and buildings of Westminster Abbey and its estates from A.D. 784; law, history, and theology. It also holds early music books dating from the 16th century and a few incunabula; photographs, prints, and drawings of Westminster Abbey.

Access: Westminster Abbey Muniment Room and Library are open to visiting scholars on written application and by appointment only. Inquiries should be addressed to the Keeper of the Muniments. The hours are Monday to Friday, 10:00 A.M. to 1:00 P.M., 2:00 P.M. to 4:30 P.M.

Publications: The Transactions of the Royal Historical Society, 4th series, vol. 19 (1936) gives a description of the muniments.

Duplication: Full-size copying services are provided on demand. Micro-copying orders must be processed elsewhere and may require a period of several weeks.

Services: The library contains an ultra-violet lamp for reading manuscripts. Photographs of manuscripts and printed books are provided.

LONDON

174	Institution	Westminster City Libraries, Public Library
	Address	Marylebone Road, London NW1 5PS
	Telephone	01-828 8070, ext. 4025

Underground   Baker Street, Marylebone

                              (Note: this collection is not held together as a
                              unit but is scattered among several branches.
                              Those of interest to the social scientist are
                              Central Reference Library [St. Martin's Street,
                              London WC2H 7HP; telephone: 01-930 3274;
                              underground: Trafalgar Square]; the Victoria
                              District Library [Buckingham Palace Road, Lon-
                              don SW1W 9UD; telephone: 01-730 0446; under-
                              ground: Victoria]; and Marylebone Library
                              [Marylebone Road].)

Holdings   1, 927, 000 books and other materials, of which
                              the Central Reference Library contains: 448, 000
                              books; 1, 195 periodicals; 54, 000 microforms;
                              25, 000 maps.
                              Victoria District Library contains: 126, 000
                              books; 135, 000 archives

Subject Coverage: The Central Reference Library houses
publications of learned societies and the Public Record Office,
all HMSO publications since 1947, and an almost complete set
of Parliamentary Papers from 1826.   It is a depository library for publications of the European Communities.   It contains a wide range of author and subject bibliographies, foreign language dictionaries, biographical dictionaries, abstracts,
and indexes.

Victoria District Library maintains a local history collection
and is an archives repository for the City of Westminster.
Also included in this collection are parish registers, the
Gillow Archives, and other business and estate records.

Marylebone Library also maintains a local history collection
and is a repository for the archives of Paddington and St.
Marylebone; the Ashridge Collection (local topography), and
the Sherlock Holmes Collection.

Access: Visiting scholars are welcome to use the library for
reference purposes.   Lending services are available to those
resident, employed, or attending educational institutions in the
City on application to the Librarian.   The library accepts all
other tickets.   The hours are as follows: Central Reference
Library, Monday to Friday, 10:00 A. M. to 7:00 P. M. ; Saturday, 10:00 A. M. to 5:00 P. M. ; District Libraries, Monday
to Friday, 9:30 A. M. to 7:00 P. M. ; Saturday, 9:30 A. M. to
5:00 P. M.

Publications: Printed Catalogue of Books and Pamphlets
Added to the Libraries of the Former City of Westminster,
1952-1964; Union List of Periodicals Held by Westminster
City Libraries; Catalogue of the Preston "Blake" Library;

Eight Views of Westminster.

Duplication: Full-size copying facilities are available at the Central Reference Library, Marylebone and Victoria District Libraries at a moderately high cost. Copies are normally provided at the time of request.

Services: Reference books do not circulate.

LONDON

> Institution   Wiener Library
>   See: LONDON, Institute of Contemporary History and Wiener Library (Reference No. 127)

MAIDSTONE

175 Institution   Kent Archives Office
    Address   County Hall, Maidstone, Kent ME14 1XQ
    Telephone   0622-54321
    Holdings   books; pamphlets; periodicals; microforms; 7,000,000 records; topographical prints

Subject Coverage: The office contains official records of the County Council, Quarter Sessions of some borough and district councils, and Boards of Guardians. There are some parish records, some tithe maps, probate records, and records of the Dean and Chapter of Rochester. It also holds unofficial estate and family records.

Access: The office is open to the public. Inquiries should be directed to the Keeper of the Records. An appointment is advisable. The hours are Monday to Friday, 9:00 A.M. to 4:30 P.M.

Publications: Guide to the Kent County Archives Office, ed. by Felix Hull (1958); First Supplement, 1957-1968, ed. by Felix Hull (1971); Handlist of Kent County Council Records, 1889-1945, by Felix Hull; Catalogue of Estate Maps, 1590-1840, ed. by Felix Hull (1974); Kentish Maps and Map-Makers, 1590-1840, ed. by Felix Hull (1974); selected studies of the archives.

Duplication: Full-size copying facilities are available. Limited arrangements can be made with outside firms for photographs and microfilms.

Services: Short searches in connection with postal and telephone inquiries will be made. No material is available on loan.

MANCHESTER

176   Institution   Co-operative Union Library
       Address   Holyoake House, Hanover Street, Manchester
                        M6O 0AS
       Telephone   061-834 0975
       Holdings   10,000 books; 5,000 pamphlets; 100 periodicals;
                        manuscripts; newspapers

Subject Coverage: Information on the co-operative movement
in Britain and elsewhere is found in this library. It is strong
in co-operative history and is a center for foreigners seeking
information about the co-operative movement. The library
contains collections of Robert Owen, George Jacob Holyoake,
and Edward Owen Greening.

Access: Admission is granted to personnel of co-operative
organizations, and to research workers, scholars, and students wishing to use the material. The library is open Monday to Friday, 10:00 A.M. to 5:00 P.M.

Publications: Accessions Lists; Checklists of Historical
Printed Books; Checklists of Periodicals.

Duplication: Copies of documents can be provided on request.
Photostat equipment is available.

Services: The library is a member of International Co-operative Alliance Working Party of Librarians. There is staff
available to assist researchers working on questions concerning the co-operative movement. Information is given by telephone or mail. Book loans can sometimes be arranged.

MANCHESTER

177   Institution   John Rylands University Library of Manchester
       Address   Oxford Road, Manchester M13 9PL
       Telephone   061-273 3333
       Holdings   2,000,000 books; 250,000 pamphlets; 10,000
                        periodicals; 400,000 microforms; 750,000 manu-
                        scripts

Subject Coverage: The library is a merger between the John
Rylands Library and The University of Manchester Library.
It is strong in 18th and 19th century French history, English
local history, the Middle Ages, British railway history, history of medicine, classical Renaissance of Italy and France,
and history of the United States. It also contains manuscripts,
papyri (Egyptian, Coptic, Arabic, Greek, and Latin), and
Aldine Press books. The manuscripts are in fifty-three different languages and contain 750,000 family and business records. Among the special collections are: Bullock (16th cen-

tury Italian books), Arnold Library on Roman history, the
Hager Memorial Library on Greek law and Teutonic philology,
the Jevons Collection on economics, the Muirhead Library on
law, and the Partington Collection of history of chemistry.

Access: A reader's ticket, which must be obtained in advance
from the Librarian, is required to use the collection.   During
the academic year, the library is open Monday to Friday,
9:00 A. M. to 9:30 P. M. ; Saturday, 9:30 A. M. to 1:00 P. M.
During vacation, the hours are Monday to Friday, 9:30 A. M.
to 5:30 P. M. ; Saturday, 9:30 A. M. to 1:00 P. M. (but closed
Saturday in the summer vacation).

Publications: Catalogue of the Christie Collection (1915);
Bulletin of the John Rylands Library (semi-annual); Annual
Report; Accessions Lists; Latin Manuscripts, by M. R. James
(1921); Arabic Manuscripts, by A. Mingana (1934); Catalogues,
Printed Books and Manuscripts, 3 vols. (1899); English Incunabula (1930); English Books to 1650 (1895); English Bible,
by R. Lovett (1899); Arabic Papyri, by D. S. Margoliouth
(1933); and Domotio Papyri, 3 vols., by F. L. Griffiths
(1909).

Duplication: Full-size copies and micro-copies are available
at high cost.   The time necessary for duplication varies from
one week onward, depending on the nature of the request.

Services: Books do not circulate to non-members of the university.   Inquiries can be made by telephone or mail.   The
library is an approved borrower of the British Library Lending Division.

MANCHESTER

178   Institution   Manchester Public Libraries
      Address   Central Library, St. Peter's Square, Man-
                      chester M2 5PD
      Telephone   061-236 9422
      Holdings   1, 926, 780 books; 4, 500 periodicals; microforms;
                      prints, illustrations

Subject Coverage: The library contains a wide spectrum of
material including strong holdings in the social sciences.
Among the many important special collections are Crofton
manuscripts; European Common Market; Farrer deeds and
manuscripts; Thomas Greenwood; Hampden Club Papers;
Jewish Collection; Neville Laski Collection; Manchester Cham-
ber of Commerce Archives; Manchester Regiment Records;
private press books; and Wilson papers.   In addition, many
learned societies have deposited their libraries here.

Access: The library is divided into subject departments.

Scholars are welcome to use the collection.   Inquiries should
be made to the Director of Libraries.   The hours are Monday
to Friday, 9:00 A. M. to 9:00 P. M.; Saturday, 9:00 A. M. to
5:00 P. M. except the General Readers' Library which is open
Monday to Friday, 9:00 A. M. to 8:00 P. M.; Saturday, 9:00
A. M. to 5:00 P. M.

Publications: Manchester Review (irregular); Annual Report;
The Local History Library: A Guide to its Resources; Commercial Information: A Guide to the Commercial Library are
among the many publications issued by the library and its departments.

Duplication: Full-size and micro-copying facilities are available.

Services: Readers holding tickets of any library authority in
the United Kingdom are allowed to borrow books.

MATLOCK

179   Institution   Derbyshire Record Office
      Address   County Offices, Matlock, Derbyshire DE4 3AG
      Telephone   0629-3411, ext. 7327
      Holdings   books; records; maps

Subject Coverage: The collection includes official records of
the county; parish and poor relief records; family and estate
papers; business records (including lead and coal mining); and
maps.

Access: The office is open to the public.   Inquiries should
be directed to the Archivist.   The hours are Monday to Friday, 9:30 A. M. to 1:00 P. M. , 2:00 P. M. to 4:45 P. M.

Publications: Annual reports are found in the Derbyshire
Archaeological Journal (1962-   ); Report of the Archivist,
1962-1973 (1974).

Duplication: Full-size copying facilities are available.   Photography by searchers is permitted.

Services: Postal inquiries about material available on specific
subjects are answered.   The material can be used only on the
premises.

NEWCASTLE UPON TYNE

180   Institution   The Literary and Philosophical Society of New-
                         castle upon Tyne
      Address   Newcastle upon Tyne NE1 1SE

Telephone   0632-20192
Holdings   100, 000 books; 400 periodicals

Subject Coverage: The library is strongest in history, bi-
ography, local history, and topography. The counties of
Northumberland and Durham and the city of Newcastle upon
Tyne are covered.

Access: Scholars are permitted to use the collection for reference by appointment only. Inquiries should be directed to
the Librarian. A letter of introduction is recommended.

Publications: Annual Report; Occasional Papers.

Duplication: No copying facilities are available.

Services: The collection circulates to members only.

NEWCASTLE UPON TYNE

181 Institution   Newcastle upon Tyne City Libraries
     Address   Central Library, P. O. Box 1 MC, New Bridge
                      Street, Newcastle upon Tyne NE99 1MC
     Telephone   0632-610691
     Holdings   399, 450 books; 7, 500 pamphlets; 950 periodicals

Subject Coverage: The library has a good collection of local
history resources; British Government publications; British
patents and standards; atomic energy reports from Britain,
America, and European countries. Among the special collections are the Joseph Cowen, Thomas Bewick, Seymour Bell,
and the Thomlinson Collections.

Access: The library is open to the public. Inquiries should
be directed to the Librarian. The hours are Monday to Friday, 9:00 A. M. to 9:00 P. M.; Saturday, 9:00 A. M. to 5:00
P. M.

Publications: Local Government Information Service (monthly
index); Local History Printed Catalogue (1932); Bewick Catalogue (1904); Calendar of the Greenwell Deeds (1927); Current Information Lists (produced by the City Information Service).

Duplication: Full-size copying facilities (self-service) are
available at moderate cost.

Services: Books circulate only to ticket holders, but tickets
of other library authorities will be accepted.

NEWCASTLE UPON TYNE

182   Institution   Northumberland Record Office
      Address   Melton Park, North Gosforth, Newcastle upon
                       Tyne NE3 5QX
      Telephone   089426-2680
      Holdings   2, 500 books; 200 pamphlets; 40 periodicals; 300
                       microforms; 15 rooms of records; 60 tape re-
                       cordings

Subject Coverage: The office contains Quarter Sessions, county, district, and parish council records; tithe maps; register
of wills after 1858; infirmary records; family, estate, and
business records, including papers dealing with mining and
agriculture; maps; plans; enclosure papers; and police records.
Among the family records held are those of Ridley of Blagdon,
Middleton of Belsay, Swinburne of Capheaton, Blackett of Mat-
fen, Allgood of Nunwich.   These record the use made of land
and the day to day management of estates.   Occasionally accounts of industries or commercial enterprises are included.
The Delaval Manuscripts contain information about salt making,
coal mining, and glass works.   In recent years, the office has
conducted an oral history program, recording the recollections
of knowledgable older Northumbrians among whom are miners,
craftsmen, farmers, and other country people.   There is also
a small reference library.

Access: The office is open to the public.   Inquiries should
be addressed to the County Archivist.   The hours are Monday
to Thursday, 9:00 A. M. to 5:00 P. M. ; Friday, 9:00 A. M. to
4:30 P. M. ; second Monday in each month, 9:00 A. M. to 9:00
P. M. ; last Saturday in each month, 9:00 A. M. to 12 noon.
The use of some 20th century records is restricted.

Publications: The Northumberland Record Office, 1958-1974;
Northumberland History: A Brief Guide to Records and Aids
in Newcastle upon Tyne (1962); Education in Hexham, by S. D.
Thomson (1964).

Duplication: Full-size copying facilities are available at moderate cost.   Photographic reproduction is also provided.

Services: Telephone and postal inquiries are answered.   Material does not circulate.   There is a photographic slide lending service.   Talks are given by staff members.

NEWCASTLE UPON TYNE

183   Institution   University of Newcastle upon Tyne Library
      Address   Newcastle upon Tyne NE1 7RU
      Telephone   0632-28511
      Holdings   418, 000 books; 49, 000 pamphlets; 4, 440 peri-

odicals; microforms; photographs

Subject Coverage: The library, in addition to supporting the
faculties of the university, has several important special collections. Among these are the Pybus Collection (medical history); Gertrude Bell (Middle Eastern archaeology); Robert
White (English literature, border history, and antiquities); the
Heslop Collection (English dictionaries); and the Runciman and
Trevelyan papers.

Access: Visiting scholars are permitted to use the collection
with permission of the Librarian. Written application in advance is necessary. The library is open Monday to Friday,
9:00 A. M. to 9:00 P. M. ; Saturday, 9:00 A. M. to 4:30 P. M.
during the academic year. In vacation, the hours are Monday
to Friday, 9:00 A. M. to 5:00 P. M.

Publications: The library issues Library Publications.

Duplication: Efficient full-size copying facilities are available
at low cost. The library contains a Photographic Department,
which is well equipped to deal with most requests for photographs of microcards, documents, illustrations, or slides.

Services: The collection circulates only to members of the
university and other local professional groups, e. g. , North
Regional Hospital Board.

NORTHALLERTON

184   Institution   North Yorkshire County Record Office
      Address   County Hall, Northallerton, North Yorkshire
                     OL7 8AD
      Telephone   0609-3123, ext. 455
      Holdings   records

Subject Coverage: Records include the official records of the
county (Quarter Sessions, County Council, District Council,
Parish Council), family and estate papers, and parish records.

Access: The office is open to the public. Inquiries should be
directed to the County Archivist. The hours are Monday,
Tuesday, Thursday, 9:00 A. M. to 1:00 P. M. , 2:00 P. M. to
4:50 P. M. ; Wednesday, 9:00 A. M. to 1:00 P. M. , 2:00 P. M.
to 8:50 P. M. ; Friday, 9:00 A. M. to 1:00 P. M. , 2:00 P. M. to
4:20 P. M. It is advisable for persons wishing to use the record office after 5:00 P. M. on Wednesday evenings to make
prior arrangements with the staff for the production of documents and to seek their advice on access to the office when
it is normally closed. Although the office is closed at lunch-
time, it is usually possible for those who have been working
there during the morning and wish to continue working between

1:00 P. M. and 2:00 P. M. to make special arrangements with
the Search Room staff to do so.   No documents can be produced after 4:30 P. M. (8:30 P. M. on Wednesday and 4:00 P. M.
on Friday).

Publications: Hird's Annals of Bedale; Copper-Mining in Rich-
mondshire.

Duplication: Full-size and micro-copying facilities are available.

Services: Exhibition material will be loaned, but researchers
must use the collection only on the premises.   The staff gives
talks about archival services.   Postal inquiries are answered.

NORTHAMPTON

185   Institution   Northamptonshire Record Office
      Address   Delapre Abbey, Northampton NN4 9AW
      Telephone   0604-62129
      Holdings   1, 000 books; 1, 500 pamphlets; 10 periodicals;
                       250 microforms; 1, 000, 000 manuscript documents

Subject Coverage: The records in the record office contain information about estates, businesses, persons and organizations
connected with Northamptonshire and the Soke of Peterborough.
There are also resources covering archives and manuscripts,
including their maintenance and conservation.

Access: Visiting researchers are permitted to use the collec-
tion.   Inquiries should be directed to the Chief Archivist.   A
letter of introduction is recommended.   The hours are Monday,
Tuesday, Wednesday, Friday, 9:15 A. M. to 1:00 P. M. , 2:00
P. M. to 4:45 P. M. ; Thursday, 9:15 A. M. to 1:00 P. M. , 2:00
P. M. to 7:45 P. M. ; Saturday, 9:00 A. M. to 12:15 P. M.

Publications: Annual Report.

Duplication: Full-size and micro-copying facilities are available.   The time necessary for processing is twenty-one days.
Cost of microfilming is high.

Services: Inquiries made by telephone or mail will be answered.

NORTHAMPTON

186   Institution   Northamptonshire Record Society
      Address   Delapre Abbey, Northampton NN4 9AW
      Telephone   0604-62297
      Holdings   4, 000 books; 2, 000 pamphlets; 12 periodicals

Subject Coverage: The resources of the society center around English history and historical records, especially works relating to Northamptonshire.

Access: Books in the library of the society are available for use by bona fide students and researchers who visit the Northamptonshire Record Office (County Archives), which is also situated in Delapre Abbey.   Only members of the Northamptonshire Record Society may use books either in the library or the Northamptonshire Record Office Students Room (which is next door).   Inquiries should be directed to the Secretary. The hours are Monday, Tuesday, Wednesday, Friday, 9:15 A.M. to 1:00 P.M., 2:00 P.M. to 4:45 P.M.; Thursday, 9:15 A.M. to 1:00 P.M., 2:00 P.M. to 7:45 P.M.; Saturday, 9:00 A.M. to 12:15 P.M.

Membership in the society is available to individuals and institutions at nominal cost.   The membership fee includes a copy of the society's annual journal, Northamptonshire Past and Present.

Publications: Northamptonshire Past and Present (annual); volumes of records (relating to the history of Northamptonshire).

Duplication: Full-size copying facilities are available at the record office.   The cost is moderate.

Services: There is a catalog in the library for use by borrowers, but there is no published guide.   Books can be borrowed by members.

NORWICH

187   Institution   Norfolk County Library
      Address   County Library Headquarters, County Hall,
                       Martineau Lane, Norwich NR1 2DH
      Telephone   0603-22288, ext. 309
      Holdings   1, 406, 385 books; 660 periodicals; press clippings;
                       maps; photographs

Subject Coverage: The Norfolk County Library is comprised of four divisional libraries as follows:

Norwich Divisional Library
Central Library, Bethel Street, Norwich NR2 1NJ

Eastern Divisional Library
Central Library, Tolhouse Street, Great Yarmouth NR30 2SH

Western Divisional Library
Public Library, London Road, King's Lynn PE30 5EZ

Central Divisional Library
County Library Headquarters, County Hall, Martineau Lane,
Norwich NR1 2DH

The Norwich Divisional Library contains the Colman and Rye
Libraries of local history (press cuttings, photographs, broadsides, maps, prints); City Library (incunabula); Norfolk Record Office; American Memorial Library. King's Lynn Public
Library holds the St. Margaret's Collection (15th to 19th century books); Stanley Collection (18th to 19th century books).
At Thetford Branch Library may be found the Thomas Paine
Collection (pamphlets and ephemera) and the Duleep Singh Collection (local history).

Access: All of the divisional and branch libraries except the
Central Divisional Library are available to the public. The
hours vary, but all are open Monday to Saturday. Inquiries
should be directed to the County Librarian.

Publications: Bibliotheca Norfolciensis (1896); Catalogus Li-
brorum in Bibliotheca Norvicensi (1883); A Bibliography of
Norfolk History, ed. by Elizabeth Darroch and Barry Taylor
(1975); City of Norwich Libraries: History and Treasures, by
Philip Hepworth and Mary Alexander (1965).

Duplication: Photocopying facilities are available at the Norwich Central Library and King's Lynn Public Library.

Services: Only registered readers may borrow books, but
tickets from other libraries are accepted.

NORWICH

188   Institution   Norfolk County Record Office
      Address   Norwich City Library, Bethel Street, Norwich
                       NR2 1NR
      Telephone   0603-22233, ext. 643
      Holdings   2,000,000 to 3,000,000 documents

Subject Coverage: The collection contains the records of both
Norfolk County and the city of Norwich. A separate record
office was established in 1963, but the records it holds date
from a much earlier time.

Access: Visiting scholars may use the records and indexes.
Inquiries should be directed to the County Archivist. The
hours are Monday to Friday, 9:00 A. M. to 5:00 P. M.; Saturday, 9:00 A. M. to 12 noon.

Publications: Guide to Great Yarmouth Borough Records
(1972); Guide to Norwich Records (1898); Norfolk Record Office:
Notes for the Assistance of Genealogists (1966).

<u>Duplication</u>: Full-size and micro-copying facilities are available at moderately high cost. Processing takes from two to three weeks for full-size copies and up to two or three months for micro-copies.

<u>Services</u>: Only brief inquiries are answered. The staff will advise on source material, but cannot conduct a search.

NOTTINGHAM

189 Institution   Nottinghamshire Record Office
     Address   County House, High Pavement, Nottingham NG1
                        1HR
     Telephone   0602-54524
     Holdings   5,000 books; pamphlets; microforms; records

<u>Subject Coverage</u>: The records include the official records of the county (Quarter Sessions, etc.); family and estate papers; Archdeaconry of Nottingham; wills proved in Exchequer Court at York; transcripts of bishops' registers, hearth tax, and forest records; enclosure awards and tithe awards. Records recently transferred from Borthwick Institute, York, cover the period c. 1583-1858. Eighty per cent of the parish registers in the Diocese of Southwell are deposited in the Nottinghamshire Record Office.

<u>Access</u>: The office is open to the public, but records and printed books may only be consulted in the Search Room. Researchers are advised to write before visiting the record office. Inquiries should be directed to the Principal Archivist. The hours are Monday, Wednesday, Thursday, 9:00 A.M. to 4:45 P.M.; Tuesday, 9:00 A.M. to 7:30 P.M.; Friday, 9:00 A.M. to 4:15 P.M.; the first and third Saturday of each month, 9:30 A.M. to 12:30 P.M.

<u>Publications</u>: An <u>Annual Report</u> and accession lists are published.

<u>Duplication</u>: Full-size copying facilities are available at moderate cost. There is little delay in fulfilling orders.

<u>Services</u>: No material is available on loan, but telephone and limited postal inquiries are answered.

NOTTINGHAM

190 Institution   University of Nottingham Library
     Address   Nottingham NG7 2RD
     Telephone   0602-56101
     Holdings   404,367 books; 123,000 pamphlets; 4,200 periodicals; 84,000 microforms; 1,000,000 manuscripts

Subject Coverage: The library holds several special collections,
including those devoted to the history and topography of the
East Midlands; the W. E. Briggs Collection of early children's
school books; the Cambridge Drama Collection (mainly 19th
century); and the Porter Collection of bird books.

The library Manuscripts Department houses the collection of
many distinguished local families, including the Galway, Man-
vers, Middleton, Newcastle, and the Duke of Portland muniments.   It has also acquired literary manuscripts (including an
important D. H. Lawrence collection); ecclesiastical papers
(Archdeaconry of Nottingham); administrative archives (Harfield
Chase Corporation); and business and trade union records.

Access: Visiting scholars must apply to the Librarian for permission to use the library.   The hours are Monday to Friday,
9:00 A.M. to 10:00 P.M.; Saturday, 9:00 A.M. to 12:30 P.M.,
during the academic year.   In August, the library is open
Monday to Friday, 9:00 A.M. to 5:00 P.M.; Saturday, 9:00
A.M. to 12:30 P.M.

Publications: Accessions lists, guides to the library and to
subject areas are issued by the library.

Duplication: Full-size and micro-copying facilities are available.

Services: Inquiries can be made by telephone or mail.   Books
and other material circulate liberally.   The library cooperates
with the British Library Lending Division.

OXFORD

191   Institution   Bodleian Library
       Address   University of Oxford, Oxford OX1 3BG
       Telephone   0865-44675
       Holdings   3, 500, 000 volumes of printed material; periodi-
                         cals; microforms; 50, 000 volumes of manuscripts

Subject Coverage: The Bodleian is one of the great libraries
of the world.   As such, it has in-depth resources in all aspects of the social sciences.   Any summary of the contents
would necessarily omit important collections.   The library
has been a copyright library since 1610, even before other
major libraries became copyright libraries.   Its finest collections relate to its special manuscript and book treasures.   The
Bodleian holdings do not focus on contemporary economic, historical, and political material, although it contains many works
in these fields.   Among the strongest holdings are works in
medieval studies, British topography and local history, and
16th and 17th century diplomatic history.   The library also
contains British Government publications and has some, al-

though not complete, publications of foreign governments. The Bodleian (Rhodes House) receives the most important U. S. and Commonwealth official publications. The library also has substantial collections on Latin American, modern Slavonic, and eastern European studies and is a depository library for the United Nations publications.

Access: A visiting scholar must write in advance to the Librarian concerned for permission to use this library or any other library of Oxford University. Those who plan to conduct research at Oxford in the summer vacation are advised to write well ahead of time. A letter of recommendation from the home institution is required. During the academic year, the library is open Monday to Friday, 9:00 A. M. to 10:00 P. M.; Saturday, 9:00 A. M. to 1:00 P. M. During vacation, the hours are Monday to Friday, 9:00 A. M. to 7:00 P. M.; Saturday, 9:00 A. M. to 1:00 P. M. The library is closed the week beginning the late summer bank holiday and December 24 to 31.

The Bodleian group is not centralized in one place, but is dispersed in several buildings. This group forms the Oxford University Central Library System. Some books in the Bodleian are under separate specialist administration.

The group of libraries which are either sections of the Bodleian or dependent upon it are Bodleian Law Library, Indian Institute Library, Radcliffe Science Library, and Rhodes House Library. In addition, there are libraries outside the Bodleian group, which are located in colleges, halls, faculties, institutes, departments, and museums of the university.

Publications: Bodleian Library Record (one or two a year); The History of the Bodleian Library, 1845-1945, by Sir Edmund Craster (1952); Current Foreign and Commonwealth Periodicals in the Bodleian Library and in Other Oxford Libraries; and readers' guides to the library and to separate departments and collections.

Duplication: Extensive facilities are available for full-size and micro-copying.

Services: The Bodleian Library does not lend to individuals, but participates in interlibrary lending through the British Library Lending Division. There is no general subject catalog, but there are subject guides to certain subjects and collections on open access shelves.

OXFORD

192   Institution   Libraries outside the Bodleian, University of
                          Oxford

Although the Bodleian Library has the largest collection of books at the university (exceeding all other Oxford University libraries combined), enormous collections of books, manuscripts, periodicals, and microforms are available in the many other libraries at the university.

The non-Bodleian collection consists of two categories: 1) College and Hall Libraries, and 2) Faculty, Departmental, Institute, and other libraries. College libraries are, in general, open only to members except for special material. Nuffield College and St. Antony's College have important social science collections. St. Antony's is a center for Latin American and Mid-Eastern studies. All Souls (Codrington Library) contains legal material. The hours and conditions for admission vary. Most of these libraries require prior appointments and recommendations, which should be sent to the Librarian of each institution. Many of these libraries are closed for various periods during the summer. Some of these libraries permit borrowing. The following is a complete list of College and Hall Libraries and a partial list of Departmental Libraries (chosen because of their social science holdings):

I.   College and Hall Libraries
     All Souls (Codrington Library)   New College
     Balliol College   Nuffield College
     Blackfriars Priory   Oriel College
     Brasenose College   Pembroke College
     Campion Hall   The Queen's College
     Christ Church   Regent's Park College
     Corpus Christi College   St. Anne's College
     Exeter College   St. Antony's College
     Greyfriars   St. Edmund Hall
     Hertford College   St. Hilda's College
     Jesus College   St. Hugh's College
     Keble College   St. John's College
     Lady Margaret Hall   Sommerville College
     Lincoln College   Trinity College
     Magdalen College   University College
     Manchester College   Wadham College
     Mansfield College   Wolfson College
     Merton College   Worcester College

II. Faculty, Departmental, Institute, and Other Libraries
     Ashmolean Museum of Art and Archaeology
     Department of the History of Art
     History Faculty Library
     Institute of Agricultural Economics
     Institute of Economics and Statistics
     Institute of Social Anthropology (Tylor Library)
     Museum of the History of Science
     Philosophy Library
     Pitt Rivers Museum (Balfour Library)
     Social Studies Faculty Library
     Taylor Institution
     University Archives

An excellent and indispensable guide to the collections in each of these libraries can be found in Oxford Libraries Outside the Bodleian: A Guide, by Paul Morgan (Oxford: Oxford Bibliographical Society and the Bodleian Library, 1973).

OXFORD

193 Institution   Oxfordshire County Record Office
    Address   County Hall, Oxford OX1 1ND
    Telephone   0865-49861, ext. 202
    Holdings   books; pamphlets; periodicals; microforms;
                     records; manuscripts; maps

Subject Coverage: The manuscript records include Oxfordshire County Council, Oxfordshire Court of Quarter Sessions from 1687, and privately deposited papers. The last group consists of deeds, family and estate papers, maps, sale catalogs, and business records. The Quarter Sessions papers contain records of crimes and of the administrative business of the court (about two hundred enclosure awards and land tax assessments). There are several thousand books and several hundred pamphlets mainly on local history.

Access: The office is open to the public. Inquiries should be directed to the Archivist. A prior appointment is appreciated. The hours are Monday to Thursday, 9:00 A.M. to 1:00 P.M., 2:00 P.M. to 5:00 P.M.; Friday, 9:00 A.M. to 1:00 P.M., 2:00 P.M. to 4:00 P.M. Researchers have only limited access to the Oxfordshire County Council records.

Publications: The Oxfordshire County Record Office and Its Records (1938); A Handlist of Inclosure Acts and Awards Relating to the County of Oxford, 2d rev. ed. (1975); A Handlist of Plans, Sections and Books of Reference for the Proposed Railways in Oxfordshire (1964); Summary Catalogue of the Privately-Deposited Records in the Oxfordshire County Record Office (1966); Catalogue of an Exhibition of Heraldic Seals (1967); The Oxfordshire Election of 1754.

Duplication: Full-size copying facilities are available. Arrangements can be made with the Bodleian Library, Oxford for photostatic copies, but there is a delay of up to two months.

Services: The collection can be used only on the premises. Telephone and postal inquiries are answered. Talks with small exhibitions are arranged on request.

PLYMOUTH

194 Institution   West Devon Record Office
    Address   14 Tavistock Place, Plymouth PL4 8AN

Telephone   0752-28293
Holdings   books; pamphlets; microforms; records

Subject Coverage: The office holds the official records of
Devonport and Stonehouse (including County Council, Quarter
Sessions, Petty Sessions, commissioners minutes, corporation records, and the records of local boards); deposits from
land owners, solicitors, commercial undertakings, and parishes.

Access: The office is open to the public. Inquiries should
be addressed to the Archivist. The hours are Monday to Friday, 9:00 A. M. to 5:00 P. M.

Publications: A Guide to the Archives Department of Plymouth City Libraries, pt. I (1962); Plymouth City Charters,
1439-1935 (1962).

Duplication: Full-size and micro-copying facilities are available.

Services: None of the material is available on loan. Telephone and postal inquiries are answered.

PORTSMOUTH

195 Institution   City Record Office
     Address   3 Museum Road, Portsmouth PO1 2LE
     Telephone   0705-29765
     Holdings   books; pamphlets; records; maps; plans; photo-
                      graphs

Subject Coverage: The collection includes both the official
records of Portsmouth and a large collection of public and
private records, maps, plans, and photographs relating to
Portsmouth. Among the holdings are Royal Charters and Letters Patent from 1313, manorial records of Portsea and Cop-
nor from 1380, court books from 1576, records of poor law
administration from 1737, records of Portsmouth and Portsea
burial boards from 1854. The family records include those
of the Hewetts and Andersons of Titchfield, Hulberts and Jack-
sons of Waterlooville, and Wiltshires of Hayling Island (from
1536). There are large collections of local title deeds and
Acts of Parliament relating to Portsmouth and the surrounding
area. The church records contain the archives of the Anglican Diocese of Portsmouth and the records of most of the
parishes in the deaneries of Alverstoke, Havant, and Portsmouth (from the 16th century). There are also non-conformist and Roman Catholic records. There are a small reference
collection and three special collections of printed books. These
are the Cogswell (architectural and antiquarian), the Halton-
Thomson (scientific and technological), and the Norster (legal
and antiquarian).

Access: Church records and printed books are currently housed at the Guildhall Record Office (Guildhall, Portsmouth PO1 2AL; telephone: 0705-21771). The offices are open to the public, but as Search Room space is limited, both request an appointment beforehand. The hours of the City Record Office are Monday to Friday, 10:00 A.M. to 12:30 P.M., 2:00 P.M. to 4:30 P.M. The Guildhall Record Office is open Monday to Friday, 9:30 A.M. to 12:30 P.M., 2:00 P.M. to 4:45 P.M. (3:45 P.M. on Friday). All inquiries should be directed to the City Archivist.

Publications: No publications have been issued by the record office, but it has taken part in the publication of Portsmouth Papers and Portsmouth Record Series. Lists of holdings are included in publications of the Hampshire Archivists Group.

Duplication: Full-size copying and photography are available. Difficult requests may take some time to complete.

Services: The record office staff will advise researchers on the availability of records and methods of searching, but cannot undertake the research itself. Material can be used only in the Search Rooms.

PRESTON

196   Institution   Lancashire Record Office
      Address   Bow Lane, Preston PR1 8ND
      Telephone   0772-51905
      Holdings   10,000 books; 75 periodicals; maps; 7,000,000
                       documents

Subject Coverage: The record office contains general information, local history, and documents dating from 1150. These include archives of the Justices of the Peace, Quarter Sessions, land tax assessments, Guardians of the Poor, school boards, boards of health, and borough police. Parish records contain registers of christenings, marriages, burials, and the accounts of churchwardens. Archives of the Society of Friends in Lancashire and the Roman Catholic Archdiocese of Liverpool (before 1894) are also held, as are wills and inventories for the whole county (15th to 19th centuries). There are many family and estate records including those of the Earls of Derby, Bradford, and Lathom, and Lords Hesketh, Chesham, and Shuttleworth. Other resources include probate records and account books. Among the special collections is the G. E. H. Allen Collection (principally British maps and atlases).

Access: Visiting researchers are permitted to use the records. Inquiries should be directed to the County Archivist. The hours are Monday to Friday, 9:00 A.M. to 5:00 P.M.

Publications: Guide to the Lancashire Records Office (1962);
Handlist of Genealogical Sources.

Duplication: Full-size copying facilities are available at moderate cost.   Photographic service can also be provided.

Services: The office contains an ultra-violet lamp for use in
reading older documents.   The collections can be consulted
only on the premises.   Exhibitions and talks are provided on
written request with sufficient notice.

READING

197 Institution   Berkshire Record Office
     Address   Shire Hall, Reading RG1 3EE
     Telephone   0734-55981, ext. 230
     Holdings   books; records

Subject Coverage: The office is a repository for historic records of the Royal County of Berkshire which include Quarter
Sessions (from 1703); records of some boroughs and small
towns within the county and records of other official and semi-
official bodies.   It is the Diocesan Record Office for parishes
within the Archdeaconry of Berkshire, and records of most
parishes in the county have been deposited there.   These consist of registers of baptisms, marriages, and burials.   Other
parish records, mainly of the 18th and 19th centuries, include
poor relief records, Poor Law Guardians records (after 1834),
and records for each union in the county.   The records of private families and individuals form one of the largest classes
of papers and include title deeds (medieval and modern), records of manorial courts, maps of farms and family estates,
accounts, letters, and diaries.

Access: The office is open to the public.   Researchers are
requested to make a preliminary inquiry to the County Archivist.   The hours are Monday to Wednesday, 9:00 A. M. to 5:30
P. M.; Thursday, 9:00 A. M. to 7:30 P. M.; Friday, 9:00 A. M.
to 4:30 P. M.   The office is closed daily from 1:00 P. M. to
2:15 P. M.

Publications: Descriptive leaflets on various types of records
are issued.

Duplication: Full-size and micro-copying facilities are available at moderate cost.   Processing takes from one to two
days.   Arrangements can usually be made to supply photographic copies of suitable documents.

Services: The collection can be consulted only on the premises.   Sets of photocopies of records are available for sale.

READING

198 Institution   University of Reading, Institute of Agricultural
                         History and Museum of English Rural Life
     Address   Whiteknights, Reading RG6 2AG, Berkshire
     Telephone   0734-85123, ext. 475
     Holdings   5,000 books; 3,500 pamphlets; 70 periodicals;
                         microforms; 700 manuscripts and items of printed
                         ephemera; 250,000 photographs and negatives;
                         1,100 reports and guide books

Subject Coverage: The archival collections include records
from the Country Landowner's Association, National Farmer's
Union, National Union of Agricultural and Allied Workers,
Royal Agricultural Benevolent Institution, Royal Agricultural
Society of England, Agricultural Co-operative Society; the trade
records of twelve agricultural engineering firms (including Ran-
somes, Sims and Jefferies of Ipswich, John Fowler of Leeds,
Nalder and Nalder Ltd. of Challow, and R. Hunt of Earls
Colne) and publicity material of two thousand firms. The li-
brary also contains two thousand printed pamphlets on land re-
form collected by the United Committee for the Taxation of
Land Values.

Access: Application must be made by letter to the Keeper to
use the resources housed in the museum. A prior appointment
is required, and a letter of introduction is recommended. The
permanent exhibition is open to all visitors, Tuesday to Saturday, 10:00 A.M. to 1:00 P.M., 2:00 P.M. to 4:30 P.M.

Publications: Agrarian Changes in Nineteenth Century Italy, by
Giuliana Biagioli; West Country Friendly Societies, by Margaret Fuller (published by Oakwood Press for the University of
Reading, 1964); G. E. Fussell: A Bibliography of His Writings
on Agricultural History (1967); Ransomes of Ipswich: A History of the Firm and a Guide to the Records, by D. R. Grace
and D. C. Phillips (1975); Estate Villages: A Study of the
Berkshire Villages of Ardington and Lockinge, by M. A. Havin-
den (published by Lund Humphries for the Museum of English
Rural Life, 1966); Historical Farm Records (a summary guide
to the manuscripts and other material in the University Library
collected by the Institute of Agricultural History and Museum
of English Rural Life, published by the Library, University of
Reading, 1973); The English Farm Wagon, by J. Geraint Jen-
kins (reprinted by David and Charles, 1973); Museum Procedure, pt. 8: Trade Record Collection (1973); The Blacksmith's
Ledgers of the Hedges Family of Bucklebury, Berkshire, 1736-
1773, by Felicity A. Palmer; The London Milk Trade, 1900-
1930, by E. H. Whetham; A Bibliography of Roman Agriculture (1970).

Duplication: Full-size copies and photography (including microfilm) are available through the University of Reading Library.

Prices are supplied on application.   Photographic services require two weeks.

Services: The collections can be consulted only on the premises.

READING

199   Institution   University of Reading Library
      Address   Whiteknights, Reading, Berkshire RG6 2AE
      Telephone   0734-84331
      Holdings   500, 000 books; 40, 000 pamphlets; 4, 000 periodicals; 4, 400 microforms; 1, 360 manuscripts

Subject Coverage: The library is fairly strong in social sciences.   Among the special collections are the Cole Library (works on early medicine); Henley Parish Library (history, philosophy, literature); Overstone Library (economics, history, topography, and literature); Turner Collection (French Revolution).

Access: Visiting academics must have permission to use the collection.   Inquiries should be directed to the Librarian.   A prior appointment is desirable.   A letter of introduction is recommended.   The hours are Monday to Thursday, 9:00 A. M. to 10:15 P. M.; Friday, 9:00 A. M. to 7:00 P. M.; Saturday, 9:00 A. M. to 6:00 P. M.; Sunday, 2:00 P. M. to 6:00 P. M. during the academic year.   During vacation, the hours are Monday to Friday, 9:00 A. M. to 5:00 P. M.; Saturday, 9:00 A. M. to 12:30 P. M.

Publications: Catalogue of the Cole Library (1969).

Duplication: Full-size and micro-copying facilities are available at low cost.   Postal charges are made if material must be mailed.

Services: The collection circulates only to members of the university.   The library cooperates with the British Library Lending Division.

RIPON

200   Institution   Ripon Cathedral Library
      Address   The Cathedral, Ripon, Yorkshire HG4 2LA
      Telephone   0765-2072 (Librarian, 2658)
      Holdings   3, 000 books; 100 pamphlets

Subject Coverage: The library contains works on archeology, theology, liturgy, ecclesiastical history, and the Lindisfarne Gospels.   Parish Registers, local history, topography, medieval manuscripts, incunabula (including Boethius' De Consolatione Philosophiae printed by William Caxton), foreign octavos, and folios from the 16th century can also be found.

Access: The collection is made available to researchers (for consultation) on special request. Inquiries should be directed to the Canon Librarian. The library is open Monday to Saturday, 10:00 A.M. to 12 noon, 1:15 P.M. to 4:45 P.M.

Publications: Ripon Ministers, by E. L. Smith; Ripon Cathedral Organ, by C. H. Moody; Guide to Ripon, by J. R. Walbran; Guide to Ripon and Fountains Abbey, by J. R. Walbran; Ripon Cathedral Guide, by W. E. Wilkinson.

Duplication: No copying facilities are available at the library, but arrangements can be made for copying material.

Services: Certain volumes may be borrowed, but most of the collection can be consulted only on the premises.

ST. ANDREWS

201   Institution   University of St. Andrews Library
      Address   St. Andrews, Fife KY16 9TR
      Telephone   St. Andrews 4333
      Holdings   600,000 books; 30,000 pamphlets; 3,000 periodicals; 1,700 manuscripts; 2,500 maps; 150 incunabula

Subject Coverage: The library collects material covered by the faculties of the university, e.g., Arts, Science, and Divinity. It contains works in early 19th century British history, early 20th century East European history, and 16th and 17th century Scottish history. The library is strong in 19th century British periodicals and political pamphlets. It was a copyright library from 1710 to 1837. Of interest to visiting American academics are the special collections, which include Beveridge, Forbes, Von Hugel, Bishop Low, Donaldson, and McGillivray.

Access: The library is open to visiting academics with permission of the Librarian. A letter of introduction is required. The hours are Monday to Friday, 9:00 A.M. to 10:00 P.M.; Saturday, 9:00 A.M. to 12:15 P.M. when the university is in session. In summer vacation, the library is open Monday to Friday, 9:00 A.M. to 4:00 P.M. During Christmas and Easter vacations, the library hours are Monday to Friday, 9:00 A.M. to 5:00 P.M.; Saturday, 9:00 A.M. to 12:15 P.M.

Publications: The library has published an Index to the correspondence and papers of James David Forbes (1809-1868) and also to some papers of his son, George Forbes. In addition, there are several catalogs including Catalogue of the

Library (1826); Catalogue of Mathematical Works (1883); Catalogue of Additions, 6 vols. (1867-1900); Catalogue of Books
Added, 1925-1933; Catalogue of Some Books Printed in the 15th
and 16th Century (1925), and Catalogue of Incunabula (1956).
Other publications include Library Bulletin, 1901-1925, 10 vols.
(1904-1925); Collections Towards a Bibliography of St. Andrews, by J. H. Baster (1926); James Gregory Tercentenary
Record, by H. W. Turnbull and G. H. Bushnell (1939); Henderson's Benefaction, by G. H. Bushnell (1942); Current Serials (1974-75).

Duplication: Full-size and micro-copying facilities are available.

Services: Books circulate only to members of the university
or on interlibrary loan. Information is given by telephone or
mail to all inquirers.

SALISBURY

202   Institution   The Diocesan Record Office
      Address   Wren Hall, 56c The Close, Salisbury SP1 2EL
      Telephone   0722-22519
      Holdings   records; maps

Subject Coverage: The Diocesan Record Office is a sub-office
of the Wiltshire Record Office. It contains three main archival
groups: diocesan records, cathedral records, and Church
Commissioners' records. The diocese has varied geographical-
ly, so that the records cover different counties or parts of
them at different times. Until 1542, Berkshire, Dorset, and
Wiltshire were included. In 1542, Dorset was transferred to
the Diocese of Bristol (except for certain parishes which were,
and remained, Salisbury Peculiars), but in 1836, it was transferred back to Salisbury, the Archdeaconry of Berkshire at the
same time going to the Diocese of Oxford; and in 1837, the
Deaneries of Cricklade and Malmesbury in the north of Wiltshire were transferred to the See of Gloucester and Bristol.
The Bishop's Registers (from 1297) are kept at the registry,
not at Wren Hall. Among the best known of the records are
the transcripts of parish registers (dating mainly from the
early 17th century).

The cathedral records include several important series, such
as the Act Books, which recorded the official acts of the Chapter, and the accounts of the Communar, who administered the
common fund of the cathedral, both dating from the 14th century; the accounts of the Clerk of the Fabric (from the 15th
century); accounts and deeds of the Choristers, chiefly 15th
and 16th centuries; and deeds, surveys, and papers.

The Church Commissioners' records consist of deeds and

manorial and estate records, including some maps, relating
to the former estates of the bishop, dean, chapter, prebendar-
ies in Wiltshire, Dorset, Berkshire, Devon, Hampshire, and
other counties dating mostly from the 17th to the 19th centuries, with a few 16th century and a very few earlier.

Access: The office is open to the public. Because of staff
limitations, it is wise to write first to the Assistant Diocesan
Archivist. The hours are Monday to Friday, 10:30 A. M.
(earlier by arrangement) to 12:30 P. M. , 1:30 P. M. to 4:00
P. M.

Publications: The Wiltshire County Record Office has published
Guide to the Records of the Bishop, the Archdeacons of Salis-
bury and Wiltshire, and Other Archidiaconal and Peculiar
Jurisdictions, and to the Records from the Bishop of Bristol's
Sub-Registry for Dorset (Guide to the Wiltshire County Record
Offices, pt. IV).

Duplication: Arrangements for the copying of documents by
photographic and other means can be made at the Wiltshire
County Record Office, Trowbridge. The cost is moderate.

Services: The collection does not circulate. Most of the records are listed, but some sections and classes are in much
greater detail than others. The lists may be consulted at
Wren Hall.

SHEFFIELD

203   Institution   Sheffield City Libraries
      Address   Central Library, Surrey Street, Sheffield S1 1XZ
      Telephone   0742-734711/3
      Holdings   1, 603, 360 books; 1, 658 periodicals; manuscripts;
                       newspapers; maps; photographs

Subject Coverage: The library is organized into a number of
divisions and sections. Those of most interest to the social
scientist are the Arts and Humanities Library, Local Studies
and Archives Sections, Business Library, and Science and
Technology Library.

The Arts and Humanities Library contains special collections
of private press books and of books printed in England from
1765 to 1779.

The Local Studies and Archives Sections include the Sheffield
Collection of printed books and manuscripts, including Went-
worth Woodhouse Muniments (papers of Earl of Stafford, Marquis of Rockingham, and Edmund Burke's correspondence) and
Duke of Norfolk's Sheffield Estate Muniments; Fairbank Collection of local maps; local newspapers from the 18th century;

Edward Carpenter's Library; manuscripts and letters.

The Business Library and the Science and Technology Library
contain in-depth collections of commerce and law (certain aspects of law are covered by the Arts and Humanities Library).

Access: The library is open to the public.   Inquiries should
be addressed to the Director of Libraries.   A letter of introduction would be useful.   The hours differ among the various
divisions.   The Central Lending Library is open Monday to
Friday, 10:00 A. M. to 8:00 P. M. ; Saturday, 9:30 A. M. to
4:30 P. M.   The Arts and Humanities Library is open Monday
to Friday, 9:00 A. M. to 9:00 P. M. ; Saturday, 9:00 A. M. to
8:30 P. M.   The Local Studies Library is open Monday to Friday, 9:00 A. M. to 5:30 P. M. ; Saturday, 9:00 A. M. to 5:00
P. M.   The hours of the Business Library are Monday to Friday, 9:00 A. M. to 5:30 P. M; Saturday, 9:00 A. M. to 4:30
P. M.   The Science and Technology Library is open Monday to
Friday, 9:00 A. M. to 9:00 P. M. ; Saturday, 9:00 A. M. to 8:30
P. M.

Publications: A Bibliography of Edward Carpenter; Catalogue
of the Arundel Castle Manuscripts; Catalogue of Business and
Industrial Records; The City Libraries of Sheffield 1856-1956;
Descriptive Catalogue of the Jackson Collection; Letters from
a Yorkshire Emigrant, Joseph Wainwright of Pittsburgh,
U. S. A. ; Guide to the Manuscript Collections (with two supplements).

Duplication: Full-size and micro-copying facilities are available at moderate cost.   Processing for full-size copies usually takes a day except in the Science and Technology Library
where a coin-operated machine is available.

Services: Only ticket holders are allowed to borrow books.
Books not held in the libraries' collections may be acquired
through interlibrary loan.

SHEFFIELD

204   Institution   Sheffield City Museums
      Address   Weston Park, Sheffield S10 2TP
      Telephone   0742-27226/7
      Holdings   5, 000 books; 1, 000 pamphlets; 22 periodicals

Subject Coverage: The museum contains resources document-
ing the museum collections.   These relate to pre-history and
social and industrial history and include source material for
antiquities of Derbyshire, North Staffordshire, and Yorkshire.

Access: Researchers are permitted to use the resources by
arrangement during office hours only.   Inquiries should be ad-

dressed to the Director. A letter of introduction is recommended. The museum hours are Monday to Friday, 10:00 A. M. to 5:00 P. M.; Sunday, 11:00 A. M. to 5:00 P. M. except for summer months. During June, July, and August, the hours are Monday to Friday, 10:00 A. M. to 8:00 P. M.

Publications: The museum issues slides, postcards, booklets, and information sheets relating to the region and catalogs of special exhibits and of the permanent collection.

Duplication: Photographs can be prepared of objects in the collection on a fee basis. A document-copying facility exists for items over which the department has copyright control.

Services: The reference collection may only be used on the premises.

SHEFFIELD

205	Institution	University of Sheffield Library
	Address	Western Bank, Sheffield S10 2TN
	Telephone	0742-78555
	Holdings	600,000 books; 41,000 pamphlets; 4,800 periodicals; 6,000 microforms

Subject Coverage: The library resources support the faculties of the university with strong holdings in law, economics, and social studies.

Access: Visiting scholars must make application to use the collection and are permitted to do so at the Librarian's discretion. A letter of introduction is recommended. The hours are Monday to Friday, 9:00 A. M. to 9:30 P. M.; Saturday, 9:30 A. M. to 12:30 P. M. during the academic year. During vacation, the hours are Monday to Friday, 9:00 A. M. to 5:00 P. M.; Saturday, 9:00 A. M. to 12:30 P. M.

Publications: Brief guides to the library and selected subject areas are available.

Duplication: Full-size and micro-copying facilities are available. Time necessary for duplication varies from one to five days.

Services: The collection circulates only to members of the university and selected foreign borrowers.

SHREWSBURY

| 206 | Institution | Salop Record Office |
| | Address | Shirehall, Abbey Foregate, Shrewsbury, Shropshire SY2 6ND |

Telephone   0743-222405/222407
Holdings   books; microforms; records

Subject Coverage: The record office contains county and some borough records of Quarter Sessions, Town Court for Shrewsbury and Ludlow, Manor Court, Overseers of the Poor, the police (from the 19th century), the parish, and business. Coroners' records from the 17th century for Ludlow Borough and from the 18th century for the county are also held. References to medical treatment and to individual doctors may be found in deeds, correspondence, and papers. Certain documents of the Shrewsbury and Atcham Borough Council have been transferred (on loan) to the care of the Salop Record Office. A small reference library of local history is maintained.

Access: Researchers are permitted to use the records. Inquiries should be directed to the County Archivist. The hours are Monday to Thursday, 9:00 A.M. to 5:00 P.M.; Friday, 9:00 A.M. to 4:00 P.M.

Publications: Guide to the Shropshire Records (1952); Shropshire Parish Documents (1903); List of Inclosure Awards; List of Canal and Railway Plans Deposited with the Clerk of Peace; List and Partial Abstracts of Contents of Quarter Sessions Rolls (three parts); Abstract of Quarter Sessions Orders; Abstract of the Quarter Sessions Rolls, 1820-1830 (1974); Shropshire Peace Roll, 1400-1414, ed. by E. G. Kimball (1959); Printed Maps of Shropshire, 1577-1900, by G. C. Cowling (1959); Gazetteer of Shropshire Place Names, by H. D. G. Foxall, 2d ed.

Duplication: Full-size and micro-copying facilities are available. The cost is moderate, and the time necessary for processing is one week.

Services: The collection may only be used on the premises. An ultraviolet lamp is available to aid reading older documents. A card index of places is provided.

SLEAFORD

207   Institution   Royal Air Force College Library
       Address   Cranwell, Sleaford, Lincolnshire NG34 8HB
       Telephone   04006-201
       Holdings   100,000 books; 2,000 pamphlets; 300 periodicals; 15,000 reports

Subject Coverage: The library contains resources in military history (emphasis on air power), economics, defense, history of the Royal Air Force, aircraft, and air warfare. There is a special collection of works by or about T. E. Lawrence.

Access: Visiting scholars must seek permission to use the collection and are subject to security regulations.   Inquiries should be directed by letter to the Librarian.   A letter of introduction is recommended.   The hours are Monday to Friday, 8:15 A.M. to 5:00 P.M.

Publications: Subject bibliographies and booklists are available for internal use only.

Duplication: Full-size and micro-copying facilities are available.

Services: The library engages in interlibrary cooperation with other government departments and with the British Library Lending Division.

SOUTHAMPTON

208	Institution	Hampshire County Library, Southampton District Libraries
	Address	Central Library, Civic Centre, Southampton SO9 4XP
	Telephone	0703-23855
	Holdings	320,011 books; 335 periodicals; 747 microforms; 2,456 maps; 42,000 illustrations of local subjects

Subject Coverage: The library contains material on economic history, the economics of labor, shipping, foreign and domestic trade, and socialism.   There is a biographical collection which covers socialists, marxists, trade unionists, merchants, and economists.   Among the special collections are the Pitt Collection of 17th and 18th century scientific books and works on Ireland; and a local history collection.

Access: Scholars are welcome to use the library, but a letter of introduction is recommended.   Inquiries should be addressed to the City Librarian.   The hours are Monday to Friday, 10:00 A.M. to 7:00 P.M.; Saturday, 10:00 A.M. to 5:00 P.M.

Publications: Catalogue of the Pitt Collection; various HATRICS bibliographies; Local Government Information Bulletin (monthly); Southampton's History: A Guide to the Printed Resources; several select bibliographies.

Duplication: Only full-size copying facilities are available. The cost is moderate.

Services: The collection circulates to those who hold library tickets, but it is possible for others to make special arrangements.   Telephone and mail inquiries are answered.

SOUTHAMPTON

209   Institution   Southampton City Record Office
       Address   Civic Center, Southampton SO9 5NH
       Telephone   0703-23855, ext. 251
       Holdings   books; records; maps; prints; photographs

Subject Coverage: The record office contains a small reference
library for use by staff and searchers.   Included are the publications of edited texts by the Southampton Record Society and
Records Series.   The most important records are the city's
official archives from 1199 (including memoranda and minute
books from the 13th century); other classes of material from
the 15th century (including accounts of treasurers, petty customs, and brokers); and family and business records for the
parish.   The holdings include a prints and photographs collection.

Access: The record office is open to the public.   Inquiries
should be directed to the Archivist.   Researchers may use the
collection only on the premises.   The hours are Monday to
Friday, 9:00 A.M. to 1:00 P.M., 1:30 P.M. to 5:00 P.M.

Publications: Guide to the Records of the Corporation and
Absorbed Authorities (1964); The Southampton Record Office:
A Description of the Office and Its Archives (1966); Southampton in 1620 and the Mayflower (1970); Transport in Hampshire and the Isle of Wight: A Guide to the Records, by Hampshire Archivists' Group (1972); Southampton Maps from Elizabethan Times, by Edwin Welch (1964); The Southampton Police
Force, 1836-1856, by Anne Cookes (1972); maps, papers, and
directories.

Duplication: Full-size copies are generally available, but at
moderately high cost.   Other photographic services can be provided by special arrangement.

Services: Telephone and mail inquiries are answered.

SOUTHAMPTON

210   Institution   University of Southampton Library
       Address   Highfield, Southampton SO9 5NH
       Telephone   0703-556331
       Holdings   476,000 books and pamphlets; 6,100 periodicals;
                        10,500 microforms

Subject Coverage: In addition to supporting the faculties of the
university, the library boasts several special collections.
Among these are the Ford Collection of Parliamentary Papers
(from 1801); the Parkes Library on relationships between Jews
and non-Jews (including books, pamphlets, and ephemera on

Middle Eastern history, history of Jewish communities in exile,
Jewish society and ethics, and anti-Semitism); Cope Collection
on Hampshire and the Isle of Wight; the Perkins Agricultural
Library with books on British and Irish agriculture published
before 1901. The library also contains publications on American and Latin American studies, history of anti-Semitism,
criminology, strategic studies, and demography.

Access: Researchers are welcome to use the collection. In-
quiries should be addressed to the Librarian. The hours are
Monday to Friday, 9:00 A. M. to 10:00 P. M. ; Saturday, 9:00
A. M. to 5:00 P. M. ; Sunday, 2:30 P. M. to 6:00 P. M. during
the academic term. The hours during vacation are Monday to
Friday, 9:00 A. M. to 5:00 P. M. ; Saturday, 9:00 A. M. to 12:30
P. M.

Publications: Abstracts of Theses (annual); Handlist of Current Periodicals; Library Leaflets (on various collections);
Catalogue of the Perkins Agricultural Library.

Duplication: Full-size copying facilities are available. Duplication can usually be accomplished on demand at low cost.
Micro-copying is available through the Photographic Unit (not
the library), and the cost of processing is high.

Services: The collection is available to those with special
study requirements who have made proper application. Inquiries are handled by telephone and through the mail.

STAFFORD

211 Institution   Staffordshire County Record Office
     Address   Eastgate Street, Stafford ST16 2LZ
     Telephone   0785-3121, ext. 156
     Holdings   books; pamphlets; periodicals; 100 microforms;
                     records

Subject Coverage: The records include official records of the
county, family and estate papers, parish records, mining papers, business and industrial records, censuses, the Dart-
mouth Collection (formerly housed in the William Salt Library).

Access: Researchers can use the collection only on the premises. Application should be made to the County Archivist. The
hours are Monday to Thursday, 9:00 A. M. to 1:00 P. M. , 2:00
P. M. to 5:00 P. M. ; Friday, 9:00 A. M. to 1:00 P. M. , 2:00
P. M. to 4:30 P. M. On Saturday, record office documents
can be consulted at the William Salt Library, if previous arrangements have been made.

Publications: None.

Duplication: Full-size copying facilities are available. Copying cannot be done immediately, but the cost is moderate. Arrangements can be made for microfilming.

Services: No material is available on loan. Postal and telephone inquiries are answered. The record office is operated in conjunction with the William Salt Library and in close association with the Lichfield Joint Record Office.

STAFFORD

212   Institution   William Salt Library
        Address   19 Eastgate Street, Stafford ST16 2LZ
        Telephone   0785-52276
        Holdings   books; pamphlets; periodicals; manuscripts;
                    newspapers; maps; prints and drawings

Subject Coverage: The library is chiefly a local history reference library and was originally based on the collections of William Salt. The collection is uncatalogued. The resources relate to the history of Staffordshire and other parts of England. Salt commissioned the copying of Staffordshire documents held in other repositories, and these manuscripts form an important part of the collection. There are, in addition, several Anglo-Saxon charters, the earliest being 956; Staffordshire maps from the 16th century; a comprehensive set of royal proclamations; the Compton Census of 1676 (religious census of the province of Canterbury); the Staffordshire Advertiser (newspaper) from 1795; many antiquarians' notes (e.g., Stebbing Shaw).

Access: The library, which is open to the public, is operated in close association with the Staffordshire Record Office and the Lichfield Joint Record Office. Inquiries should be directed to the Librarian. The hours are Tuesday to Saturday, 10:00 A.M. to 12:45 P.M., 1:45 P.M. to 5:00 P.M.

Publications: None.

Duplication: Full-size and micro-copying facilities are available through the County Record Office.

Services: The collection can be used only on the premises.

SURBITON

213   Institution   Ministry of Overseas Development, Directorate
                    of Overseas Surveys
        Address   Kingston Road, Tolworth, Surbiton, Surrey KT5
                    9NS
        Telephone   01-337 8661
        Holdings   14,000 books and pamphlets; 550 periodicals;

80,000 maps; 2,000,000 air photographs

Subject Coverage: The directorate is concerned with the production by photogrammetric methods of topographical maps of
the Commonwealth countries of Africa, the Caribbean, and the
Far East, British dependent territories, and some foreign
countries.

The library collections are held in the Technical Services section, which is divided as follows:

Map Library: contains an extensive collection of maps with
topographical, road, and place-name data; all maps produced
by the directorate (including superseded issues), and some
maps of historic interest.

Survey Data Library: contains original field observations; results of surveys by local survey departments; profiles of railways; information on names and road classification.

Air Photo Library: contains vertical air photography flown for
mapping purposes; contact prints, together with detailed index
diagrams.

Book Library: contains items on geodesy, land surveying,
cartography, and photogrammetry; land tenure; survey legislation; geographical background of the areas mapped.

Access: An appointment is required to use the collection. The
library is open Monday to Friday, 9:30 A.M. to 4:30 P.M.

Publications: Catalogue of Maps (1960), supplements appear
in Technical Co-operation; Proceedings of the Conference of
Commonwealth Survey Officers (quarterly); Survey Review
(quarterly); Annual Report (HMSO).

Duplication: Copying facilities are not available.

Services: Air photographs, lists of co-ordinates and descriptions of survey stations are supplied only with the written authority of the survey departments of the countries concerned.

SWANSEA

214 Institution   University College of Swansea Library
     Address   Singleton Park, Swansea SA2 8PP
     Telephone   0792-25678, ext. 368
     Holdings   250,000 books; 50,000 pamphlets; 3,500 periodi-
                      cals; 320 microforms; 30,000 manuscripts and
                      archives

Subject Coverage: The library holds works in economics, social sciences, pure and applied sciences, humanities, and a collection of Celtic material.

Access: The library is open to members of the university, accredited scholars, and members of the public for special reference problems. Inquiries should be directed to the Librarian. A letter of introduction is recommended. During the academic year, the hours are Monday to Friday, 9:00 A.M. to 10:00 P.M.; Saturday, 9:00 A.M. to 5:00 P.M.; Sunday, 2:00 P.M. to 6:00 P.M. During vacation, the hours are Monday to Friday, 9:00 A.M. to 5:00 P.M.; Saturday, 9:00 A.M. to 12 noon.

Publications: The library issues an Annual Report, a Handbook, and subject guides for readers.

Duplication: Both full-size and micro-copying facilities are available.

Services: Books circulate only to members of the university. The library cooperates with the British Library Lending Division and the Wales Regional Library Bureau.

TAUNTON

215   Institution   Somerset Record Office
      Address   Obridge Road, Taunton, Somerset TA1 4DY
      Telephone   0823-87600
      Holdings   2,500 books and pamphlets; 10 periodicals;
                       4,000,000 records

Subject Coverage: The manuscript holdings of the record office consist of the official records of the County Council, including records of the Court of Quarter Sessions, the diocesan records of Bath and Wells, parish records for over two hundred parishes, records of many former local councils or public local authorities, and a mass of privately deposited material relating to Somerset families, estates, and businesses. A small reference library consists largely of HMSO Calendars of Public Records and other works of reference to be used in the interpretation of the manuscript holdings.

Access: The collection is open to the public. An initial inquiry by letter to establish the availability of relevant material is advisable. Inquiries should be directed to the County Archivist. The hours are Monday to Thursday, 9:00 A.M. to 12:45 P.M., 1:45 P.M. to 5:00 P.M.; Friday, 9:00 A.M. to 12:45 P.M., 1:45 P.M. to 4:30 P.M.

Publications: "Annual List of Main Manuscript Accessions" is published in the Proceedings of the Somerset Archaeological Society. Off-prints are available.

Duplication: A full-size copying machine is located on the premises. Processing costs are moderately high, but work may be completed immediately.

Services: The resources can be used only on the premises. Information on availability of records and the answers to limited specific questions can be given in response to telephone or postal inquiries, but return postage is requested.

TROWBRIDGE

216 Institution   Wiltshire County Record Office
    Address   County Hall, Trowbridge, Wiltshire BA14 8JG
    Telephone   02214-3641
    Holdings   books; pamphlets; periodicals; microforms;
                   records

Subject Coverage: The record office is the official repository for Wiltshire records, whether public or private. It contains Quarter Sessions records from 1563, of which the most important are the Great Rolls and enclosure awards; records of private estates and families; probate records of the local ecclesiastical courts covering Wiltshire from the 16th century to 1857; tithe apportionments from c. 1840; the records of parishes. The Wiltshire County Record Office is also responsible for the Diocesan Record Office in Salisbury. There is a small library of reference books useful to people studying the documents.

Access: The record office is open to the public. Inquiries should be directed to the Archivist. Students wishing to use the collection for extensive research should give advance notice. The hours are Monday to Friday, 8:45 A. M. to 12:30 P. M., 1:30 P. M. to 5:15 P. M.; Wednesday, 6:00 P. M. to 9:30 P. M.

Publications: Guide to the Records in the Custody of the Clerk of the Peace for Wiltshire (Guide to the County and Diocesan Record Offices, pt. I); Guide to County Council, Poor Law and Other Official Records in the Wiltshire County Record Office (Guide to the County and Diocesan Record Offices, pt. II).

Duplication: Full-size copying facilities are available. The cost is moderate. Microfilming and photographic services can also be provided.

Services: All records and book material must be consulted on the premises. Telephone and postal inquiries are answered.

TRURO

217 Institution   Cornwall County Record Office

Address   County Hall, Truro, Cornwall TR1 3HG
Telephone   0872-3698
Holdings   books; pamphlets; records

Subject Coverage: The records include some official records
of the county; family and private estate papers; parish and
diocesan records (including tithe maps); wills of the former
Archdeaconry of Cornwall from 1600 to 1858 and of Bodmin
district probate registry from 1858 to 1941; business records
(including those relating to mines). A small reference library
of a few thousand books and several hundred pamphlets is
available for use on the premises for staff and researchers.

Access: The office is open to the public. Application should
be directed to the County Archivist. If extensive research is
planned, a letter a few days in advance of a visit is appreciated. The hours are Monday to Friday, 9:00 A. M. to 1:00
P. M., 2:00 P. M. to 5:00 P. M.; Saturday (except before Bank
Holidays), 9:00 A. M. to 12 noon.

Publications: Typewritten quarterly accession lists are provided.

Duplication: Limited full-size copying and photographic facilities are available. Processing takes a few days, depending on
the size and shape of the material to be copied. Microfilming
is sometimes possible through arrangements with another section.

Services: Mail inquiries are answered, but only on specific
points. Material does not circulate.

WARWICK

218 Institution   Warwickshire County Record Office
     Address   Priory Park, Cape Road, Warwick CV34 4JS
     Telephone   0926-43431, ext. 2506/2507/2508
     Holdings   5,000 books; 2,000 pamphlets; 6 periodicals;
                   records; manuscripts; newspapers; maps

Subject Coverage: The office contains maps of Warwickshire;
Quarter Sessions records from 1625; Birmingham and Coventry
Diocesan records; parish registers; topography resources and
other deposited records; local newspaper files.

Access: The office is open to the public. Inquiries should be
directed to the County Archivist. The hours are Monday to
Friday, 9:00 A. M. to 1:00 P. M., 2:00 P. M. to 5:30 P. M.;
Saturday, 9:00 A. M. to 12:30 P. M.

Publications: Warwick County Records; The Printed Maps of
Warwickshire, 1576-1900 (1959); Sir William Dugdale, 1605-

1686: A List of His Printed Works and of His Portraits...,
by M. D. Styles and A. Wood.

Duplication: Full-size and micro-copying facilities are available.

Services: The collection can be used only on the premises.

WIGAN

219	Institution	Wigan Record Office
	Address	Leigh District Office (Wigan Metropolitan Borough County), Lancashire WN7 1DY
	Telephone	05235-72421, ext. 65/66
	Holdings	3,500 books; 1,100 pamphlets; 8 periodicals; microforms; records

Subject Coverage: The Search Room Library contains local society transactions and reference books for public and staff use. Collections cover fourteen local authority records; Wigan courts from 1618, including Leet; Quarter Sessions; family, parish, and estate papers; Edward Hall International Collection of Diaries, 1658-1945.

Access: Researchers may use the collections on the premises or on temporary transfer to repositories in England under acceptable standards of security and accommodation. Application should be made to the Archivist. The record office is open Monday to Friday, 8:45 A.M. to 4:45 P.M.

Publications: Annual Reports; Accessions Lists; Handlist 1975; Archive Teaching Units. Catalogs of specific collections are published from time to time, e.g., the Edward Hall Diary Collection.

Duplication: Full-size copying facilities are available at varying cost, depending on the size and character of the original documents. The time necessary to copy a document depends on the condition of the document. Photographs and microfilms can be arranged subject to copyright restrictions, and only for purposes of scholarship.

Services: Telephone and mail inquiries are answered. Project work has been arranged with local universities.

WINCHESTER

220	Institution	Hampshire County Record Office
	Address	20 Southgate Street, Winchester, Hampshire SO23 9EB
	Telephone	0962-63153

Holdings   books; pamphlets; periodicals; microforms;
                30,000 linear feet of records; manuscripts; maps

Subject Coverage: The collection includes records on the history of Winchester since 1155 in all aspects, especially administrative, legal, financial, sanitary, and ecclesiastical;
parish records concerning poor relief; documents illustrating
the history of Hampshire. A printed reference library is also
available.

Access: The record office is open to the public. Inquiries
should be directed to the Archivist. Prior notice of a visit
is appreciated. The hours are Monday to Friday, 9:15 A.M.
to 4:30 P.M.; second and fourth Saturday of each month (except public holiday week-ends), 9:15 A.M. to 12 noon.

Publications: Poor Law in Hampshire Through the Centuries
(1970); Transport in Hampshire and the Isle of Wight (1973).

Duplication: Full-size and micro-copying facilities are available at moderate cost.

Services: Documents can be consulted only on the premises.
Postal and telephone inquiries are answered.

WORCESTER

221 Institution   The County Council of Hereford and Worcester
                      Record Office
     Address   Headquarters: Shirehall, Foregate Street, Wor-
                      cester WR1 1DS; Hereford: The Old Barracks,
                      Harold Street, Hereford HR1 2QX
                      See also: HEREFORD, County Council of Here-
                      ford and Worcester Record Office (Reference No.
                      71)
                      St. Helen's: Fish Street, Worcester WR1 2HN
     Telephone   0905-23400, ext. 458
     Holdings   books; pamphlets; periodicals; 4,000,000 records

Subject Coverage: The County of Hereford and Worcester
Record Office is divided into three sections: Headquarters,
Hereford, and Worcester. Headquarters contains the archives
of the Worcestershire Quarter Sessions, the Worcestershire
County Council, and the County Council of Hereford and Worcester. The Hereford Section holds the archives of the Herefordshire Quarter Sessions, the Herefordshire County Council,
certain district and parish councils originating in Herefordshire, the Diocese of Hereford, other ecclesiastical bodies
and persons associated with Herefordshire, together with other
records pertaining to Herefordshire. The Worcester Section
contains the archives of certain central and regional bodies,
district and parish councils originating in Worcestershire,

the Diocese of Worcester, other ecclesiastical bodies and persons associated with Worcestershire, together with other records pertaining to Worcestershire. Because of shortages of space for official records at the Headquarters at Worcester, some documents have been moved temporarily to St. Helen's.

Access: The offices are open to the public. Inquiries should be addressed to the County Archivist. An appointment is suggested. The hours for the three offices are Monday to Friday, 9:15 A.M. to 4:45 P.M.

Publications: Annual Report.

Duplication: Full-size and micro-copying facilities are available. The cost and time necessary for processing vary depending on the size of the work to be copied.

Services: Questions not requiring extensive searchers will be answered, but the inquirer must deal with more difficult problems. The collection can be used only on the premises. Other services include cooperation with educational establishments, lectures, exhibitions, and paleographical assistance.

YORK

222	Institution	University of York, Borthwick Institute of Historical Research, Gurney Library
	Address	St. Anthony's Hall, Peasholme Green, York YO1 2PW
	Telephone	0904-59861, ext. 274
	Holdings	9,500 books, pamphlets, periodicals

Subject Coverage: The Gurney Library is a working library for use in connection with the deposited archive collections. The library contains resources in English ecclesiastical history, particularly of the northern province, archive and ecclesiastical administration, canon law, and palaeography. The institute is the record office for the archives of the Archbishopric of York.

Access: Scholars are permitted to use the collections, but an advance appointment is necessary. Inquiries should be addressed to the Director. The institute is ordinarily open Monday to Friday, 9:30 A.M. to 1:00 P.M., 2:00 P.M. to 5:00 P.M. It is closed on public holidays, for a short period at Easter and Christmas, the week preceding the August bank holiday, and the week beginning the first Monday in October.

Publications: Borthwick Papers; Borthwick Texts and Calendars; Borthwick Wallets; Borthwick Institute Bulletin (annual); a guide to the archive collections.

Duplication: Photographs and full-size and micro-copies of the archives can be obtained under certain conditions. A list of charges is available on request.

Services: The institute is an archive repository and a research institute, and its aim is to make the contents of the archive collections on deposit more readily accessible for research. The documents can be consulted only on the premises.

YORK

223 Institution   University of York, J. B. Morrell Library
     Address   Heslington, York YO1 5DD
     Telephone   0904-59861
     Holdings   220,000 books and pamphlets; 2,500 periodicals

Subject Coverage: The library contains resources in history, economics, politics, sociology, and social work; collections from the libraries of Lord Beveridge, Professor Henry Carter Adams, and Seebohm Rowntree.

Access: Visiting academics are permitted to use the collection. Inquiries should be addressed to the Librarian. A letter of introduction is recommended. During the academic year, the library is open Monday to Friday, 9:00 A.M. to 10:00 P.M.; Saturday, 9:00 A.M. to 5:00 P.M. During vacation, the hours are Monday to Friday, 9:00 A.M. to 5:15 P.M.

Publications: Library guides are issued.

Duplication: Full-size copying facilities are available on demand at low cost. Micro-copying is also provided, but the processing time varies depending on the type of work.

Services: The collection circulates only to members of the university.

YORK

224 Institution   York City Archives Department
     Address   Public Library, Museum Street, York YO1 2DS
     Telephone   0904-55631
     Holdings   several thousand books; 200 pamphlets; 15 micro-
                   forms; several thousand records

Subject Coverage: The collection includes City Charters (from the 12th century); Council Minute Books (from 1476); Chamberlains' Books and Rolls of Account (although incomplete, these exist from the 14th century); lists of freemen (from 1272); guild records; Quarter Sessions (from 1520); family and business records and plans relating to property in York.

Access: The archives department is open to the public.   Inquiries should be directed to the Archivist.   The hours are Monday to Friday, 9:00 A. M. to 12:30 P. M. , 2:00 P. M. to 6:00 P. M.

Publications: Catalogue of the City Records, by William Giles (1908); York City Archives, by Rita J. Green (1971).

Duplication: Photocopying facilities are available in the Reference Library.   Photography and microfilming can be arranged through York University.   The time necessary for processing is one to two weeks.

Services: The collection can be used only on the premises. Telephone and postal inquiries are answered.

Chapter 3

BRITISH SOCIETIES, ASSOCIATIONS
AND POLITICAL PARTIES

The American researcher in Britain might wish to
join societies and professional associations related to his
area of expertise. A variety of such organizations exists in
Britain in such fields as history, politics, economics, sociology and genealogy. The visiting scholar might find that
these organizations provide services worthy of his attention.
Such associations and societies conduct meetings and discussion groups, arrange contacts between American and British
scholars working in similar academic disciplines, publish
journals and provide specialized library resources. Not every
organization provides all of these services, but the visiting
American researcher has many opportunities available to him.

This chapter lists some of the British associations and
societies. The name, address, telephone number, officer to
whom inquiries should be made and an indication of the general services and specific benefits for visiting Americans are
provided for each organization. Some professional associations have links with their American counterparts and this
fact is recorded. Because their primary value is in their libraries, some societies are entered in Chapter 2. Chapter
3 includes entries for political parties, which are a source
of information to scholars working in British political studies.

AFRICAN STUDIES ASSOCIATION OF THE UNITED KINGDOM
The Hon. Secretary, c/o Centre of West African Studies,
University of Birmingham, P.O. Box 363, Birmingham B15
2SD
Telephone: 021-472 1301, ext. 2263

The principal aims of the association are to advance

African studies in the United Kingdom and to develop facilities for the interchange of information.   Membership is open to anyone professionally concerned with African studies upon completion of an application form and admission by the Council.   Associate membership is open to individuals and bodies with an interest in African studies.   Associates have the same privileges as full members with the exception of voting rights.   Honorary members are elected from time to time from among persons who have made an outstanding contribution to African studies.   Student and corporate memberships are also available.

The association holds a major conference, lasting several days every other year and a one-day symposium on a specific subject in the intervening years.   Participation is open to all classes of members.

African Research and Documentation is published three times a year by the association.   A Directory of African Studies in the United Kingdom and the Proceedings of the first symposium have been published by Cambridge University Press and are available to members at a concessionary rate.   Conference proceedings are also issued, appearing either as a single volume or as journal articles.

No special services are provided for visiting scholars nor is the association prepared to arrange meetings.

ANCIENT MONUMENTS SOCIETY
Hon. Secretary, 33 Ladbroke Square, London W11 3NB
Telephone: 01-221 6178

The Society was founded for the study and preservation of monuments and buildings of historic or architectural importance.   Membership is open to all interested individuals and institutions upon payment of the moderate annual subscription.

Members receive the Transactions of the Society and reports of the work of the society.   A general meeting is held annually.

This society is of interest to those concerned with the preservation of historic sites.   No special services are provided for social scientists, but contacts are maintained with most schools of architecture in the United Kingdom. A visiting scholar would be provided those contacts if he so desired.

THE ASSOCIATION OF GENEALOGISTS AND RECORD AGENTS
Hon. Secretary/Treasurer, 123 West End Road, Ruislip, Middlesex HA4 6JS
Telephone: 71-37138

The purpose of the association is to promote the science and skill of genealogical, biographical, and topographical research and the competent use of records, manuscripts and muniments.

Membership, which is selective, is by application and is subject to the approval of the Council of the Association. Before being accepted for membership, individuals must have experience and be able to convince the council of their ability and integrity.   Most members are genealogists, but several are also historians with varied interests.   An annual meeting is held by order of the council.

A list of experienced genealogists and record agents is maintained.   A professional journal and such literature as may further the objects of the association are issued. Members receive the journal without charge.

An American researcher visiting Great Britain can make contact with members of the association for aid in genealogical research or for other matters of mutual interest. Meetings between visiting Americans and others in their field of study are arranged whenever possible.

THE BIBLIOGRAPHICAL SOCIETY
Rooms of the British Academy, Burlington House, Piccadilly, London W1V 0NS
Communications to: Hon. Secretary, British Library, London WC1B 3DG

The main purpose of the society is to encourage research in historical, analytical, descriptive and textual bibliography and in the history of printing, publishing, bookselling, collecting and bookbinding.

The society's membership is international and is open to all who are concerned with bibliography.   Acceptance is conditional upon election by the council.   Candidates should be proposed by a member and their names submitted through the Hon. Secretary.   A prospective candidate not acquainted with a member should write to the Hon. Secretary informing him of the circumstances and mentioning his bibliographical interests and any bibliographical works he has compiled.   Libraries and institutions may also become members.   An annual subscription is charged.

Meetings of the society are ordinarily held at University College, London, on the third Tuesday of each month from October to March.   An annual meeting is held in March or April after the conclusion of the ordinary monthly meeting. Papers are read at the meetings.

The official transactions of the society are The Library.   There is also an annual monograph on a bibliographical subject.   Members receive The Library (quarterly) and the monographs without charge.   The society's library is housed at University College, London.   Books may be borrowed by members at any time the college library is open.

No special services are provided for American scholars, but the society could informally arrange for researchers to meet British scholars working in the same field.

THE BRITISH CARTOGRAPHIC SOCIETY
Hon. Secretary, 11 Hope Terrace, Edinburgh EH9 2AP
Telephone: 031-447 6261

The object of the society is the promotion of the study of cartography by facilitating exchange of information and ideas, publishing periodicals and books, arranging and participating in national and international conferences.

Membership is open to individuals interested in cartography.   Organizations, universities or government departments may become corporate members.   The Council can designate honorary members as it sees fit.   There is a moderate annual subscription.

An annual weekend symposium is held at a university at which papers by members and speakers of international repute are presented and discussed.   Between symposia, technical papers are presented to members at regular meetings held in London, Southampton, Edinburgh, Taunton and occasionally at other locations.   There are a Cartography Teachers' Group which serves as a forum for the special interests of members engaged in teaching, a Map Curators' Group which concerns itself with matters of interest to archivists and curators of map collections and an Automation in Cartography Group for those interested in all aspects of automated or computer-assisted cartography.

The society publishes The Cartographic Journal twice a year.   This journal holds a leading position in world cartographic literature and serves as a record of the society's activities.   Members receive the journal without charge.   A Newsletter on matters of current interest is issued to members several times each year.   A booklet, Careers in Car-

tography, is published to assist young people in the choice
of a career. Automated Cartography, containing papers presented at a symposium on the subject, is the first in a series
of special publications.

The society's library and map collection are housed
in the Edinburgh Public Library. Items are available for
loan to members. No special services are offered to visiting scholars, but the society is prepared to introduce researchers to members working in a similar field.

THE BRITISH INSTITUTE OF INTERNATIONAL AND COM-
PARATIVE LAW
Director, 32 Furnival Street, London EC4A 1JN
Telephone: 01-405 4051/3

The institute was founded in order to bring together
and expand the work of the Society of Comparative Legislation and International Law and the Grotius Society. The institute provides an international center for studying the practical application of public international law, private international law and comparative law. Membership is open to individuals, firms and corporations without restriction of nationality. There is a moderately high annual membership fee
which is reduced for students. Larger firms and corporations are invited to become corporate members at an in-
creased annual fee. Corporate members have advantages regarding receipt of all the institute's publications and participation in conferences.

The institute organizes a wide range of lecture meetings, seminars and conferences and conducts and promotes
research. Among its publications are The International and
Comparative Law Quarterly, British Practice in International
Law, the Bulletin of Legal Developments and monographs in
the institute's fields of interest. Members receive The International and Comparative Law Quarterly without charge.
A Newsletter on the activities of the institute is also issued
to members.

Members are entitled to consult the professional staff
of the institute on legal questions of general interest, to
make use of the institute's Commonwealth Legal Advisory
Service and to use the Barnett Shine Reading Room and Library. There are no special services for visiting American
scholars who are not members of the institute. The institute
can undertake to arrange meetings between British and American scholars, but only if one of them is a member of or is
known to the institute.

BRITISH RECORDS ASSOCIATION
Hon. Secretary, The Master's Court, The Charterhouse,
Charterhouse Square, London EC1M 6AU
Telephone: 01-253 0436

The association serves as a link between all who are
concerned with the ownership, custody, preservation, study
and publication of records. It furthers the use of records
as historical material, particularly through the medium of
publication and seeks to develop informed opinion on the necessity for preserving records of historical importance.

Membership is open to individuals and institutions interested in the aims of the association. A moderate annual
subscription is charged.

An annual two-day conference is held, usually in December. Papers are read on a variety of topics and an opportunity for discussion is provided.

The association's journal, Archives, is published bi-
annually and is available to members at a reduced rate. An
Annual Report of the Council, a monographic series Archives
and the User and reports on various subjects are issued.

The association will advise visiting American scholars
on the location of documents or will direct them to the proper
organization to do so. The association is also prepared to
put American archivists in touch with their British counterparts.

THE BRITISH SOCIOLOGICAL ASSOCIATION
Hon. General Secretary, 13 Endsleigh Street, London WC1H
0DJ
Telephone: 01-387 3627

The association seeks to promote interest in sociology,
to advance its study and application in Britain, and to bring
together workers in relevant fields by arranging lectures,
conferences, study groups and publications.

Membership is open to anyone working within the broad
area of sociology. The association consists of Members,
Student Members and Overseas Associate Members. They
are elected by the Executive Council and must be sponsored
by two members. The association is affiliated with the International Sociological Association.

Meetings and one-day conferences for the reading of
papers and for discussions are organized periodically on special topics. A major residential conference is held annually,
designed to provide maximum opportunity for membership

participation.   The association endeavors to keep the membership informed of research being carried out by other
members.   Sociology, the association's journal, and Sociological Review are available to members at a reduced rate.
British Journal of Sociology is made available to members
by the publishers at a concessionary rate.
        No special services are provided for visiting Ameri-
can scholars, but the association does try to put visitors in
touch with people working in particular fields of interest.

COMMUNIST PARTY
16 King Street, London WC2E 8HY
Telephone: 01-836 2151
(See also: LONDON, Marx Memorial Library, Reference
No. 139)

        The Communist Party does not maintain a research
department at its offices.   It will refer inquirers to the
Marx Memorial Library which contains material on communist affairs.   The party will, however, refer academicians
to Communist Party officials and sympathizers.

CONSERVATIVE PARTY
Research Department, 24 Old Queen Street, London SW1H
9HX
Telephone: 01-930 1471
(See also: LONDON, Conservative Research Department Li-
brary, Reference No. 102)

        The Conservative Party Research Department will
assist visiting academics conducting advanced research, provided this research will lead to a publication.

THE ECONOMIC ASSOCIATION
General Secretary, Room 340, Hamilton House, Mabledon
Place, London WC1H 9BH
Telephone: 01-387 6321

        The association seeks to promote the study of eco-
nomics and kindred subjects in schools and colleges, to provide means for the exchange of views and to act as a representative body on occasions when the educational interests of
economics are involved.   Although there are no restrictions
on membership, the association is primarily composed of

economics teachers.   A moderate annual subscription is required.

There are at present nine branches of the association, each of which holds meetings.   An annual Schools' Conference is held at which professors give the main lecture, and eminent men of business join the discussion panels.   The association's publications include the journal Economics which is received by members without charge, occasional book lists, monographs and pamphlets.

Meetings are arranged between visiting scholars and members of the association.   These are usually at the request and with the cooperation of the British Council.

ECONOMIC HISTORY SOCIETY
Hon. Secretary, Keynes College, The University, Canterbury, Kent CT2 7NP
Telephone: 0227-66822

The society was founded to encourage the teaching and study of economic history.   Its functions are primarily to organize an annual conference and to publish the Economic History Review.   Membership is open to all interested individuals on payment of the annual subscription.

The society does not provide services to visiting scholars and is not prepared to arrange meetings between American academics and their British counterparts.

THE FOLKLORE SOCIETY
Hon. Secretary, c/o University College London, Gower Street, London WC1E 6BT
Telephone: 01-387 5894

The original purpose of the society was the systematic comparative study of oral traditions and cultures.   Today it also includes the study of material culture, song and dance.

Membership is granted after election by committee and on payment of the current subscription.   There are monthly meetings from October to June, usually on the third Wednesday of the month.   These are open to the public and are held at University College, London.

Members receive Folklore, the society's journal.   A complete list of publications is available from the society's office.   Members may borrow from the society's library and use the general library of the University College, London. Books are not lent overseas.   Visiting researchers may use

the library on the premises and are welcome to attend the
society's lectures.

As the staff is limited, little assistance can be provided to visiting scholars. Introductions between American
and British scholars are not arranged, but a Central Register
of Researchers in different fields is maintained and this list
is available to visitors on request.

THE GEOGRAPHICAL ASSOCIATION
Hon. Secretary, 343 Fulwood Road, Sheffield S10 3BP
Telephone: 0742-661 666

The association was founded to further the knowledge
and teaching of geography in all categories of educational institutions. Membership is open to all those interested in
geography or its teaching. Details of subscription charges
are available on request.

The association arranges courses, conferences and
summer schools for its members and operates an information
service. There are branches throughout Great Britain which
carry out much of the association's active work. A library
is maintained which contains about 15,000 books and 220 foreign geography periodicals. Members may borrow from the
collection and non-members may use the resources on the
premises Monday to Friday, 9:00 A.M. to 5:00 P.M.

No special services are available to visitors, but the
association will offer help in introducing Americans to British
scholars researching the same field.

THE HARLEIAN SOCIETY
Hon. Secretary, Church Cottage, Thames Ditton, Surrey KT7
0NN

The society is not a professional association but is engaged solely in publishing the heraldic visitations of counties,
parish registers and manuscripts relating to genealogy, family
history and heraldry.

There are two sections, one concerned with heraldic
visitations and manuscripts, the other with parish registers.
In general, the membership is comprised of institutions. A
moderate annual subscription is charged. Copies of the publications of the society, which are valuable for genealogical
reference, are supplied only to members. Only recent volumes are still in print. These include Catalogue of the Earl
Marshal's Papers, The Life of William Bruges, a new edi-

tion of the Visitation of London, 1568, and Aspilogia II, Rolls of Arms of the Reign of Henry III.

THE HISTORICAL ASSOCIATION
The Secretary, 59A Kennington Park Road, London SE11 4JH
Telephone: 01-735 3901

The aims of the Historical Association are to advance the study and teaching of history at all levels and to increase public interest in all aspects of the subject. Membership is open to all who are interested in history. Colleges, schools and libraries may become corporate members on the same terms as individuals. A nominal annual subscription is charged. There are over a hundred branches in the United Kingdom and overseas.
An annual conference is held, usually in April, which includes lectures, reports and discussions on recent historical work, excursions and receptions. Branches arrange lectures, discussions, excursions to places of historical interest and studies of local history.
A library is maintained from which members may borrow, either personally or by post. Visiting American researchers may use the collection on the premises. A printed catalogue is available for a small fee.
The association publishes a General Series, an Annual Report and an Annual Bulletin which members receive without charge. History, Teaching History, Helps for Students of History and Teaching History Pamphlets are available to members at a reduced cost. A complete list of publications is provided.
The association is prepared to give information to visiting American scholars and to arrange introductions to British scholars working in the same field of specialization.

INSTITUTE OF JEWISH AFFAIRS (in association with the World Jewish Congress)
13-16 Jacob's Well Mews, George St., London W1H 5PD
Telephone: 01-935 1436

The institute's main concern is with Jewish affairs throughout the world. An effort is made to be continually informed about current events particularly those dealing with Jewish matters.
A prospective member must be proposed and seconded by two members of the institute. He should be a genuine

researcher in the specialized fields of the institute and should be interested in its activities.

The institute sponsors a lecture series annually and engages in several continuing research projects. Among its publications are LJA News Bulletin, Patterns of Prejudice, Christian Attitudes on Jews and Judaism, Research Reports and several monographs.

A library is maintained and visiting scholars are permitted to use the resources for material they cannot otherwise obtain. The institute is prepared to arrange meetings between British and American scholars working in the same field of interest.

THE IRISH GENEALOGICAL RESEARCH SOCIETY
82 Eaton Square, London SW1A 9AQ
Telephone: 01-265 4164

The society was formed to promote and encourage the study of Irish genealogy, both Gaelic and Anglo-Irish. Replacement of genealogical material lost as a result of the destruction of the Public Records Office in Dublin in 1922 is one of the aims of the society.

Membership is open to those with an interest in Irish genealogy and preferably those with Irish ancestors. The entrance fee is nominal. The annual subscription is moderate for which members receive The Irish Genealogist. They may submit short queries to this publication at no extra charge. The spouse of a member is admitted without an entrance fee and at half the subscription of an ordinary member.

An excellent reference library is maintained at the society's address. Members may use the collection without charge, but non-members must pay £1 per visit. The library is open Tuesday, 2:30 P.M. to 6:00 P.M. and Saturday, 2:30 P.M. to 5:30 P.M. Short postal inquiries will be answered for members at no charge, but those wishing an extensive search should write to the Secretary for a list of charges.

The society is not prepared to undertake lengthy research on behalf of individuals or to provide special services to visiting academics. Meetings between British and American scholars will not be arranged, but a list of professional genealogists in London and in Ireland will be supplied on request.

THE JEWISH HISTORICAL SOCIETY OF ENGLAND
Hon. Secretary, 33 Seymour Place, London W1H 5AP
Telephone: 01-723 4404

The society was founded with the object of promoting
the study of the history of the Jews of the British Empire.
Its work is not limited to research, but includes promoting
knowledge of the history of the Jewish people and the particular historical role they have played in the United Kingdom
and the Commonwealth.

There are no restrictions on membership. Both individuals and institutions may become members.

Monthly meetings are held from November to June or
July. Original papers and popular presentations are delivered
on various aspects of Anglo-Jewish history. Conferences are
held from time to time and occasionally the society invites
an eminent personality to deliver the Lucien Wolf Memorial
Lecture on a subject related to Lucien Wolf's interests.

The society's publications include the Transactions,
which contain many of the papers delivered to the society,
and Miscellanies, which carries basic research material,
membership lists and shorter contributions. Four volumes of
the Exchequer of the Jews have been published in addition to
pamphlets and monographs.

The society maintains a library and museum (the Mocatta Library at University College, London) for the preservation of archives of Anglo-Jewish congregations and institutions and of documents, books, prints and other objects of
Jewish historical interest (Anglo-Jewish Archives).

Visiting researchers are welcome to use the Mocatta
Library and to contact historians who are members of the
society's council through the Chairman of the Research Committee.

LABOUR PARTY
Transport House, Smith Square, London SW1P 2JA
Telephone: 01-834 9434
(See also: LONDON, Labour Party Library, Reference No.
129)

The Labour Party will provide information about its
past and present activities. If the visiting scholar is interested in current matters, he should write or telephone the
Information Officer. For information of past years the Librarian should be consulted.

LIBERAL PARTY
7 Exchange Court, The Strand, London WC2R 0PR
Telephone: 01-240 0701

The Liberal Party office has press clippings, pamphlets and books dealing with party matters as well as official policy statements and news releases.   There is a
small staff with limited resources.   Assistance concerning
sources of Liberal Party information will be provided.   Inquiries should be addressed to the Information Officer.

THE LIBRARY ASSOCIATION
Information Officer, 7 Ridgmount Street, Store Street, London
WC1E 7AE
Telephone: 01-636 7543
(See also: LONDON, British Library, Library Association
Library, Reference No. 94)

The purposes of the Library Association are the fol-
lowing: to establish and improve libraries, to promote legislation, to encourage research, to improve the training of librarians and to serve the personal benefit of its members.
Membership is open to all librarians, library science students and those interested in librarianship.
An annual one-week conference is held, usually in
September.   The papers read are reported in the Library
Association Record, which members receive without charge.
Only some of the papers are reproduced in full.   Groups and
sections of the association, which serve the specialized interests of members, hold conferences and meetings throughout the year.
The Library and Information Department offers an information service on the professional problems of members.
The association's publication program attempts to insure that
needed works are published even when commercial success
is doubtful.   A current-awareness service is provided for all
branches of the profession through the monthly publications,
the Record and Liaison.   Other publications include British
Humanities Index, British Technology Index and Library and
Information Science Abstracts (with Aslib).
The association is prepared to help visiting American
scholars interested in librarianship or information science.
It will also attempt to arrange meetings with British scholars
having similar interest.

LONDON RECORD SOCIETY
Hon. Secretary, c/o Leicester University Library, University Road
Leicester LE1 7RH

The society was founded to stimulate interest in archives relating to London and to publish transcripts, abstracts and lists of primary sources for the history of London.

Membership is open to any individual or institution. A nominal annual subscription is charged. Members receive one copy of each volume published by the society during the year. Previously published works are available to members at reduced cost.

Informal assistance within the capability of the society is offered to visiting American scholars, and names of the members would be provided to bona fide scholars working on London history.

MILITARY HISTORICAL SOCIETY
Centre Block, The Duke of York's Headquarters, Chelsea, London SW3
Secretary: 7 East Woodside, Leighlands; Bexley, Kent DA5 3PG
Telephone: 29-27476

The aim of the society is to encourage research into the history, traditions, uniforms, badges, etc. of the armed forces of Great Britain and the Commonwealth. Membership is open to those interested in these matters. A small subscription is charged.

Informal meetings are held once a month at the society's headquarters. A visit to European battlefields, led by lecturers of international repute, is organized each spring.

An extensive military library is maintained at the headquarters from which members may borrow. The society's archives are available to members (by correspondence for overseas members) for reference. The collection contains unpublished material on Commonwealth and some foreign forces, e.g., almost complete lists of most Commonwealth units from the earliest times and many brief histories. The collection of Rev. Cannon W. Lummis, consisting of individual files on all who have been awarded the Victoria Cross and publications on the subject, is also available for reference.

The society publishes a quarterly Bulletin which

members receive without charge.   A special publication was
issued in 1968 which gives full details of all Regular Infan-
try Colours since 1881.   This and many back numbers of
the Bulletin are available to members at moderate cost.   A
Directory of Members is also available which gives the
names, addresses and interests of all members.

PLAID CYMRU (Welsh Nationalist Party)
8 Queen Street, Cardiff CF1 1DZ
Telephone: 022-31944
(See also: CARDIFF, Plaid Cymru, Reference No. 29)

        The party will assist scholars conducting advanced
research by directing visitors to library resources, Plaid
Cymru officials and individuals with specialized information.

POLITICAL STUDIES ASSOCIATION OF THE UNITED
KINGDOM
The Secretary, Institute of Local Government Studies, Uni-
versity of Birmingham, P. O. Box 363, Birmingham B15 2TT

        Full membership in the association is open to any per-
son holding an appointment in political studies or allied subjects in a university or polytechnic of the United Kingdom or
colonies.   Associate membership is open to any person holding an appointment in political studies or allied subjects in a
university in a foreign country.   At the discretion of the
Executive Committee, any person whose participation in the
association would be advantageous to political studies may be
admitted to membership.   A resolution has been put forward
for debate at an annual meeting that anyone who wishes to
join the association should be allowed to do so.
        An annual conference is held and specialist study
groups are arranged (e. g. , American Politics, Political
Sociology, the Study of Public Policy Making).   Members
receive copies of the journal Political Studies and a newsletter on current developments in the profession.   For persons who wish to visit British universities, the association
makes available a brief directory which indicates those universities willing to accept visitors and which lists the facilities of each.
        The association will provide information and encour-
agement to visiting American scholars who wish to meet
British counterparts working in the same field of study.
Any scholar requiring information should contact the Secre-

tary of the association, who will attempt to put him in touch
with the appropriate university department.

THE ROYAL ECONOMIC SOCIETY
Information Secretary, 48 Kidderminster Road, Hagley,
Stourbridge, West Midlands DY9 0QD
Telephone: 056-286 4788

The society was established to promote the general
advancement of economic knowledge. It is one of the oldest
associations of economists in the world.
Membership is open to anyone with an active interest
in economic questions. The majority of members are professional economists in business, government service or
higher education.
The society publishes Economic Journal quarterly
which members receive without charge. There is also an
important monographic series which includes the Collected
Writings of John Maynard Keynes, Collected Works of Ri-
cardo and Papers and Correspondence of William Stanley
Jevons. Members may purchase society publications at a
concessionary rate. There is also a quarterly Newsletter
which contains information about scholarships; fellowships;
facilities for study abroad; scholars visiting the United Kingdom with details of where they are visiting, approximate
dates and research interests; forthcoming events of interest
to economists, e. g. , conferences, lectures and special
courses with dates and details. Members may receive the
Newsletter without charge on application to the Information
Secretary. Non-members may receive it at nominal cost.
The American researcher will be assisted in Britain
by the information contained in the Newsletter. The society
will also help in contacting British scholars working in the
same field.

ROYAL HISTORICAL SOCIETY
Executive Secretary, University College London, Gower
Street, London WC1E 6BT
Telephone: 01-387 7532

The principal object of the society is to promote the
study of history. Fellows are elected and candidates should
have published some substantial historical work based on
original research. This contribution may be in the form of
books or learned articles. Associates are also elected and

candidates must either be preparing some work of this nature for publication or be helping the study of history in some other active way.   The teaching of history is not by itself regarded as sufficient qualification.   Applications for both classes of membership must be supported by two Fellows who have personal knowledge of the applicant.   A nominal annual subscription is charged.

Documentary material, bibliographical and reference works are published.   Once a month, except during vacations, a paper is read before the society.   These papers appear in the society's Transactions.   A list of members is also printed in the Transactions.   Fellows and Associates receive as part of their membership an annual volume of the Transactions and Fellows also receive the Camden Series and the Guides and Handbooks Series.   These may be purchased by Associates at a reduced price.   Bibliographies of British History and Writings on British History are available to members at a reduced cost.   A full list of the society's publications is printed each year in the Transactions.   The society maintains a library for the use of Fellows.

Subscribing libraries are admitted to membership upon payment of an annual fee.   They receive the same publications as Fellows.

THE ROYAL INSTITUTE OF INTERNATIONAL AFFAIRS
Administrative Director, Chatham House, 10 St. James's Square, London SW1Y 4LE
Telephone: 01-930 2233
(See also: LONDON, Royal Institute of International Affairs, Reference No. 151)

The objects of the institute are to advance the scientific study of international politics, economics and jurisprudence, to facilitate the exchange of information on these subjects and to provide a means to accomplish these ends.

Membership in the institute is open only to British and Commonwealth citizens.   Other nationals may become Foreign Associates.   Candidates must be proposed and seconded by members to whom they are known personally.
They should be persons who are active in or have special knowledge of international affairs.   They should also be able to show evidence that they can contribute to the activities of the institute.   Organizations may become corporate members without going through the formalities of election.

The institute conducts general meetings devoted to subjects of general interest and private discussion meetings,

which are attended by invitation only. Study groups and conferences are organized to bring together both British and foreign experts to consider international problems. Research
into international questions--political, economic, legal, cul-
tural--is undertaken by members of the permanent staff of
the institute.

A library of over 130, 000 books and pamphlets and
600 periodicals is maintained. It is one of the leading specialized collections in Britain of material dealing with international affairs from 1918.

Visiting Americans are occasionally admitted as Foreign Associates. Membership will not normally be granted
to foreign students studying only temporarily in the United
Kingdom nor to members of foreign missions. It is possible
that meetings could be arranged between British and American
scholars with similar interests.

ROYAL INSTITUTE OF PUBLIC ADMINISTRATION
Director General, Hamilton House, Mabledon Place, London
WC1H 9BD
Telephone: 01-388 0211

The institute was founded to promote the study of public administration. Membership is open to civil servants, officers of local authorities, the health services, public corporations and teachers and students of public administration.
The Executive Council may also elect as a member any other
person considered to be actively concerned in the practice
or study of public administration.

The institute provides a meeting ground for officials
of various public services and encourages the exchange of
new ideas and practical experience. It undertakes research
assisted by study groups comprising university teachers and
those who hold responsible administrative posts in the public
services. Lectures are arranged in major administrative
centers on topics of current interest to which members are
invited without charge.

The publications include the journal Public Administration, which is available to members without charge, conference reports and a number of monographs. A list is available from the institute. A library is maintained which includes books, pamphlets, official publications and many British and foreign periodicals. A loan and bibliographical service is provided to members. The library also serves as
the basis of an information service which members may use.
Only members may borrow from the collection.

The institute has always been pleased to welcome visiting scholars in public administration from the United States
and to offer them the use of the institute's library. Advice
will be given to visitors about British scholars it would be
helpful for them to meet, but actual introductions would be
arranged only for members.

ROYAL STATISTICAL SOCIETY
Secretary, 21 Bentinck Street, London W1M 6AR
Telephone: 01-935 7638

The society is concerned with the development of statistical theory and methodology and the application of statistical methods in many fields, e. g. , medicine, industry, agriculture and government.

Fellowship in the society is attained by election. A
candidate must be proposed by two or more Fellows who will
vouch for his qualifications and eligibility. Upon election the
current subscription must be paid. Corporate bodies and institutions may become Associated Members. They may nom-
inate a representative who is subject to Council approval, but
need not be a Fellow.

There are four sections of the society, all of which
normally meet in London. These are: Research Section,
Medical Section, Industrial Application Section and General
Application Section. There are also several local groups
which serve statisticians in their area. Membership in the
sections and local groups is open to Fellows without charge.
Representatives of Associated Members may attend meetings
and conferences of the society, its sections and local groups.
Fellows and representatives may introduce guests to meetings, receive all the society's journals and have full use of
the library.

Meetings are held monthly, October to June. Papers
are read at these meetings and discussions invited from Fellows, representatives and visitors. One-day conferences are
organized by the sections from time to time. Usually two
residential conferences of about three days duration are arranged by one or more of the sections each year.

The society publishes three Journals: Series A (General), Series B (Methodological), Series C (Applied Statistics). Papers read at ordinary meetings of the society are
included in the journals. Other papers, whether by Fellows
or not, may also be submitted for publication.

A library is maintained which contains a large and
unique collection of statistical books and basic source ma-

terial. The collection is available to Fellows and accredited
members of sections and local groups.

The society does not provide specific services for
visiting researchers, but there is considerable overlap of
membership with the American Statistical Association and
there is cooperation between statisticians in the United States
and Great Britain. The society will encourage and facilitate
such cooperation in any way possible.

SCOTS ANCESTRY RESEARCH SOCIETY
Director, 20 York Place, Edinburgh EH1 3EP
Telephone: 031-556 4220

The society was established to assist persons of Scottish ancestry to trace facts about their forebears in Scotland.
It is solely a research organization and has no membership.
The offices are only for administrative purposes as the research is carried out in the original records, housed in various record offices. There are no library facilities.

Serious research scholars in the genealogical field are
welcome, and advice is given on sources and facilities available for research in Scottish records. The office is open
Monday to Friday, 10:00 A.M. to 12:15 P.M., 2:15 P.M. to
4:00 P.M.

Forms are provided for those desiring help in tracing
Scottish ancestry. A fee is charged for the actual research
work and report, and for registration.

THE SCOTTISH GENEALOGY SOCIETY
Hon. Secretary, 21 Howard Place, Edinburgh, Scotland EH3
5JY

The society's aims are to promote research into Scottish family history and to undertake the collection, exchange
and publication of material relating to genealogy. The society is academic and consultative and does not engage in
record searching. A list of members who are professional
searchers is available from the Secretary. Membership is
by election and a small annual subscription is charged.
Meetings are held monthly from September to April, ordinarily on the fifteenth.

A library service is maintained for members residing
in the United Kingdom. The collection includes printed
books, manuscripts and foreign periodicals which are received in exchange for the Scottish Genealogist.

No specific services are provided for visiting American researchers, but from time to time meetings have been arranged for American groups. The society is willing to arrange meetings between scholars.

THE SCOTTISH HISTORY SOCIETY
Hon. Secretary, c/o National Library of Scotland, George IV Bridge, Edinburgh EH1 1EW
Telephone: 031-226 4531

The society was founded for the purpose of discovering and printing unpublished documents pertaining to the history of Scotland. Membership is open to anyone interested in Scottish history and to libraries and other institutions who wish to receive the publications. There is a small annual subscription in return for which members receive a hard cover volume on a topic of Scottish history. An annual meeting is held at which a presidential address is delivered.
The society is not prepared to offer any special services to visiting academics, but is willing to put any researcher in touch with another scholar in the same field.

SCOTTISH NATIONAL PARTY
6 North Charlotte Street, Edinburgh EH2 4HR
Telephone: 031-226 5722
(See also: EDINBURGH, Scottish National Party, Reference No. 52)

The Press Officer can introduce visiting academics to individuals involved in the Scottish National Party. He can also direct the visitor to university library resources which contain information about various aspects of Scotland.

SELDEN SOCIETY
Secretary, Faculty of Laws, Queen Mary College, Mile End Road, London E1 4NS
Telephone: 01-980 4811, ext. 584

The society was founded to encourage the study and advance the knowledge of the history of English law. Membership is unrestricted upon payment of the annual subscription.
Lectures are held from time to time and the society collaborates in the organizing of legal history conferences.

The office of the secretary acts as a channel of information on activities in the legal history field and helps to publicize conferences, meetings, forthcoming publications, etc.

The society produces at least one large volume every year (sent to all members), an annual report, lectures, a handbook and other occasional literature.

No special services are provided for visiting scholars. The society would, however, help arrange meetings between American and British scholars working in the same field.

SELECT LIST OF BRITISH UNIVERSITIES

ENGLAND

University of Aston in Birmingham, Gosta Green, Birmingham.
  Telephone: 021-359 3611
University of Bath, Claverton Down, Bath. Telephone: 0225-6941
University of Birmingham, P. O. B. 363, Birmingham. Telephone:
  021-472 1301
University of Bradford, Bradford 7, West Yorkshire. Telephone:
  0274-33466
University of Bristol, Bristol. Telephone: 0272-24161
Brunel University, Uxbridge, Middlesex. Telephone: 89-37188
University College at Buckingham, Buckingham. Telephone: 028-
  02 3737
University of Cambridge, Cambridge. Telephone: 0223-58933
  (Registry)
    Colleges of the University of Cambridge
    Christ's College, Cambridge. Telephone: 0223-67641
    Churchill College, Cambridge. Telephone: 0223-61200
    Clare College, Cambridge. Telephone: 0223-58681
    Clare Hall, Cambridge. Telephone: 0223-63330
    Corpus Christi College, Cambridge. Telephone: 0223-59418
    Downing College, Cambridge. Telephone: 0223-59491
    Emmanuel College, Cambridge. Telephone: 0223-65411
    Fitzwilliam College, Cambridge. Telephone: 0223-58657
    Girton College, Cambridge. Telephone: 0223-76219
    Gonville and Caius College, Cambridge. Telephone: 0223-
      53275
    Hughes Hall, Cambridge. Telephone: 0223-52866
    Jesus College, Cambridge. Telephone: 0223-57536 (lodge);
      0223-61345/6 (office)
    King's College, Cambridge. Telephone: 0223-50411
    Lucy Cavendish Collegiate Society, Cambridge. Telephone:
      0223-63409
    Magdalene College, Cambridge. Telephone: 0223-61543
    New Hall, Cambridge. Telephone: 0223-51721
    Newnham College, Cambridge. Telephone: 0223-62273
    Pembroke College, Cambridge. Telephone: 0223-52241
    Peterhouse, Cambridge. Telephone: 0223-50256
    Queens' College, Cambridge. Telephone: 0223-65511

St. Catharine's College, Cambridge. Telephone: 0223-59445
St. Edmund's House, Cambridge. Telephone: 0223-50398
St. John's College, Cambridge. Telephone: 0223-61621
Selwyn College, Cambridge. Telephone: 0223-62381
Sidney Sussex College, Cambridge. Telephone: 0223-61501
Trinity College, Cambridge. Telephone: 0223-58201
Wolfson College, Cambridge. Telephone: 0223-64811
University of Durham, Old Shire Hall, Durham. Telephone: 0385-64466
University of East Anglia, Earlham Hall, Norwich. Telephone: 0603-56161
University of Essex, Wivenhoe Park, Colchester. Telephone: 0206-44144
University of Exeter, Exeter. Telephone: 0392-77911
University of Hull, Cottingham Road, Hull. Telephone: 0482-46311
University of Keele, Keele, Staffordshire. Telephone: 078-271 371
University of Kent at Canterbury, Canterbury, Kent. Telephone: 0227-66822
University of Lancaster, Bailrigg, Lancaster. Telephone: 0524-65201
University of Leeds, Leeds. Telephone: 0532-31751
University of Leicester, University Road, Leicester. Telephone: 0533-50000
University of Liverpool, P. O. B. 147, Liverpool. Telephone: 051-709 6022
University of London, Senate House, London. Telephone: 01-636 8000

> Schools of the University of London
>
> Bedford College, Inner Circle, Regent's Park, London. Telephone: 01-486 4400
> Birkbeck College, Malet Street, London. Telephone: 01-580 6622
> Chelsea College, Manresa Road, Chelsea, London. Telephone: 01-352 6421
> Imperial College of Science and Technology, South Kensington, London. Telephone: 01-589 5111
> King's College, Strand, London. Telephone: 01-836 5454
> London School of Economics and Political Science, Houghton Street, Aldwych, London. Telephone: 01-405 7686
> Queen Elizabeth College, Campden Hill Road, London. Telephone: 01-937 5411
> Queen Mary College, Mile End Road, London. Telephone: 01-980 4811
> Royal Holloway College, Egham Hill, Egham, Surrey. Telephone: 389-4455
> School of Oriental and African Studies, Malet Street, London. Telephone: 01-637 2388
> University College, Gower Street, London. Telephone: 01-387 7050
> Westfield College, Kidderpore Avenue, Hampstead, London. Telephone: 01-435 7141

Loughborough University of Technology, Loughborough, Leicestershire. Telephone: 050-93 63171

Victoria University of Manchester, Oxford Road, Manchester. Telephone: 061-273 3333

University of Newcastle upon Tyne, Newcastle upon Tyne. Telephone: 0632-28511

University of Nottingham, University Park, Nottingham. Telephone: 0602-56101

University of Oxford, University Register, Oxford. Telephone: 0865-48491

Colleges of the University of Oxford

All Soul's College, Oxford. Telephone: 0865-22251

Balliol College, Oxford. Telephone: 0865-49601

Brasenose College, Oxford. Telephone: 0865-48641

Campion Hall, Oxford. Telephone: 0865-40861/2

Christ Church, Oxford. Telephone: 0865-42201

Corpus Christi, Oxford. Telephone: 0865-49431

Exeter College, Oxford. Telephone: 0865-44681

Greyfriars, Oxford. Telephone: 0865-43694

Hertford College, Oxford. Telephone: 0865-41434

Jesus College, Oxford. Telephone: 0865-49511

Keble College, Oxford. Telephone: 0865-59201

Lady Margaret Hall, Oxford. Telephone: 0865-54353

Linacre College, Oxford. Telephone: 0865-43526

Lincoln College, Oxford. Telephone: 0865-42580

Magdalen College, Oxford. Telephone: 0865-41781

Mansfield College, Oxford. Telephone: 0865-43507

Merton College, Oxford. Telephone: 0865-49651

New College, Oxford. Telephone: 0865-48451

Nuffield College, Oxford. Telephone: 0865-48014

Oriel College, Oxford. Telephone: 0865-41651

Pembroke College, Oxford. Telephone: 0865-42271

The Queen's College, Oxford. Telephone: 0865-48411

Regent's Park College, Oxford. Telephone: 0865-59887

St. Anne's College, Oxford. Telephone: 0865-57417

St. Antony's College, Oxford. Telephone: 0865-59651

St. Benet's Hall, Oxford. Telephone: 0865-55006

St. Catherine's College, Oxford. Telephone: 0865-49541

St. Cross College, Oxford. Telephone: 0865-43182

St. Edmund Hall, Oxford. Telephone: 0865-45511

St. Hilda's College, Oxford. Telephone: 0865-41821

St. Hugh's College, Oxford. Telephone: 0865-57341

St. John's College, Oxford. Telephone: 0865-47671

St. Peter's College, Oxford. Telephone: 0865-48436

Somerville College, Oxford. Telephone: 0865-57595

Trinity College, Oxford. Telephone: 0865-41801

University College, Oxford. Telephone: 0865-41661

Wadham College, Oxford. Telephone: 0865-42564

Wolfson College, Oxford. Telephone: 0865-56711

University of Reading, Reading, Berkshire. Telephone: 0734-85123

University of Salford, Salford, Lancashire. Telephone: 061-736 5843

University of Sheffield, Sheffield. Telephone: 0742-78555

University of Southampton, Highfield, Southampton. Telephone: 0703-559122

University of Stirling, Stirling. Telephone: 0786-3171
University of Surrey, Guildford, Surrey. Telephone: 0483-71281
University of Sussex, Falmer, Brighton, Sussex. Telephone:
   0273-66755
University of Warwick, Coventry, Warwickshire. Telephone: 0203-
   24011
University of York, Heslington, York. Telephone: 0904-59861

SCOTLAND

University of Aberdeen, Aberdeen. Telephone: 0244-40241
University of Dundee, Dundee. Telephone: 0382-23181
University of Edinburgh, Edinburgh. Telephone: 031-667 1011
University of Glasgow, Glasgow. Telephone: 041-339 8855
Heriot-Watt University, Edinburgh. Telephone: 031-225 8432
University of St. Andrews, Fife. Telephone: St. Andrews 4411
University of Strathclyde, George Street, Glasgow. Telephone:
   041-552 4400

WALES

University of Wales, Cathays Park, Cardiff. Telephone: 0222-
   22656
   Colleges of the University of Wales
   University College of Wales, Aberystwyth. Telephone: 0970-
      2711
   University College of North Wales, Bangor. Telephone: 0248-
      51151
   University College, Cardiff, P. O. B. 78, Cardiff. Telephone:
      0222-44211
   University College of Swansea, Singleton Park, Swansea.
      Telephone: 0792-25678
   St. David's University College, Lampeter, Cardiganshire.
      Telephone: Lampeter 422351
   University of Wales Institute of Science and Technology, King
      Edward VII Avenue, Cardiff. Telephone: 0222-42522

NORTHERN IRELAND

New University of Ulster, Coleraine, Co. Londonderry. Telephone:
   0265-4141
Queen's University of Belfast, University Road, Belfast. Telephone:
   0232-45133
The Presbyterian College, Botanic Avenue, Belfast. Telephone:
   0232-78312
Ulster College, The Northern Ireland Polytechnic, Jordanstown,
   Newtownabbey, Co. Antrim. Telephone: Whiteabbey 65131

Appendix B

ALPHABETICAL LIST OF LIBRARIES AND ARCHIVES

(Numbers referred to are entry numbers)

Shaw, Stebbing 214
Sheepscar Library 97
Sheffield Collection 207, 208
Sheffield Estate Muniments 207
Sherlock Holmes Collection 184
Shiffner Archives 100
Shipping See: Ships and
  Shipping
Ships and Shipping 75, 105,
  146, 149, 174, 211
    History 149, 157, 174
Shiskin Papers 47
Shrewsbury Local History 210
Shrewsbury Papers 144
Shrievalty 50
Shuttleworth, Lord 201
Sierra Leone Newspapers 37
Sikorski Museum 160
Simms, Samuel, Collection 44
Sims and Jefferies of Ipswich
  203
Slavonic Studies 97, 197
Smith, Adam, Library 44
Smith, Charles Lesingham,
  Collection 53
Smith, William Robertson,
  Library 54
Social Activities 138
Social-Democratic Federation
  152
Social History 90, 170, 174,
  208
Social Party 152
Social Science 47, 60, 70,
  75, 76, 85, 99, 115, 135,
  148, 150, 164, 181, 187,
  198, 204, 209, 215
    Africa 179
    Asia 179
Social Security Library 121
Social Services 144
Social Work 78, 222
Socialism 144, 150, 152, 211
    Manuscripts 98
Socialist Labour Party 152
Societies 25, 224
Society for the Diffusion of
  Useful Knowledge 172
Society of Friends 43, 58,
  80, 86
    Lancashire 201
    See also: Quakers
Sociological Association, The

British 229
Sociology 57, 82, 98, 173,
  174, 222, 229
Soke of Peterborough 192
Somerset 40
Sons of the Clergy 129
South Asia See: Asia
South Asian Studies 140
Southampton, Lord 129
Southampton Local History 211
Southampton Record Society 212
Southwark 129
Southwark, Diocese of 169
Southwell, Diocese of 195
Soviet Studies Collection 52, 85
Spain 177
    Civil War 152
    Collection 55
Spectator 9
Speer Ministry 138
Sports 123
Stafford, Earl of 207
Stafford Local History 214
Stalin, Joseph, Collection 152
Standards 41, 49, 189
    British 58
Stanford, (Sir) Charles Thomas
    See: Thomas-Stanford, (Sir)
    Charles
Stanley Collection 194
Stationery Supplies 13
Statistical Society, Royal 242
Statistics 57, 80, 103, 107,
  109, 135, 146, 150, 158,
  159, 161, 162, 168, 174
Stepney Manor 129
Stevenson, Robert Louis 75
Stirling-Maxwell Collection 84
Stokes, Whitley, Library 172
Stone, (Sir) Benjamin, Collec-
  tion 46
Stonehouse 200
Storrs, R., Papers 55
Strategic Studies 143, 213
Stuart, C., Papers 55
Stuart Studies 67
Styring Collection 157
Sudan Archive 73
Suffrage 147
Surrey, Court of 129
Surrey Dispensary 129
Surveying 122
Sussex Collection 48